Robert W. Allan

THE MIRACLE ON WASHINGTON SQUARE

NEW YORK UNIVERSITY

"I can think of no other way in which a young man coming to this terrific city as I came to it could have a more comprehensive and stimulating introduction to its swarming life, other than through the corridors and classrooms of Washington Square."

—Thomas Wolfe

THE MIRACLE ON WASHINGTON SQUARE
NEW YORK UNIVERSITY

JOAN MARANS DIM

NANCY MURPHY CRICCO

LEXINGTON BOOKS

Lanham • Boulder • New York • Oxford

LEXINGTON BOOKS

Published in the United States of America
by Lexington Books
4720 Boston Way, Lanham, Maryland 20706

12 Hid's Copse Road
Cumnor Hill, Oxford OX2 9JJ, England

British Library Cataloguing in Publication Information Available

Library of Congress Cataloging-in-Publication Data

Dim, Joan Marans.
 The miracle on Washington Square : New York University / Joan Marans Dim,
Nancy Murphy Cricco.
  p. cm.
 Includes bibliographical references (p.) and index.
 ISBN 0-7391-0216-8 (alk. paper)
  1. New York University. I. Title: Miracle on Washington Square. II. Cricco,
Nancy Murphy. III. Title.

LD3835.D56 2000
378.747'1—dc21

00-063560

Printed in the United States of America

♾ ™ The paper used in this publication meets the minimum requirements of American
National Standard for Information Sciences—Permanence of Paper for Printed Library
Materials, ANSI/NISO Z39.48–1992.

Design, layout, and photo restoration: Leonard Levitsky

ON THE COVER: A photographic rendering of Washington Square Park.

FRONTISPIECE: Interior of the chapel in the old University Building. An unsigned watercolor, most often attrib-
uted to architect James Dakin, is considered the best early representation of the Gothic-style chapel.
Photo: Collection of the New-York Historical Society.

*Photographs in this book without credit lines are from the NYU Archives with the exception of the
still-life photos at the beginning of each chapter, which were taken by Eric Jacobson.*

Dedicated to Dr. L. Jay Oliva,
whose integrity, leadership, and
commitment helped make this
miracle possible, and to
Naomi Levine, who inspired and
championed this project.
Without her fire, guidance, and
full support, this volume
simply would not be.

Contents

FOREWORD:
A PRESIDENT'S PERSPECTIVE
—past, present, future
L. Jay Oliva

I*t is rare that the president of a university has the privilege and pleasure of spending over 40 years at one institution. It is still rarer that the president of a university observes in his lifetime the kind of academic and physical transformation that has occurred at NYU. It is a transformation that to me is nothing short of a miracle.*

Each night as I leave my office atop Bobst Library on Washington Square South, I see through the windows behind my desk the skyline of New York City—thousands of lights on the huge skyscrapers silhouetted against the dark—a scene that never fails to fill me with awe. For me, it represents the magnificent power of what men and women can do as they reach toward the heavens to fulfill their dreams. It is also the story of New York University, an institution always looking upward and moving forward with vigor, creativity, and drive. It is no accident that NYU shares these same quintessential characteristics with New York City.

Indeed, the ascent of New York City to its present status as the acknowledged capital of the world parallels the ascent of NYU from a solid, urban, research university into an institution of learning and research that is today acclaimed as truly global and of extraordinary quality and distinction.

Clearly, no part of the University has been left unexamined in our process of change, and we can take great pride in the result. In fact, so extraordinary have been our gains that even the *New York Times* recognized this "Miracle on Washington Square."

The *New York Times*, March 20, 1995, reported:

...the administration, doing some long-range planning, decided that being the safety school was not good enough. So in 1984, it began a brash campaign aimed at moving the school into the nation's top tier of universities. And according to academics around the country who have looked on with envy, the strategy worked....

The strategies and programs that led to New York University's dramatic rise are elaborated on fully in the words and pictures of this volume. All I shall do is summarize them to give you a very brief picture of this "miracle" as a backdrop for the pages that follow.

THE TASK
OF REBUILDING

Our metamorphosis did not occur by accident. It was the result of a deliberate plan developed by NYU's trustees and academic leaders.

A major factor in our efforts was the decision in 1985 to conduct a 15-year billion-dollar campaign. Our goal was explicit—to build a better University both physically and academically.

Incredibly, we raised $2 million a week for 500 weeks and achieved our billion-dollar objective in only 10 years. This daunting task of fund-raising was eased by a series of major gifts. In 1988, the Tisch family made a $30-million donation. That same year Leonard Stern contributed $30 million. In 1991, Paulette Goddard left a $25-million legacy. NYU achieved its billion-dollar goal, moreover, without even counting what may well be the largest single gift ever given to an American university—La Pietra, the late Sir Harold Acton's estate in Florence.

Many people share the responsibility for our fund-raising success. They include our benefactors, both alumni and friends of the University; our trustees, led by former Chairman Laurence A. Tisch, current Chairman Martin Lipton, and Development Committee Chairman George Heyman; President Emeritus John Brademas; Senior Vice President for External Affairs Naomi Levine, the University's chief development officer; and the deans and faculty who create the programs that attract support and who also involve themselves directly in the development effort.

One lesson I have learned, however, is that one cannot rest on one's laurels. Progress demands continued effort; to stand still is to fall backward. To remain at the top, NYU must intensify its efforts and build on its successes. For this reason, NYU has launched a second billion-dollar campaign, to be completed in 2002, in which our goals are to increase scholarships and endowed professorships, to further support our faculty, to continue the enhancement of student life, and to carry on the expansion of interdisciplinary and research programs.

REPUTATION, APPLICATIONS, AND SAT SCORES SOAR

We were always focused and persistent in our ambitions. As a result of the original Billion-Dollar Campaign, NYU has accomplished much:

- Spent $600 million for academic expansion
- Endowed 88 chairs
- Raised $109 million for scholarships and fellowships
- Completed a more than $600-million building and renovation effort using private gifts and construction bonds
- Increased its endowment from $384 million in 1984 to $1 billion in 1999

Our professional and academic schools—long well regarded—have over the last decade become recognized as among the best in the country.

In 1998, NYU Hospitals Center and Health System became full clinical partners with Mount Sinai Medical Center, creating Mount Sinai-NYU Health. Through this historic agreement, two of the premier medical centers in the nation joined to provide a powerful base of medical research and clinical care. Mount Sinai-NYU Health also includes affiliations with the two medical schools (NYU School of Medicine and Mount Sinai School of Medicine) and more than 40 clinical affiliates throughout the region. Surely enormous intellectual opportunities for University-wide growth in science and health care will result from such alliances.

Our successful fund-raising in a competitive market made possible the energetic recruitment of stellar new faculty. Indeed, the list of our distinguished faculty could fill this report. Some of these include Michael C. Alfano, an educator and health industry leader, who became dean of the NYU College of Dentistry; Jo Ivey Boufford, who served as principal deputy assistant secretary for health in the U.S. Department of Health and Human Services prior to being named dean of the Robert F. Wagner Graduate School of Public Service; John Freccero, a distinguished Dante scholar, who came from Stanford; Russell Hardin, a leading expert on the role of morality in politics, who came from the University of Chicago; Larry Kramer, a distinguished authority on the Constitution, who left the University of Chicago to join the School of Law; Peter Lennie, formerly chair of the Department of Brain and Cognitive Science at the University of Rochester, who joined NYU as a professor of neural science and dean for science in the Faculty of Arts and Science; Diane O'Neill McGivern, a leading educator in nursing, who came from the University of Pennsylvania and Hunter College; David W. McLaughlin, a mathematician, who left Princeton University to become director of the Courant Institute of Mathematical Sciences; J. Anthony Movshon, a leading specialist in neuroscience and founding director of the Center for Neural Science, who chose to come to NYU rather than accept an offer from MIT; Andrew Ross, who left Princeton to chair NYU's Program in American Studies; Zelda Fichandler, founder of the Arena Stage and a winner of the 1996 National Medal of the Arts, joined NYU's Tisch School as chair of the Graduate Acting Program after four decades of theatrical trailblazing in Washington, DC; Matthew S. Santirocco, a classicist tapped from the University of Pennsylvania, joined the College of Arts and Science as dean; and Catharine R. Stimpson, who was director of the MacArthur Foundation Fellows Program before joining the Graduate School of Arts and Science as dean.

Examples of our international faculty include literary critic Denis Donoghue, Henry James Professor of English and American Literature, who left his beloved Ireland to come to NYU; Menachem Elon, retired deputy president of the Supreme Court of Israel, who became the Gruss Visiting Professor of Talmudic Civil Law and a member of the Global Law School Program faculty; and Marti G. Subrahmanyam, Charles E. Merrill Professor of Finance, who came from India to pursue his doctoral work at MIT and subsequently joined the Stern faculty.

Clearly, this influx of faculty—both national and international—has immeasurably enriched us as we constantly seek to redefine and reshape the University.

The Scholastic Assessment Test scores of entering students have risen from 1200 in 1990 to 1334 in 2000, which places NYU among the most selective of universities.

All this good news, apparently, traveled quickly.

In 2000, NYU received more than 30,000 applications for its entering class. We admitted only 29 percent of those applicants—our lowest-ever acceptance rate.

The 3,400 freshmen enrolled in 2000 included candidates from all 50 states and

43 foreign countries. Some 60 percent were women; some 40 percent were men. Nearly 40 percent were people of color.

Undoubtedly many of these students were attracted not only by the academic stan dards of NYU but by the excitement of New York City and NYU's proximity to Wall Street, Broadway, and Silicon Alley. Indeed, no other place in the world offers as much access to the dazzling array of professional opportunities as the Big Apple.

THE BUILDING BOOM

During the last decades, we embarked on one of the largest building and renovation programs undertaken by an urban university in the 20th century. The results have been nothing short of amazing.

The deluge of student applications from around the country and world created a demand for more residence halls, and NYU responded. In the last decade, NYU has nearly doubled the number of undergrad-uates in student housing from some 4,000 to nearly 8,000. And in fall 1999, approximately 10,000 graduate and undergraduate students resided in University housing. Thus, in one of the world's most expensive cities, where space is singularly dear, NYU has met the nearly impossible task of providing safe, comfortable, and affordable housing for its students.

THE EMERGENCE OF THE GLOBAL UNIVERSITY

Becoming an international university has always been a fundamental objective for NYU. For a long time, this objective was deferred because of the University's need to concentrate on the more pressing work of rejuvenation. During the last decade, however, a new level of institutional strength permitted us to pursue the establishment of the global university.

Our plans were greatly accelerated by the gift of La Pietra, now the home of the League of World Universities, an organization I chair. La Pietra, the spectacular Tuscan estate with its endowment and magnificent artworks, was left to NYU by Sir Harold Acton. The acquisition of La Pietra meant that NYU now had a center for international study, a locus for global faculty inquiry, and an anchor for our worldwide conferences.

One of the dreams I expressed at my inauguration in 1991 was to make it possible for every student to spend at least one semester abroad without the usual bureaucratic difficulties that accompany many study abroad programs. I am pleased to report that we are making steady progress toward this goal. In fact, more than 1,000 NYU students annually spend at least one semester in study abroad programs. The NYU 2000 Summer Study Abroad offered over 35 programs in more than 20 sites in Europe, Asia, Africa, and Latin America, with more than 700 students currently participating in these programs.

In addition to our extensive programs abroad, we express our internationalism in numerous other ways:

- The overwhelmingly international character of our student body and faculty
- Our leading role in the global exchange of knowledge, which draws distinguished international faculty and students to Washington Square and sends NYU students and faculty abroad
- The focus of each of our schools and departments on its own unique programs of international scholarship and our ever-expanding set of international houses and centers
- Our leadership in the League of World Universities

THE LEAGUE OF WORLD UNIVERSITIES

One of the clear themes of our history has been our willingness to associate, indeed, to be immersed, in the life of the city in which we make our home. As our global vision for NYU expanded, we began to think even more about the University's role and obligation to its city. We also began thinking about those other urban universities throughout the world that, like us, were at the epicenter of cultural, social, and political ferment. From these thoughts came our concept of creating an alliance—to be called the League of World Universities—of major metropolitan universities from around the world whose representation would meet regularly to address the pressing issues we have in common.

At the first meeting in 1991 of the League of World Universities, some 30 rectors, presidents, and chancellors from the world's most renowned urban universities established an open dialogue that quickly echoed our similar tensions, tasks, and missions.

The Second Conference of the League of World Universities in 1993 focused on "Large City Universities and the Public School System," and the Third

Conference in 1995, on "The Image of the University." At the Fourth Conference of the League of World Universities in 1997, members discussed ways to enable students from member institutions to access classes and faculty throughout the world. Additional meetings and planning sessions have also taken place at NYU Villa La Pietra and at the National Autonomous University of Mexico in Mexico City.

At this writing, some 35 student and faculty exchange agreements have been signed by NYU and league members. The result is that our students and faculty—and those in international sister universities—now have a multitude of global exchange options from which to choose. In addition, my goal of providing a study abroad opportunity for every NYU student is moving one step closer to reality.

In less than a decade, the League of World Universities has united the world's great urban universities with a common vision and purpose while accelerating NYU's mission of globalization.

THE TRADITION OF PUBLIC AND COMMUNITY SERVICE

A university's description of itself too often describes unfulfilled dreams. But not ours. "A private university in the public service" still speaks for NYU.

Whether it is a performance of street theatre, Village Improvement Day, a soup kitchen at the Medical Center, an annual toy drive yielding more than 1,000 donations from NYU employees, or mentoring children at P.S. 63 (to name just a few examples), public and community service performed by students, faculty, and staff has always been an NYU tradition.

Senior Vice President Debra James* led our efforts to support this tradition. In fall 1996, we created a centralized Office of Community Service to promote a continued expansion of our efforts throughout the University. Among the 130 community-wide projects are the President's C-Team, a group of student volunteers who work with eight settlement houses on the Lower East Side and in Greenwich Village, and the America Reads program, a community-based literacy campaign with the national goal of ensuring that every child in America is able to read by the end of the third grade.

An especially exhilarating moment for all was a visit by First Lady Hillary Rodham Clinton in 1997, who said:

Debra James passed away July 19, 2000.

The University has set an exemplary standard for what can be accomplished when opportunities to serve are provided. So whether it's AmeriCorps/Project SafetyNet, or any other program, what I see and hear is that the spirit of service has imbued the University and has given meaning to the experience here for so many of you.

WHERE PHYSICS, NOT PHYSIQUES, DOMINATE

I believe that sports play a significant role in the life of the academy and have greatly enjoyed the privilege of participating in its regeneration at NYU. Where else but on the playing field can young men and women in college today share the experience that puts their talents and egos on the line, learn the meaning of team play, and come to appreciate the need and value of balancing good sportsmanship and competition?

Though sports deliver the purest form of joy and comradeship that I know, I also know that sacrificing academic excellence for a great sports team does a great disservice to our student athletes. It is a notion that I have worked hard to guard against.

Like many others more than a decade ago, I was mystified, angered, and ashamed by the state of college athletics in the United States and considered it a burden to all who attended to the academic tradition. To ensure that payoffs, grade fixing, and relaxed eligibility practices found no home at NYU, we adopted a Division III approach to athletics. We set basic guidelines for *all* of our student athletes, which meant regular admissions procedures, no athletic scholarships, need- and academic merit-based aid as with other students, and competition with other schools who shared a similar commitment.

In 1986, NYU was a founding member of the University Athletic Association (UAA), a group of urban universities that endorses strong academic goals while offering opportunities to compete against the nation's leading universities.

Our covenant with our students and the UAA paid off magnificently on March 27, 1997, when NYU's women's basketball team won their first NCAA Division III Championship. It was a night to remember. As pandemonium reigned in Coles Sports Center, more than 1,900 fans watched the thrilling win. The score was tied at 70-70 as NYU Violet Marsha Harris dribbled the ball the length of the court, blew past two defenders, and laid the basket in with just one and a half seconds left against Wisconsin-Eau Claire.

Soon after, Mayor Giuliani welcomed the Violets to City Hall, and the team rang the bell to open trading at the New York Stock Exchange.

NYU displayed a competitiveness and a desire that is a trademark of New York City teams and New Yorkers. This is a team that is as diverse as the University it represents, with players from as far away as Georgia and Wyoming, and as near as Queens and the Bronx.

—Rudolph Giuliani

The victory by NYU's Violets marked the first women's collegiate basketball title for New York City and the metropolitan area. The victory was doubly sweetened by the knowledge that our student champions were also exemplary scholars. The team's grade point average was nearly 3.5. And I am additionally pleased to report that Marsha Harris, still an exemplary student, is now in her second year of study at NYU's School of Medicine.

THE FUTURE

As I review the past decades, I think about how far we have come and how blessed I have been.

Today, I can say this with enormous confidence—NYU enters the 21st century well prepared to meet the challenges and responsibilities it will face. To visit our campus today, to stroll around Washington Square, to experience the energy of the University and the range and enthusiasm of its student body and faculty, is to see a microcosm of New York City—and a microcosm of the world.

For all of this and more, I thank the University's students, alumni, trustees, friends, faculty, and staff who make up that remarkable entity called "the NYU family." Proudly, I remain a part of that family.

And I hope as you read through the pages that follow, you will not only enjoy the saga of NYU's amazing journey but that you, too, will feel a part of this extraordinary family.

L. Jay Oliva

ALBERT GALLATIN, FIRST
PRESIDENT OF THE
UNIVERSITY COUNCIL

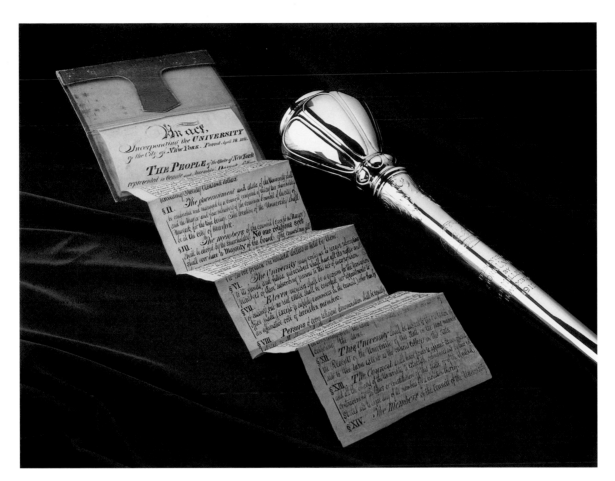

New York University was founded on April 18, 1831. It came into existence during a time when a young nation was embroiled in intensive discussions concerning the best ways to provide a useful and practical education for its populace. The discussions were not theoretical. The Industrial Revolution had dawned, and social and economic changes would soon transform the nation from an agrarian society into great, urban-based factory centers.

In the early 19th century, American colleges existed exclusively under religious auspices and focused rigidly on classical and sectarian subjects. But during this same period in Vienna, Berlin, and Paris, a remarkable experiment occurred. Institutions of higher learning began to devote themselves not only to the classics and religion but also to modern languages, philosophy, history, political economy, and physical science—subjects at the core of a modern university's curriculum.

In October 1828, a university in London opened and embraced this novel notion. Designed for young men of the middle class, the university accentuated a practical education at a reasonable rate. It was this *new* University of London that became the paradigm for a group of daring and ambitious New Yorkers interested in the city's future.

A THIRST FOR KNOWLEDGE

DeWitt Clinton, governor of New York State, talked of improving the common schools. Philip Hone, mayor of New York City, was instrumental in opening the Mercantile Library in 1821, which served the city's clerks and mechanics. The New York Athenaeum, opened in 1824, provided monthly lectures for men and women with the goal of "advancing science, art, and literature." The feeling that there was a

need for a skilled and educated citizenry to buttress a new age prevailed.

Awash in this spirit of progress, nine local citizens, including John Delafield, a merchant and banker with a strong voice for nonsectarian education, and Dutch merchant Myndert Van Schaick, met in December 1829 to discuss the formation of a different kind of university in New York City. To them, the classical curriculum offered at American colleges seemed out of touch with the needs of the working classes. Something more modern and useful was required. The notion of "utilitarianism" would shape the ensuing debates surrounding the creation of the new university.

The founders' innovative approach

JOHN DELAFIELD, FIRST SECRETARY OF THE UNIVERSITY COUNCIL, 1831-1833

well fit New York City's changing times. Indeed, the city was undergoing a tremendous transformation in terms of its structure, size, and wealth. With a swelling population of 200,000, the city was already America's leading metropolis—the "London of America."

On January 6, 1830, the founders issued a manifesto entitled "Expediency and Means of Establishing a University in the City of New-York." This document proclaimed the urgency of educating young men in modern languages, history, political economy, and natural science so they might become merchants, mechanics, farmers, manufacturers, architects, and civil engineers—that is, productive members of society.

In 1829, New York City had only one other institution of higher education, Columbia College, later renamed Columbia University. The oldest educational institution in New York City, Columbia was founded in 1754 as King's College. The new university would be strikingly different from Columbia College, which had the full support of the Anglican Church and offered the sons of the wealthy a classical education.

Educating the Sons of the Metropolis

From its inception, this new university, as envisioned by the 1830 manifesto, was different.

Because this new institution would not have a religious affiliation, the founders decided to finance it privately through the sale of stock costing $25 per share. Setting up a joint stock company, an idea modeled after the University of London, would prevent any self-interested group or religious denomination from dominating the affairs of the institution. The founders hoped to raise $100,000 by August 1, 1830. In time, 175 subscribers—merchants, lawyers, bankers, clergymen, artisans, and tradesmen—purchased stock.

In October 1830, a 32-member governing council was chosen. The council elected one of the city's most accomplished and eminent citizens, Albert Gallatin, as its president. Gallatin believed that the mission of the new university should be to elevate standards of learning and render knowledge more accessible to the community. He proposed a school with an English-based curriculum that did not require the study of Greek and Latin. For Gallatin, an English-based education was just as worthy as the classic curriculum.

The University would educate the sons of the great metropolis, whose talents would then advance the reputation and stature of the city of New York. Other new American colleges might reflect pride in their states, regions, or denominations; this university uniquely symbolized the aspirations of a city.

New York University and the City
by Thomas J. Frusciano and Marilyn H. Pettit

On April 21, 1831, the New York State Legislature passed an act incorporating the University of the City of New-York—a name the institution bore until 1896, when it became New York University.

THE DOORS OPEN

The program of instruction was innovative. Students could enroll for regular course work leading to a diploma, or they could elect to take individual courses according to their means and convenience, a philosophy anticipating today's schools of continuing education. No specific qualifications were required for part-time instruction. The course work leading to a diploma also was innovative. Two regular courses of study were offered. The more unusual was the English and scientific course, championed by Gallatin, for which no knowledge of Greek or Latin was required. The other was the traditional classical and scientific course, which demanded the conventional requirement of Latin and Greek grammar and an acquaintance with Virgil, Cicero, and Homer.

The *Commercial Advertiser,* a newspaper, published a University prospectus as an advertisement on September 12, 1832, in which other courses such as architecture, civil engineering, astronomy, chemistry, mineralogy, sculpture, painting, and languages were offered. The writer of the prospectus noted that "in a city like ours, the scene of so many arts, and such extensive commerce," special consideration had been given to the needs of those "who are designed for the more practical pursuits of life; and who would desire to become master of those branches of knowledge most immediately connected with their respective professions, or employments."

Annual tuition was $80, and less for part-time students. Uptown at Columbia College, tuition was $90. The $80 tuition was a princely sum given that room and board in the neighborhood at the time was approximately $2 a week. The salaries of most of the first faculty members were derived directly from student fees. Among the students enrolled during the University's first year of study were Robert R.

Crosby and Clarkson F. Crosby, sons of William B. Crosby, a wealthy and distinguished citizen. At least one of the Crosby brothers, possibly both, had transferred from Columbia College. Another Crosby brother, Howard, would later serve as fourth chancellor of the University. In any case, judging from the names and addresses in the University's first Matriculation Book, most of the students came from upper-middle-class families, several from elite neighborhoods in the City Hall area. Clearly, these were not *exactly* the kind of students that the founders had in mind.

The University's first faculty consisted of five salaried professors and seven part-time instructors in art and the foreign languages. Not surprisingly, the faculty was divided between advocates of a classical education and those who favored a more modern, "American" approach.

One of the most interesting faculty members was Henry P. Tappan. A professor of philosophy, Tappan became both a controversial and a visionary figure. Indeed, his philosophy presented the image of the University as the locus of a great metropolitan home for the "learned" of the United States. To Tappan, the University was *of* the city and *in* the city.

> *By adding to the natural attractions of a metropolitan city the attractions of literature, science, and art, as embodied in a great University, students from every part of the Union would be naturally drawn together. We should thus have a fully appointed Institution where the bonds of our nationality would be strengthened by the loftiest form of education, the sympathy of scholars, and the noblest productions of literature.*

Henry P. Tappan as quoted in *New York Intellect* by Thomas Bender

HENRY P. TAPPAN, PROFESSOR OF PHILOSOPHY AND BELLES-LETTRES, 1832-1838

Embroiled in one of the University's earliest controversies in 1837, he was fired the following year, at least in part for his support of Gallatin's democratic principles and his disdain for those who championed the classical curriculum.

DAVID BATES DOUGLASS, PROFESSOR OF
NATURAL PHILOSOPHY AND CIVIL
ENGINEERING, 1832-1841

Other distinguished scholars in those early years included Henry Vethake, a professor of mathematics and astronomy, a graduate of Columbia College, and a former Princeton professor. David Douglass, a professor of natural philosophy and civil engineering, had taught at West Point and served as an engineer on the construction of the Croton Aqueduct. Inventor Samuel F. B. Morse was the obvious choice for professor of painting and sculpture. He was already a recognized artist and the president of the National Academy of Design. John Torrey, a noted botanist, was a professor of chemistry, mineralogy, and botany; and the Reverend George Bush, a professor of Hebrew and Oriental literature, later became a prominent member of the American Bible Society.

In one notable misstep, the University turned down an aspiring young poet named Henry Wadsworth Longfellow when he applied in 1834 for a teaching post. No doubt the sting of rejection by New York University was soothed in 1835 when Harvard hired him.

JOHN TORREY, PROFESSOR
OF BOTANY, 1832-1833

APPOINTMENT
OF THE
FIRST CHANCELLOR

The first chancellor of the new University, James M. Mathews, pastor of the South Dutch Reformed Church, extolled the virtues of densely populated cities as the most advantageous sites for universities. He viewed the University's place in New York City as particularly salutary because of the city's scholarly resources and its powerful cultural and commercial influence.

R. Ogden Doremus, class of '42, recalled visits by Mathews to his parents' home when Doremus was a young boy. "He was tall and handsome and in manner and address most charming, as well as commanding the respect of all those with whom he came in contact," wrote Doremus in an essay.

Mathews's inauguration in Clinton Hall on September 26, 1832, according to newspaper reports, "was filled to overflowing with an audience of the first respectability." It must have been a somber affair as the city was in the grips of one

JAMES MELANCHTHON MATHEWS, FIRST CHANCELLOR OF NEW YORK UNIVERSITY, 1831-1839

of its worst cholera epidemics from which some 5,000 perished. Notably absent from the inauguration ceremony was Albert Gallatin, who had resigned from the council a year earlier. Gallatin opposed Mathews's advocacy of a religious approach to education and the chancellor's resistance to any separation of science and morality. Two distinctly different factions argued for two very different destinies for the University. On one side was a succession of clergymen who wished to sustain the evangelical character of the University. On the other side were faculty members Samuel F. B. Morse, banker John Delafield, Dutch merchant Myndert Van Schaick, and Albert Gallatin, who argued that while religion might be a central feature of the curriculum, the University should also provide practical and inexpensive instruction in a nonsectarian setting.

"No possible injury could arise from embracing the opportunity offered by the new university, to make the fair experiment of what may properly be called an 'English college.' So long as mastery of Greek and Latin was 'the test by which the well educated man, as he is called, is distinguished from the man without education'...there is but little hope of any essential improvement in our system of education...."

—Albert Gallatin as quoted in "A University for Its Times—
The Formative Years: 1830-1870" by Bayrd Still

A PERMANENT HOME ON WASHINGTON SQUARE

During its formative years and even beyond, the University suffered repeated disappointments and financial crises. Indeed, financial insecurity was the one constant within the University. Another source of conflict and disappointment was the growing conservatism of its curriculum during the 1840s and 1850s. It seemed at times that the University had forsaken the innovative expressions of its founders. Yet, for all the unfulfilled hopes, the young institution achieved significant gains.

One important milestone was the construction of the University's first permanent home, an immense neo-Gothic building located on the northeast corner of Washington Square between Waverly and Washington Places. When the new University Building, which contained a three-story chapel, opened in 1835, the Washington Square area had only recently been considered a distant suburb. The farms that had dotted the landscape, broken by an occasional church steeple, were rapidly being divided into lots for houses. Streets were being graded and the crackling sound of rocks being blasted broke the peace. Elegant Greek revival row houses were springing up, and some of the city's richest and most prestigious families were moving into them.

The new University Building, designed by the architectural firm of Town, Davis and Dakin, sat across from Washington Square Park. The

AN INTERIOR VIEW OF ONE OF THE GREEK REVIVAL
ROW HOUSES ON WASHINGTON SQUARE NORTH

park had been converted from a burial ground and open field into a military parade ground and pastoral public park. A detailed description of the new building appears in a column entitled "City Improvements" in the September 13, 1834, edition of the weekly journal, *New-York Mirror.*

DETAIL OF ORIGINAL UNIVERSITY BUILDING

> *This edifice is built of marble from the quarries of Sing-Sing, and exhibits a specimen of the English collegiate style of architecture....The building is one hundred feet wide and one hundred and eighty feet long. In front this oblong is divided into five parts—a central building, with wings flanked by towers, one rising on each of the four corners of the edifice. This central building, or chapel, is superior to the rest of the breadth, height and character; and is somewhat similar to that of King's College, Cambridge, England—a masterpiece of pointed architecture, and the model for succeeding ages. . . . The principal entrance is under the great western window, through a richly moulded and deeply recessed portal. . . . The doors are oak, richly panelled, and filled with tracery of open work, closely studded with bronze. Entering at the west and principal door, you pass on the right to the room of the janitor, and to the apartments of the professor of chemistry and botany, or on the left to the office of the clerk of the university, and rooms for classes in the ancient and modern languages.*

Fulfilling Mathews's hopes, the new University Building became a model of collegiate neo-Gothic architecture for other academic institutions. Chancellor Mathews strongly believed that the University should have a building of its own and that it should, as he wrote in his *Recollections of Persons and Events,* "correspond with the prevailing taste in architecture." But the building's excessive grandeur would cost him dearly. His administration, under a cloud of mismanagement, was wracked by debts and riddled with faculty complaints. In 1839, he was forced to resign. In the end, Mathews's zeal had led to extravagant expansionism, which had resulted in failure, disappointment, and his departure.

Theodore Frelinghuysen, a New Jersey congressman and mayor of Newark, succeeded Mathews. During his chancellorship, Frelinghuysen unsuccessfully ran in

1844 for the vice presidency of the United States. In 1850, Frelinghuysen departed to become president of Rutgers; it would be three years before a new chancellor assumed leadership.

Despite the financial problems associated with the new University Building, it looms large in the annals of American education as a place where great men of art and science accomplished important deeds. It was there that famed inventor Samuel F. B. Morse perfected the telegraph and created some of his most memorable paintings. It was there that John W. Draper, professor of chemistry and natural history and a pioneering medical educator, produced one of the earliest daguerreotypes of the human face and also took some of the first photographs of the moon. Draper's advances in optics and photography led to analyses of the chemical composition of

sunlight. These major achievements were unmatched at the time by larger institutions.

Draper was a man of boldness and foresight. In *New York University 1832-1932,* Theodore F. Jones discusses an 1853 address by Draper to alumni. Draper chose the occasion of the University's 21st anniversary to urge New York City to do a better job of supporting the University. Draper noted that the city had benefited greatly from the economic development of Morse's telegraph and from his own work in photography. Furthermore, since its establishment in 1841, the Medical Department had trained 1,200 doctors and was treating about 2,000 destitute New Yorkers every year, he added.

Draper admonished University administrators, too:

STUDY OF JOHN W. DRAPER, PROFESSOR OF CHEMISTRY, 1839-1882

What has been done thus far, in the University, is good…having made provision for education of members of the Gospel of any religious denomination, and of physicians, and of literary men, there is next before us the great task of dealing with the true strength of New York—its commercial classes, manufacturers, engineers, and mechanics—the men who have little concern in knowing what was said or done in Athens or Rome, two thousand years ago, but who are craving for a knowledge [of] how they shall conduct the business enterprise they are to enter on to-morrow.

Draper's exhortations did not go entirely unheeded. In 1860, under the direction of the Reverend Isaac Ferris, the University's third chancellor, a new curriculum was established based on science and modern languages, which led to a Bachelor of Science degree. Yet, despite this important advance, the University continued to be dominated by the classics through the next quarter century.

BECOMING A GENUINE UNIVERSITY

At the University's inception, it was a university in name only.

That changed in 1835 when Benjamin F. Butler, attorney general in the presidential administrations of Andrew Jackson and Martin Van Buren, created a plan for a "scientific law school." Instruction began in April 1838, but was discontinued by 1840-1841. Instruction resumed once again in the late 1850s.

The Medical Department began instruction in 1841 and was an extraordinary success from the moment it opened its doors. Student enrollment grew from 239 in 1841 to more than 400 by 1848. By comparison, the undergraduate college rarely enrolled more than 150 students.

Always in the minds and hearts of the founders of the University was the desire to provide medical instruction and to improve the woefully inadequate medical care in

BENJAMIN BUTLER,
FOUNDER, NYU SCHOOL
OF LAW, 1835

THEODORE
FRELINGHUYSEN,
CHANCELLOR,
1839-1850

New York City. Dr. Valentine Mott, a leading proponent in the founding of the Medical Department and one of the University's founders, was considered New York City's leading surgeon in the 1830s. The Medical Department's initial goals were to lengthen the term of instruction, provide students the opportunity for comprehensive study of anatomy, and stress the importance of chemistry in the curriculum. Not surprisingly, John W. Draper was a critical member of the medical faculty, and his leadership led to an expanded chemistry curriculum.

Although the Medical Department prospered, the University was financially weak and in real danger of closing its doors.

AN AUTHENTIC LEADER
TAKES THE HELM

The Reverend Isaac Ferris, pastor of the Market Street Dutch Reformed Church, resigned his pastorate and took the helm in 1853 of what was surely an uncertain venture. Time would prove, however, that the struggling University was most fortunate to have Ferris's services as chancellor until his retirement 17 years later in 1870.

WASHINGTON SQUARE, 1858

(Collection of the New-York Historical Society)

Ferris's tasks were clear. First, he needed to clear the University's debt. With the help of the Dutch merchant Myndert Van Schaick, he began to solicit donations. Ferris proved an excellent fund-raiser and record-keeper. All pledges were accurately recorded, the debt cleared, and by the mid-1860s some six professor-ships were endowed in the amount of $25,000 each. Most of the gifts came from affluent families living in and around Washington Square. This largess allowed faculty salaries to climb from approximately $1,500 in 1864 to approximately $3,000 in 1869. More faculty members could be appointed, too.

ISAAC FERRIS, CHANCELLOR, 1853-1870

Ferris's second task was to bring the University more in line with the original philosophy of the founders, which was to create a "utilitarian" University that would meet the "spirit and wants of our age and country." Ferris leaned heavily on the advice of Professor Draper, who had exhorted the University to give as much attention to the "commercial classes" as to the training of clergy. The new chancellor initiated the creation of the Chemical Laboratory (which later evolved into the School of Practical and Analytical Chemistry), the School of Engineering, and the School of the Arts (later called the School of Design). The School of Practical and Analytical Chemistry was the first department within the University to award a Ph.D. degree on examination, rather than as an honorary degree. This development undoubtedly anticipated the creation of the Graduate School in 1886. Of import, too, was the fact that instruction was now offered in the evening as well as during the day. Thus, this initiative was a precursor to the University's many "night school" programs that would proliferate in later years.

A CITY ON THE MOVE

Less than a dozen blocks from the University Building on Washington Square, Niblo's Garden was the 19th century's "in" spot at Broadway and Prince Street. A saloon, theatre, and hotel complex, it was a popular gathering place for New Yorkers in search of amusement.

Charles Dickens visited New York City and published in 1842 a detailed log of his journey in *American Notes and Pictures from Italy,* in which the burgeoning metropolis was revealed. Broadway, he reported, was a great "promenade and thor-oughfare" that stretched perhaps four miles from the Battery Gardens to a simple country road.

> *Was there ever such a sunny street as this Broadway! The pavement stones are polished with the tread of feet until they shine again; the red bricks of the hous-es might be yet in the dry, hot kilns; and the roofs of those omnibuses look as though, if water were poured on them, they would hiss and smoke, and smell like half-quenched fires. No stint of omnibuses here! Half-a-dozen have gone by within as many minutes. Plenty of hackney cabs and coaches, too; gigs, phaetons, large-wheeled tilburies, and private carriages—rather of a clumsy make, and not very different from the public vehicles, but built for the heavy roads beyond the city pavement.*

EUCLEIAN ROOM IN UNIVERSITY BUILDING, 1890

By the eve of the Civil War, New York City's population had grown to more than half a million. The area around Washington Square echoed the city's mix of splendor and decrepitude. Impressive houses now stood on Washington Square North, up Fifth Avenue, and along Waverly Place. West of the square were homes of the middle class; south of the square, poorer residents lived. And not far to the east were the city's worst slums.

In addition to the growth of the University of the City of New-York, another college, the Free Academy, was founded in 1847 that provided both classics and "practical" subjects for students coming from the expanding public school system. In 1866, the Free Academy became the City College of New York.

Three years later, in 1869, the Normal and High School for the Female Grammar Schools of the City of New York, renamed Hunter College in 1914, was founded. Hunter College, which held its first classes in rented space on Broadway and West Fourth Street, operated a model school where future teachers could gain practical experience.

Critical changes were occurring elsewhere, too. Charles W. Eliot led Harvard in establishing a curriculum based on modern languages, literature, history, philosophy, and science. Princeton and Yale prospered as undergraduate schools. And in 1876, Daniel Coit Gilman organized the Johns Hopkins University in Baltimore, which offered—like German universities—advanced instruction and research opportunities. The example of Johns Hopkins University had a profound impact on the intellectual life of America and stimulated other universities to institute programs of research and graduate education.

ONE CLIFFHANGER AFTER ANOTHER

The history of the university for the first hundred years is studded with one cliff-hanging financial crisis after another. Proposals to close the school were often the order of the day, but always a miracle happened just in time and a few dollars scraped from somewhere staved off disaster for a few more months.

Power and Conflict in the University
by J. Victor Baldridge

Despite the diligent efforts of Chancellor Ferris, financial setbacks continued to plague the University. Clearly, the University had not fulfilled the goals of its founders, which was to educate not only the privileged classes but also the sons of the working classes. The reasons were several. The University's multidenominational charter blocked support from just one church. Unlike Columbia College, with its support from the Anglican Church, the University had no such generous patron. A policy of free tuition instituted in the fall of 1871 and a location in a commercial urban area also undermined the financial stability of the University.

Only a small fraction of city residents attended college—and those who did usually did so outside of New York. This point is enlarged upon by Frusciano and Pettit in *New York University and the City*:

> *And still another factor was the absence of a culture of advanced education in the United States. Anyone, if he tried hard enough, could be a teacher or merchant, and could acquire wealth without education. Minimum schooling only was required to succeed, and so higher education remained chiefly a prerogative of the elites.*

THE UNLUCKY CHANCELLOR

The policy of free tuition was a tactical error—proving the aphorism that no good deed goes unpunished. It was the brainchild of the University's fourth chancellor, Howard Crosby, a Greek scholar and Presbyterian minister, who reasoned that the policy would augment enrollment while allowing the University to better serve New York City and its citizens. Crosby also hoped that the free tuition would burnish the University's image and attract donors. The policy backfired, however, when alienated alumni viewed the now free university as a charity institution unfit for their progeny. Adding to Crosby's woes was the fact that at precisely the moment the University offered free tuition, $110,000 of the University's endowment was lost in a stock venture involving the Jersey Central Railroad.

HOWARD CROSBY,
CHANCELLOR,
1870-1881

THE CRISIS OF 1881

Another low point in the Crosby administration occurred in 1881 when enrollment suddenly plummeted and the University's finances with it. The undergraduate school, which always had sluggish enrollments, foundered even more. Crosby, seeing no other way out of this predicament, advocated closing the undergraduate school. His action caused great consternation among students, faculty, and alumni.

"We're poor, miserably poor. We have no money and can't carry on our work, and that's all there is to it," Crosby bitterly countered. When the hoopla was over, the undergraduate school remained, and Crosby resigned. In fairness to Crosby, his pessimism was not entirely unwarranted. The standards of the University's professional schools, which had once been as high as any in the country, had remained fixed, while those of other universities had advanced. The absence of postgraduate instruction was another problem. Add to that the small size of the undergraduate college, its conservatism, and lack of laboratory equipment. The problems of the University, clearly, were immense.

> *It is probable that the stagnation of the College was due to three main reasons: its presence in the midst of a business section, with no campus or athletic facilities; free tuition; and its lack of sectarian connections.*
>
> New York University 1832-1932
> by Theodore F. Jones

THE DISMAL DECADE

The University's fifth chancellor, the Reverend John Hall, one of the staunchest defenders of the undergraduate college, was unanimously elected by the council on October 24, 1881. Undoubtedly reflecting his ambivalence about his new post, he insisted on the title of acting chancellor rather than chancellor. Born in Ulster in 1829, Rev. Hall had been a teacher and missionary and was at the time the pastor of the Fifth Avenue Presbyterian Church.

Hall's caretaking decade at the University, 1881 to 1891, was fraught, like Crosby's tenure, with financial and enrollment problems. By the early 1880s, the University had shrunk some 50 percent from what it had been just six years earlier. Although the professional schools of law, medicine, and engineering thrived, the undergraduate school continued to struggle, with usually fewer than 100 students registered.

The travails of the University were in stark contrast with what Columbia College had been experiencing. Indeed, just a few decades earlier, in 1860, the University had been an equal partner with Columbia College in higher education. The two universities had shared similar resources and comparable prestige. But

JOHN HALL, D.D.,
CHANCELLOR, 1881-1891

times had changed. At Columbia College, enrollment was up. Finances were excellent. And two dynamic and influential presidents, Seth Low and then Frederick Barnard, were in charge.

In addition to the University's financial and academic concerns, fundamental changes in student attitudes were shifting in ways that would have a profound effect upon the struggling University. When the University began classes in 1832, campus life focused mainly on urban pursuits such as membership in literary and debating societies. For students, the particular joys of athletics were a remote idea—a distant, even unknown pleasure. But the wants of students were changing.

Young men selected their colleges for reasons different from those that moved their grandfathers; and New York University had nothing more to offer in the way of college life than membership in a fraternity and in the Eucleian or Philomathean literary societies, a view of Washington Square from the window of a stuffy classroom, and an occasional frolic across the river to Hoboken. With no dormitories, no campus, and no athletic teams, the University College seemed, to the average youth of 1881, a sorry place.

New York University 1832-1932
by Theodore F. Jones

Thus, the problems at the dawning of the 20th century were many and difficult. Yet, despite obvious concerns and disappointments, the University and its leaders were infused by the spirit of the new age:

New York in 1890 had a population of 1,515,301 and was fundamentally different from the city that had gone to war in 1860. Almost doubled in population, increasing streams of European immigration gave the city the unfinished, exciting quality it still retains. Additional thousands of small business establishments solidified Manhattan's ranking as America's prime manufacturing center. In 1890, New York's 25,399 factories produced 299 different industrial products, goods valued at $777 million.

American Metropolis: A History of New York City
by George J. Lankevich

Buttressed by the Industrial Revolution and the seemingly unending streams of immigration, New York City was the throbbing center of a burgeoning nation. Uptown at 1 West 72nd Street, for example, the Dakota apartment building was being built for wealthy New Yorkers. Many people wondered who would live in such a remote and unfashionable section of the city. On its completion in 1884, however, all 85 apartments were rented without benefit of advertising. The Metropolitan Opera House, seating 3,700, was built in 1883 at Broadway and 39th Street in response to a number of frustrated (and wealthy) New Yorkers who were unable to purchase boxes at the Academy of Music on 14th Street. In 1883, widely acclaimed as the "new eighth wonder of the world," John Augustus Roebling's Brooklyn Bridge connected Manhattan with Brooklyn. And by 1900, New York was the home of 69 of the nation's one hundred largest corporations. A guarded optimism ruled the day—the notions that magnificent ideas could be implemented and great institutions built were palpable.

THE REBIRTH AND ASCENT OF THE UNIVERSITY

Despite financial reverses, the University continued to grow. Indeed, it was from the near collapse during the 1870s and early 1880s that a modern university would spring. Much of the credit for rekindling the University is given to Henry Mitchell MacCracken, who from 1884 to 1910 served first as a professor of philosophy, then as vice chancellor, finally as chancellor.

MacCracken grew up in Oxford, Ohio, the son of a Presbyterian minister. At the age of 17, he graduated from Miami College and went on to the Princeton Seminary. Upon graduation from the Princeton Seminary in 1863, he assumed the pastorate of a church in Columbus, Ohio. MacCracken's worldliness was undoubtedly enhanced when, some four years later, he traveled to Europe and studied in Berlin and Tübingen. There, he learned much about the German system of graduate education.

MacCracken was a true visionary and the strong leader the University needed if it were to survive and flourish. MacCracken was the one who finally implemented the philosophy set forth by the University's founders in the manifesto, "Considerations upon the Expediency and Means of Establishing a University in the City of New-York." He established the uptown Bronx campus at University Heights.

JEROME ALLEN, PH.D., CA. 1890

He oversaw the changing of the University's name to New York University in 1896. He introduced the Graduate School of Arts and Science—one of the first in the country. He supported and strengthened scientific and technical education, created the School of Pedagogy, and organized a business school.

The growth of graduate education offered MacCracken new opportunities to recruit faculty dedicated to advanced instruction. In 1885, Daniel Webster Hering joined the University, where his leadership earned him the title of "father" of the School of Engineering in the Bronx. Abram S. Isaacs, the distinguished Hebrew scholar, joined the University in 1886. Frank Ellington, a well-known clergyman, joined in 1887 to teach comparative religion. Jerome Allen joined the faculty in 1887 and, with MacCracken, pioneered the development of the School of Pedagogy.

At the turn of the century, New York City was undergoing a transformation as its population swelled. People of means moved uptown, leaving the once fashionable and highly desirable neighborhood of Washington Square. "Thus New York University found itself no longer at the center of a charming suburb but instead crammed into a commercial metropolis," wrote J. Victor Baldridge.

In addition, the grand neo-Gothic University Building, once the pride and joy of the fledgling University, was now considered old-fashioned, drafty, and far too small to contain the expanding student body.

The bucolic days of Washington Square were over.

THE AUDACIOUS MOVE
TO THE BRONX

In 1892, Columbia University trustees approached the NYU Council to consider the possibility of a merger between the two institutions. While MacCracken saw clearly the financial advantages of such a partnership (Columbia College operated with a six-figure profit; NYU, with a six-figure deficit), he was reluctant to give up his institution's autonomy. Talks of a merger ended. MacCracken declared,

It has become evident to us that there exists an utter want of mutual desire to unite in any plan of federation. . . . If upon some accounts this separation of work is to be regretted, still there must be essential advantages in our maintaining in this city separate and competing faculties, working on different lines of thought, with differing methods, and with the zeal which friendly rivalry engenders.

New York University 1832-1932
by Theodore F. Jones

With the possibility of a "United Colleges" forever dampened, MacCracken returned to an earlier notion, which was to establish an "uptown" campus. MacCracken searched out a property in the then distant borough of the Bronx known as the Mali Estate. There he relocated the undergraduate college to provide what he considered a more pleasing college milieu than Washington Square's citified campus afforded.

MacCracken hired noted architect Stanford White, a founding partner in the legendary architectural firm of McKim, Mead & White, to design the new campus. White's portfolio includes such urban treasures as the Judson Memorial Church, the Washington Memorial Arch, and the original Madison Square Garden.

The new campus, which had spacious dormitories, generous athletic fields, and multiple classrooms and laboratories, soon had a splendid new library and the Hall of Fame, a graceful veranda studded with sculptures of America's wisest and most valiant.

One of Stanford White's less well known masterpieces is the Gould Library—a memorial to financier Jay Gould—on Fordham Heights in the Bronx. The library's circular reading room is a breathtaking exercise in Beaux Arts panache. Its sixteen rare green Connemara marble columns with gilded Corinthian capitals support an elaborate entablature which carries a balcony studded with classical statues. The sumptuous space is enclosed by a splendidly coffered dome.

STANFORD WHITE, CELEBRATED
ARCHITECT AND DESIGNER OF
GOULD LIBRARY

GOULD LIBRARY

Begun in 1896, the Gould Library became the focal point of what was the undergraduate campus of New York University. The buff-colored brick, limestone, and terra-cotta structure bears a striking resemblance to the Pantheon in Rome....

Stanford White's New York
by David Garrard Lowe

THE "GRIM, GREY PALISADES" BECKON

New York University was poised to fulfill its mission as a school of opportunity for talented and ambitious New Yorkers.

Not long after the University Heights campus was established, a new wave of immigrants—many of them Central and Eastern European Jews—arrived in the United States clinging to one powerful belief. They understood that the future of their sons and daughters in the *Goldine Madina*—the Golden Land—would be direct-

(Courtesy Museum of the City of New York)

IMMIGRANTS AT BATTERY PARK, CA. 1890

ly linked to attaining a university education. New York University, with its reasonable tuition and emerging heritage of academic distinction, provided a good and practical alternative.

By the early part of the 20th century, 280 students were in attendance at the University Heights campus—half in University College and half in the School of Applied Science, which had organized as a separate undergraduate college offering an engineering curriculum. By 1910, nearly 1,000 students were in attendance. Another growth spurt occurred between 1917 and 1918 when the Interborough Subway System expanded into upper Manhattan. There were other train routes to the University Heights campus, but the subway's great attraction was not its swiftness (about 42 minutes from 42nd Street and Broadway to University Heights, no matter what one's mode of travel), but its frequency.

The new uptown campus also acquired an alma mater, "The Palisades," written by Duncan M. Genns and dedicated to his class of 1900.

O grim, grey Palisades, thy shadow / Upon the rippling Hudson falls, / And mellow mingled tints of sunset / Illumine now our classic halls; / While students gather 'round thy altars / With tributes of devotion true, / And mingle merry hearts and voices / In praise of NYU.

These words expressed the feeling that the heart and soul of the University now resided, not in the midst of a pulsating city, but uptown in the pastoral countryside.

Clearly, the move to University Heights had a profound effect upon New York University. Though the traditions of the oldest college within the University— University College—remained intact, the University's curriculum was widened by the addition of new departments of instruction, and students could now substitute other courses of study in place of the old required classical course. The prestige of the new campus was formidable, the faculty was eager to teach uptown, and students enthu-

DORMITORY ROOM,
TURN OF THE CENTURY

SONGBOOK OF NEW
YORK UNIVERSITY, 1915

NEW YORK VNIVERSITY
SONG BOOK

siastically enrolled. The new campus was also physically attractive and uncrowded; the atmosphere was one of a small college within a great university. Favorable comparisons to such stalwart institutions as Columbia, Amherst, Williams, and Yale were often drawn. Indeed, it would be some 60 years before the focus and luster of the University would once again shift back to Washington Square.

TRANSFORMATION AT WASHINGTON SQUARE

At Washington Square, the plan was to demolish the old neo-Gothic University Building and replace it with the Main Building, which remains to this day.

Other important alterations were afoot. In 1900, the School of Commerce, Accounts, and Finance, now called the Leonard N. Stern School of Business, was established as a two-year undergraduate unit at New York University. Located in the new Main Building along with the School of Law and the School of Pedagogy, Stern's classes were offered Monday through Friday from 8 to 10 p.m.

"The timing of class schedules reflected the founders' perception of the student body to be served," wrote Abraham L. Gitlow, former dean of the undergraduate college, in his book *New York University's Stern School of Business: A Centennial Retrospective.*

The concept of collegiate education for business and the "higher accountancy," adds Gitlow, was one that met the needs and wants of the time. Enrollments, hesitant at first, burgeoned. Beginning with 60 students in 1900-1901, enrollment increased to 441 in 1905-1906 and soared to 2,190 in 1913-1914.

While most students commuted to New York University by subway (hence the term "subway university"), early bulletins advertised room and board in the Washington Square area at $6 per week. A hike in the rates to $8 per week occurred in 1913. Rates continued to increase until they stabilized in 1917.

THE ARCH, CA. 1920

In 1914, another milestone was reached—the undergraduate coeducational Washington Square College was founded. Since the turn of the century, women had been attending all the schools of the University except the undergraduate college at the Heights.

Following World War I, still another wave of immigrants settled in New York, and the children of these newcomers brought their intellects and ambitions to New York University and to the public City College. By then, New York University's reputation as an institution that provided opportunities for immigrants and their children was well established.

New York, already known as America's premier city, was admired for its great and bustling port and as the nation's locus of culture, commerce, manufacturing, and finance. Demographically, its dominant ethnic groups had shifted in the late 19th century from German and Irish to Italian and Jewish.

During the early part of the century, both the city and the University expanded in consonance with the rest of the nation. Units added during this period include the Graduate School of Business Administration, which opened its doors in 1916, the School of Retailing in 1921, the College of Dentistry (founded in 1865 as the New York College of Dentistry) in 1925, the Division of General Education in 1934, and the Graduate School of Public Administration and Social Service in 1938. New York University also acquired property on Trinity Place that became the home of the Graduate School of Business Administration. In 1988, it joined the undergraduate business school at Washington Square. Today the two divisions form the Leonard N. Stern School of Business.

DESPITE GROWTH, ANOTHER FINANCIAL DISASTER LOOMS

An immense system of individual schools and divisions was growing; each had its own power and structure, yet each was a fundamental part of the University.

After World War II, another wave of students—this time returning veterans hungry for education and advancement—entered New York University. By 1949, New York University had more than 40,000 students and a faculty of nearly 2,000. Programs flourished as New York University steadily improved as a place of learning. At the same time, New York City's population topped 7.5 million people. Remarkably, the bond between the city and the University that its founders had envisioned had grown stronger despite more than a century of upheaval.

In 1956, under the leadership of Chancellor Henry Townley Heald, the University issued the *New York University Self-Study Final Report,* a 419-page tome examining every element of the institution. The *Report* championed unification of the University rather than continuing the somewhat disengaged alliances of schools, colleges, and institutes that then constituted the University. An important marker for the future, the *Report* presaged the selling of the University Heights campus and rede-

HENRY TOWNLEY HEALD,
CHANCELLOR, 1952-1956

fined the University as an urban entity with strong attachments to the city.

THE TROUBLED '60S

As the 1960s loomed, the issues of civil rights and the war in Vietnam stirred student unrest at NYU and throughout the nation. James McNaughton Hester, at 37 the University's youngest chief administrative officer, shepherded the University through this trying period.

> *A significant tragedy of recent American history is the damage that was done to our colleges and universities by the period of student unrest that began with the Free Speech Movement at Berkeley in 1964 and effectively ended with the week of demonstrations following the invasion of Cambodia in May of 1970. The damage was of many kinds. Public respect and support of higher education was reduced. Because the protests were expressed against what was widely accepted as weaknesses in the nation's civil rights record and war policies, many faculty members were loath to take positions against student demands. Many of them believed the students had good reason to be upset and did not want to seem to defend the status quo. The revolutionary spirit flowed over from civil rights and war issues into matters of curriculum and university governance.*

STUDENT PROTEST, 1968

Some of that spirit was stimulating and healthy; some was empty posturing. Many people had difficulty distinguishing between valid and empty demands, and harmful curricular changes and other dubious arrangements resulted. The education of many students suffered because of disruption of classes and time spent in protest meetings. Much of the time and energy of administrators and faculty members was diverted from education to strategy sessions on how to deal with threats of violence.

This was true of institutions throughout the United States, and it was true of NYU....

Adventure on Washington Square: Being President of New York University, 1962-1975
by James McNaughton Hester

The student disruptions cast a pall over the University, and the once rising record of applications noted in the early 1960s began to decline seriously. By the 1970s, optimism faded as the University faced, yet again, impending financial disaster.

To ease the University's burden, President Hester orchestrated the merger of the School of Engineering and Science with Polytechnic Institute of Brooklyn, both schools founded in 1854, to form Polytechnic Institute of New York, now Polytechnic University. But the most painful and difficult decision was yet to come.

For the University to continue, the beloved University Heights campus in the Bronx had to be sold. The transaction in 1973 unified the University at Washington Square, provided some $40 million to retire the University's debts, and added $32 million to the University's endowment. Wrote Hester,

The sale of the Heights campus was an embittering experience for many of its alumni and current students....Now some of the most ardent devotees of the Heights campus point out that the university is stronger and more coherent focused on Washington Square.

ELMER HOLMES BOBST LIBRARY AND STUDY CENTER VIEWED FROM WASHINGTON SQUARE PARK

A BRIGHT MOMENT

One of the bright moments of the Hester years was the construction of the Elmer Holmes Bobst Library, which Hester considered the "symbol and embodiment of the change in the academic experience at Washington Square."

Before the building of Bobst Library, the University's book storage and reading rooms were dispersed in more than 36 spaces throughout the Main Building and other buildings at Washington Square. People and books were crowded into nooks and crannies; the space was often airless and poorly lit. In fact, so inferior was NYU's library space that many students preferred the New York Public Library.

Philip Johnson, an avant-garde architect, was chosen to design the library. The goal was to add new architecture to Washington Square that would be in harmony with the existing environment. The result was an imposing edifice of red sandstone with an interior that featured a towering 150-foot atrium rimmed by balconies and connecting stairs. A dazzling black-and-white Palladian mosaic main floor greeted the visitor. The effect was at once grand and dramatic.

Opened in 1973, Bobst Library is one of the largest open-stack research libraries in the nation. Of the total NYU Libraries collection of 4.1 million volumes, Bobst now houses more than 2.9 million. A welcome and necessary addition to the burgeoning campus, the library bears the name of its primary patron, pharmaceutical executive Elmer Holmes Bobst.

THE GREAT, MODERN URBAN UNIVERSITY EMERGES

In 1976, at the urging of President John C. Sawhill, the C. F. Mueller Company, a pasta factory owned by the Law Center Foundation in a trust fund, was sold for $115 million. Of the day of the sale, the University's new vice president for academic affairs, L. Jay Oliva, said, "It was perhaps the most historic moment since NYU's founding."

The saga of the C. F. Mueller Company begins in 1947 when the School of Law, led by Dean Arthur Vanderbilt, acquired the company. While this purchase initially involved a substantial risk, Dean Vanderbilt was, to quote a *New Yorker* magazine story about it, "a dean of pluck as well as vision." The risk paid off. The Mueller Company proved to be a profitable investment and helped pay for the building of Vanderbilt Hall, the School's Georgian colonial academic building, dubbed "Noodle Hall," on Washington Square. The income from the Mueller Company also meant that the School of Law had the financial strength to set a course for building one of the nation's finest law schools.

However, as the law school's financial position rose, thanks to the booming earnings of Mueller, NYU—its parent institution—faced hard times with rising deficits and a decline in enrollment. What followed was a decision to sell the Mueller Company and use a portion of the cash settlement to help the University. How the money would be divided between the University and the School of Law was hotly

JOHN C. SAWHILL, PRESIDENT OF THE UNIVERSITY
FROM 1975-1979

debated. The challenge was to resolve this conflict so that both parties benefited.

It is a testament to the people involved, especially to Martin Lipton, a School of Law alumnus and currently chairman of the NYU Board of Trustees, that a final resolution was reached—one that divided the Mueller money in a fashion that helped the University to reduce its deficit and embark on a grand plan to improve the academic quality of all of the University's schools, while at the same time allowing the School of Law to emerge with enough financial support to continue its own academic growth. The key to this resolution was that both parties understood they were bound by a common need—to keep the University sound. A great law school, indeed, any great professional school, could not flourish within a weakened university. This prescience produced a generous and wise compromise between University and School of Law leaders. Everyone benefited.

Still, despite this momentous step, a wrenching, cost-cutting period followed under President Sawhill, a former head of the Federal Energy Administration. An able manager, he had the thankless task of achieving fiscal stability in an atmosphere of declining student enrollment, rising inflation, and governmental cuts in education and research. Regardless of these challenges, the University issued in 1976-1977 its first balanced budget in more than a decade.

Although the University experienced deep fiscal pain during the 1970s, responsible leadership paved the way to better times. Perhaps most important, the fundamental values of the University never wavered. President Sawhill's Goals Statement, stressing the desire to raise academic standards and recruit stellar faculty, was becoming a reality.

In 1979, President Sawhill took a leave of absence and subsequently resigned.

Ivan L. Bennett, Jr., executive vice president for health affairs, provost of the NYU Medical Center, and dean of the School of Medicine and Post-Graduate Medical School, took over as acting president. Bennett continued the work of his predecessors, and by October 14, 1981, the day of John Brademas's inauguration as the University's 13th president, the University was well positioned to ascend the loftiest peaks of higher education.

President Brademas, a Democratic congressman from Indiana for 22 years, was a Washington insider with a passion for the arts (he was instrumental in the creation of the National Endowment for the Arts) and a track record of supporting issues relating to educational institutions. He was also an energetic fund-raiser.

Frusciano and Pettit wrote that President Brademas welcomed the opportunity to provide strong leadership in three ways:

DR. IVAN L. BENNETT, JR., ACTING PRESIDENT OF THE UNIVERSITY FROM 1979-1981

> *First, he would strive to build a deeper sense of community around NYU—enhancing the quality of everyday life for teachers, staff and students. Second, he would maintain the fiscal stability and financial strength of the university and wisely use those resources available to him. Third, he proposed to explore for NYU "new paths to intellectual excellence and public service."*

President John Brademas brought a visible excitement to the University. Indeed, his enthusiasm and devotion were contagious, and world leaders and renowned scholars flocked to the campus as the University's focus began to shift toward a more international view. As President Brademas became a major, nationally recognized spokesperson on issues of higher education, the profile and prestige of the University rose. Transformation was palpable.

In a 1987 speech delivered to the New-York Historical Society, he said:

Forced and painful as was the retrenchment that New York University under-
went in the 1970s, this development has paid valuable dividends in the 1980s.
For NYU today is a major, modern, progressive urban university. It is finan-
cially sound, academically strong, the largest private institution of higher
learning in the nation, and I believe, a university that is clearly on the move.

President Brademas stepped down in 1991 at age 64. His legacy would be the emergence, finally, of NYU as the great modern urban university.

JOHN BRADEMAS, PRESIDENT OF THE UNIVERSITY FROM 1981-1991

(Photo credit: Lou Manna)

"The Golden Age"

L. Jay Oliva became president of NYU on November 21, 1991. In his inaugural address, President Oliva graciously tipped his hat to all those who preceded him:

> *I stand here, therefore, on the shoulders of these giants. Few universities have kept their sights so sharply focused or enjoyed such superb leadership—it is one of the true keys to our success.*

From the beginning, he has been a different kind of leader. Unlike any other NYU president, he alone emerged from the ranks of NYU faculty to become president. Beginning in 1960 as an instructor in Russian history at the University Heights campus, he has been a witness to and active participant in the sweeping changes of the last four decades.

"A hands-on approach" is the phrase most often heard to describe President Oliva's philosophy of leadership. His interests include a genuine love of teaching and a day-to-day involvement in the life of the University and the city. He participates actively in campus life: working with students on Village Improvement Day to clean up Washington Square Park, acting in a student production of *Brigadoon,* and teaching Russian history. He is an ardent fan of NYU's basketball teams, which he roots for with the same level of devotion that others bestow on the New York Knicks. He also has been a forceful advocate for restoring a sensible balance between collegiate athletics and scholarship, has written extensively on this topic, and was a founder of the University Athletic Association, which links NYU to the major private research universities in the nation.

One of President Oliva's principal interests has been to create a critical link to the international community. The expression of this internationalism may be viewed in a multitude of ways.

> *We now have the largest number of international students affiliated with any American university—nearly 5,000. The hub of our international study is La Pietra, the breath-taking Tuscan estate with its endowment and magnificent art collection left to NYU by Sir Harold Acton. La Pietra is also a locus for global faculty inquiry and an anchor for our worldwide conferences.*
>
> *In addition, during the past decade we significantly enlarged our global vision by creating an alliance of nearly 50 major metropolitan universities from around the world in the League of World Universities, an organization committed to addressing issues central to the millennium.*
>
> —L. Jay Oliva

L. Jay Oliva, Dean of University College, September 4, 1970

A scholar, teacher, administrator, and visionary—President Oliva has skillfully guided the University through a decade of unprecedented growth and innovation unmatched by any other institution of higher education in the land.

With the painful period of retrenchment in the past, President Oliva was able to concentrate on building a superb faculty, attracting the brightest scholars, globalizing the University, revitalizing and reshaping the campus, strengthening community service, and completing a record-breaking billion-dollar campaign. So spectacularly successful has been his tenure that the period of the 1990s is now referred to as "The Golden Age" of NYU.

A SHARED DESTINY

As the city has achieved its destiny, so has New York University. From its humble beginnings in rented quarters in lower Manhattan, the founders could hardly have imagined the transformation into the nation's largest private university. While the University's first Commencement in 1833 celebrated the graduation of only three students, the Class of 2000 numbered some 8,000 students.

As a new century dawns, one wonders: What would the founders of New York

THE STORY OF NYU,
"IN FIRST RANK"
NEW YORK TIMES,
MARCH 20, 1995

*Copyright © 1995 by the
New York Times Company.
Reprinted by permission.*

University think of the modern rendering of their great notion? Could they have, even in their wildest dreams, envisioned a University of such complexity, of such spirit, of such immense reach and resource, while still fulfilling the destiny envisioned by its founders?

More than likely, they would be amazed and proud to see how much their dream has been realized, especially considering the numerous travails New York University has weathered.

The reasons for this "Miracle on Washington Square" are complicated and many. Without question, however, the University's recent successes rest in great part on the shoulders of the able leaders who have led the University during the past 40 years. These men and women, with a firm and focused grasp on the University's direction, had the courage to make critical, even painful, choices in the quest for a secure and healthy future.

To mark the millennium and the University's many achievements, this volume provides a pictorial panorama of the way we were, the way we are, and the way we hope to be. The real story is in the faces. Look at them. Study them. The photographs provide a rich panoply, a document, a testament that demonstrates the University's contributions, from its very inception, to the advancement of knowledge.

In the beginning, the University's charter proposed the birth of an educational institution that urged educating young men in modern languages, history, political economy, and natural science so that they might become merchants, mechanics, farmers, manufacturers, architects, and civil engineers—that is, productive members of society. While the notion of a university located in the city and dedicated to the academic aspirations of the people dwelling in the city does not seem startling to us now, it was a visionary idea in its day.

From the firm resolve of the founders to open the University's doors to the progeny of working Americans and the continuing stream of immigrants to the inevitable realization of the global University, from the invention of Samuel F. B. Morse's telegraph to the computer work of scientists at the Courant Institute of Mathematical Sciences . . . from Sidney Hook's philosophy lectures to Wassily Leontief's economic models . . . from the pioneering studies in physical rehabilitation medicine of Howard Rusk to Victor and Ruth Nussenzweig's search for a malaria vaccine . . . from *Sunrise Semester* to the *Virtual College* . . . from legendary football coach Chick Meehan's numerous victories to the 1997 NCAA Division III Women's Basketball Championship . . . from Thomas Wolfe's, E. L. Doctorow's, and Frank McCourt's novels to Galway Kinnell's and Sharon Olds's poetry . . . from Spike Lee's and Martin Scorsese's films to the artistry of Romare Beardon . . . from the first landmark benevolence of the Gould family to the magnificent contemporary philanthropy of the Kimmel, Skirball, Stern, and Tisch families, New York University has demonstrated a remarkable persistence of ambition. Indeed, recent history suggests that the University has had an almost unprecedented gift for managing limited resources and making courageous choices while nurturing good and supportive friends.

As the University meets the 21st century, it can take great satisfaction in its history, in its many memories, and in the knowledge that its future is inexorably linked to three critical entities. For it is New York University and New York City, New York University and the nation, New York University and the world.

TIFFANY TORCH,
GIFT OF
HELEN MILLER GOULD

UNIVERSITY OF THE CITY OF NEW-YORK.

THE Annual Course of Instruction in the Institution, will commence on Monday, the 3d of October, under the direction of the following Professors.

REV. JAMES M. MATHEWS, D. D., CHANCELLOR.

DAVID B. DOUGLASS, Professor of Civil Engineering and Architecture.
S. F. B. MORSE, Professor of the Literature of the Arts of Design.
REV. HENRY P. TAPPAN, Professor of Intellectual and Moral Philosophy and Belles-Lettres.
ROBERT B. PATTON, Professor of Greek Language and Literature.
REV. JOHN PROUDFIT, Professor of Latin Language and Literature.
CHARLES L. PARMENTIER, Professor of French Language and Literature.
LORENZO L. DA PONTE, Professor of Italian Language and Literature.
MIGUEL CABRERA DE NEVARES, Professor of Spanish Language and Literature.
CHARLES RABADAN, Associate Professor of do.
ISAAC NORDHEIMER, Acting Professor of German Language and Literature.
REV. GEORGE BUSH, Professor of Hebrew, and Oriental Languages and Literature.
CHARLES W. HACKLEY, Professor of Mathematics.
WILLIAM A. NORTON, Acting Professor of Natural Philosophy and Astronomy.
LEWIS C. BECK, M. D., Professor of Chemistry and Botany.
HON. B. F. BUTLER, Professor of Law, and Principal of the Law Faculty.*
L. D. GALE, M. D., Professor of Geology and Mineralogy.
ISAAC NORDHEIMER, Professor of Arabic, Syriac, Persian, and Ethiopic.
REV. CYRUS MASON, Professor of the Evidences of Revealed Religion.

* The other Professors in the Law Faculty will be appointed within a few weeks; and the course of legal instruction will be commenced simultaneously by Mr. Butler and the other Professors early in May, 1837.

SCHEDULE OF THE RECITATIONS, AND OTHER EXERCISES, DURING THE WEEK.—(Prayers in the Chapel at half past nine o'clock A. M.)

HOURS.	MONDAY.	TUESDAY.	WEDNESDAY.	THURSDAY.	FRIDAY.	SAT.
From 10 to 11 A. M.	Latin. Belles-lettres. Natural Philosophy. Architecture and Civil Engineering. * Geology and Mineralogy.	Latin. Belles-lettres. Natural Philosophy. Greek. Architecture and Civil Engineering. Geology & Mineralogy	Latin. Belles-lettres. Natural Philosophy. Chemistry. Architecture and Civil Engineering. Geology & Mineralogy	Latin. Belles-lettres. Natural Philosophy. Chemistry. Architecture and Civil Engineering. Geology & Mineralogy	Latin. Belles-lettres. Natural Philosophy. Chemistry. Architecture and Civil Engineering. Geology & Mineralogy	Declamation in the Chapel.
From 11 to 12 A. M.	Mathematics. Latin. Greek. Psychology and Moral Philosophy.	Mathematics. Greek. Latin. Psychology and Moral Philosophy.	Mathematics. Greek. Latin. Psychology and Moral Philosophy.	Mathematics. Greek. Latin. Psychology and Moral Philosophy.	Mathematics. Greek. Latin. Psychology and Moral Philosophy.	
From 12 to 1 P. M.	Greek. Mathematics. Logic. Philosophy of Rhetoric and Criticism. Natural Philosophy.	Greek. Mathematics. Logic. Philosophy of Rhetoric and Criticism. Chemistry.	Greek. Mathematics. Logic. Philosophy of Rhetoric and Criticism Natural Philosophy.	Greek. Mathematics. Logic. Philosophy of Rhetoric and Criticism. Chemistry.	Greek. Mathematics. Logic. Philosophy of Rhetoric and Criticism. Latin.	
From 1 to 2 P. M.	Evidences of Revealed Religion. Hebrew. New Testament as a Classic. Elementary Drawing.	Belles-lettres. Chaldaic and Syriac.	Evidences of Revealed Religion. Hebrew. Elementary Drawing.	Belles-lettres. Chaldaic and Syriac.	Evidences of Revealed Religion. Hebrew. Elementary Drawing.	
From 2 to 3 P. M.	Rabinical Hebrew.				Rabinical Hebrew.	
From 4 to 5 P. M.	Arabic.	Hebrew.	Hebrew.	Hebrew.	Arabic.	
From 7 to 8 P. M.	Persian.		Sanscrit.	Persian.	Sanscrit.	

* The class in Geology will commence in April.

NOTE.—There are also classes in French, Spanish, Italian and German, taught at such hours as will be found most convenient to the students and professors.

H
ow does New York University define itself? By the strengths of its academic programs. By the achievements of its students, alumni, and faculty. By the generosity of its patrons. By its linkages to the great city of New York, to the nation, and to the world. By fulfilling the hopes and dreams of its founders. By making the world a better place.

⸎

One purpose in assembling a pictorial history is to reveal the defining moments in the life of the University in which fateful decisions were made and great achievements attained. These are the moments that have inevitably directed the course of future events and that have had a lasting impact on the institution.

Opposite: ACADEMIC SCHEDULE, CA. 1836

It is impossible to chronicle every defining moment in a history as long and noble as the University's. The men and women pictured in this chapter—and in this book—represent literally hundreds of thousands of people who are bound to New York University and its magnificent tradition and expanding legacy.

CHANCELLORS AND PRESIDENTS OF NEW YORK UNIVERSITY*

Today New York University stands as the largest private university in the United States. The University, which includes 13 schools and colleges, occupies five major centers in Manhattan. NYU also operates branch campus and research programs in other parts of the United States, as well as study abroad programs in more than 20 countries.

1831-1839
James Melanchthon Mathews

1839-1850
Theodore Frelinghuysen

1850-1853
Faculty and Council jointly
administered the University

1853-1870
Isaac Ferris

1870-1881
Howard Crosby

1881-1891
John Hall

1891-1910
Henry Mitchell MacCracken

1910-1911
John Henry MacCracken,
Syndic, Acting Chancellor

1911-1933
Elmer Ellsworth Brown

1933-1951
Harry Woodburn Chase

1951-1952
James Loomis Madden,
Acting Chancellor

1952-1956
Henry Townley Heald

1956-1962
Carroll Vincent Newsom

1962-1975
James McNaughton Hester

1975-1980
John Crittenden Sawhill

1979-1981
Ivan Loveridge Bennett, Jr.,
Acting President

1981-1991
John Brademas

1991-
L. Jay Oliva

* In 1956, based on the *New York University Self-Study Final Report,* the office of president was created as the chief administrative post of the University, with the office of chancellor retained as chief academic officer. Beginning with Carroll V. Newsom, the title of president is used for the chief administrative officer.

Schools, Colleges, and Institutes of New York University

~

1832
College of Arts
and Science

1835
School of Law

1841
School of Medicine

1865
College of Dentistry

1886
Graduate School of Arts
and Science

1890
School of Education

1900
Leonard N. Stern
School of Business

1933
Institute of Fine Arts

1934
Courant Institute of
Mathematical Sciences

1934
School of Continuing
and Professional Studies

1938
Robert F. Wagner Graduate
School of Public Service

1960
Shirley M. Ehrenkranz
School of Social Work

1965
Tisch School of the Arts

1972
Gallatin School of
Individualized Study

Early Seal showing the Old University Building
(above)

The founders issued a manifesto entitled "Considerations upon the Expediency and Means of Establishing a University in the City of New-York" on January 6, 1830. This document proclaimed the urgency of educating young men to become productive members of society. Undoubtedly struck by the critical links between the great European universities and their cities, the founders chose to name the new institution, The University of the City of New-York. The University's original Latin motto *Perstando et praestando utilati,* "striving and excelling in useful pursuits," stressed the fledgling institution's utilitarian focus.

So many institutions keep their founding purposes as mementos; we keep ours as our contemporary and guiding themes.

—L. Jay Oliva, President

UNIVERSITY OF THE CITY OF NEW-YORK
(Above)

The University Building at Washington Square, New York University's first permanent home, was the site of many early innovations. Such illustrious professors as Samuel F. B. Morse, John William Draper, and Daniel Webster Hering, working diligently and brilliantly in that great white marble structure, forever secured the University's position in the forefront of American scientific achievement.

The new building, designed by the architectural firm of Town, Davis, and Dakin, sat across from Washington Square Park, which had recently been converted from a burial ground and open field into a military parade ground and pastoral public park. It was an immense neo-Gothic building located on the northeast corner of Washington Square.

An Englishman led unexpectedly, by moonlight, through Washington Square might, at first view of the University, imagine himself approaching King's, or Christ, or either of several other colleges at Cambridge or Oxford. . . . Let no one visit New York without a visit to this building.

—The New York American

SAMUEL F. B. MORSE
(Right)

While returning from Europe in 1832, Samuel F. B. Morse, the inventor of the telegraph and Morse code, took part in a shipboard conversation that stirred his scientific imagination. "If the presence of electricity can be made visible in any part of the circuit, I see no reason why intelligence may not be transmitted instantaneously by electricity," said Morse. Shortly thereafter, Morse took up residence in the old University Building and began the revolutionary design of an electric telegraph system. Although Morse was an accomplished artist and held the title of professor of sculpture and painting at the University, science was a major concern.

(Collection of the New-York Historical Society)

ALLEGORICAL LANDSCAPE OF NEW YORK UNIVERSITY, BY SAMUEL F. B. MORSE, 1835-1836

(Above)

Samuel F .B. Morse is remembered today as the inventor of the telegraph. Few people know that he also was an artist of national stature, an acclaimed portraitist, art theorist, and a founder and first president of the National Academy of Design.

Morse's last few works were among his best. In 1835 he began a fantastic Allegorical Landscape of New York University, *a work that coincided with his appointment as that fledgling school's first Professor in the Literature of the Arts of Design. The idea of painting a heroic picture of an educational institution was as daring iconographically as the House of Representatives and the Louvre. And like those previous works, Morse wanted to paint an ideal image of his subject.*

Samuel F. B. Morse
Essays by Paul J. Staiti and Gary A. Reynolds, Grey Art Gallery and Study Center, New York University

ART STUDIO IN THE OLD UNIVERSITY BUILDING, CA. 1890

(Left)

Samuel F. B. Morse and Winslow Homer were among the many artists who honed their craft in art studios in the old University Building.

JOHN W. DRAPER
(Right)

Samuel F. B. Morse's early telegraph device was powered by a chemical battery designed by John William Draper, one of NYU's most distinguished scientists. Draper served as the University's professor of analytical chemistry from 1838 until his death in 1882. His experiments in light reactive chemistry helped him refine French daguerreotype techniques and cut required exposure times from 45 minutes down to 50 seconds. This advance spurred the creation of practical figurative photography.

DOROTHY CATHERINE DRAPER
(Above)

Draper took perhaps the first portrait of a human face taken in the United States on the roof of the University Building in June 1839. The portrait was of his sister, Dorothy. To achieve the desired resolution, her face was caked in flour. Thus, Dorothy Catherine Draper wore the first application of "screen" makeup.

REPLICA OF MORSE'S EARLY TELEGRAPHIC DEVICE
(Right)

(Courtesy Smithsonian Institution)

MEDICAL FACULTY OF THE UNIVERSITY OF NEW YORK
AND THE FOUNDERS OF THE MEDICAL DEPARTMENT

MEDICAL DEPARTMENT

Undoubtedly one reason the Medical Department, which was established in 1841, so rapidly succeeded was its ability to provide students the critical opportunity of legally dissecting the human body.

In fact, the medical faculty, led by Dr. Martyn Paine, fought for and won legalization of dissection in New York State, through passage of the "Bone Bill" in 1854.

Medical students came from all over the United States—many from the southern states, as well as from the entire Atlantic coast, a few from Kentucky, Illinois, Missouri, and even Canada and the West Indies. One basis of the appeal of medical instruction in New York City was the availability here of bodies for dissection. It boasted that 'no city in the Union furnishes the same supply of the material for the study of Practical Anatomy as the City of New York.'

"A University for Its Times— The Formative Years: 1830-1870" by Bayrd Still

THE PRINCE OF WALES
(Left)

The Prince of Wales *(seventh from right)* in his suite at the Fifth Avenue Hotel the morning after his visit to the University. The photograph was probably taken by Matthew Brady.

The visit of the Prince of Wales to the halls of the University on October 12, 1860, was a notable highpoint. The 19-year-old bachelor prince, using one of his official titles, the Baron of Renfrew, engaged a number of eager ladies at a party and met with Professors Morse and Draper. The visit of the Prince of Wales signaled a long list of heads of state and dignitaries who would visit the University. Indeed, the stream of visitors was particularly strong in the 1980s and 1990s. Presidents John Brademas and L. Jay Oliva were both instrumental in the globalization of the University. Just a few of the memorable visitors include the late King Hussein of Jordan, President of Ireland Mary Robinson, President Bill Clinton, Vice President Albert Gore, First Lady Hillary Rodham Clinton, Prime Minister Tony Blair, Prime Minister Boris Yeltsin, King Juan Carlos I of Spain, and many, many others.

HENRY M. MACCRACKEN
(Left)

Henry Mitchell MacCracken served the University for 26 years—from 1884 to 1910—first as a professor of philosophy, then as vice chancellor, and finally as chancellor. MacCracken was a man of action, vision, and dedication—the leader who would implement the philosophy set forth by the University's founders in the manifesto, "Considerations Upon the Expediency and Means of Establishing a University in the City of New-York." His achievements include introducing, in 1886, one of the first graduate schools of arts and sciences in the United States; strengthening the scientific and technical curriculum; opening the School of Pedagogy—now the School of Education—which was one of the first in the nation to provide graduate training for school teachers; organizing the School of Commerce, Accounts, and Finance—now the Leonard N. Stern School of Business—the largest institution of its kind in the country; and establishing an extramural division, which was a precursor of today's School of Continuing and Professional Studies.

DINER & SOUPER
ALA GARTE.

RESTAURANT

GEO. EHRET'S
LAGER BEER.

WASHINGTON SQUARE AT THE TURN OF THE CENTURY
(Above)

The 60 years after the University's founding saw great changes in New York City. The population swelled to more than two million people, and the area around the great neo-Gothic University Building and Washington Square was now a crowded neighborhood teeming with tradesmen. Although pigs no longer roamed freely, most of the upper-class mercantile and banking families who had resided on the north side of Washington Square in stately row houses had moved uptown. A *New York Herald* poll revealed that in 1846 only 20 of the city's richest 200 men lived above 14th Street. By 1851, 100 of them did. This was a blow to the neighborhood. It was also a blow to the University because it had relied heavily through its for- mative years on the generosity of these families. Thus, the tenor of the neighborhood—struggling to cope with the influx of immigrants and the rise of crime and poverty—discouraged students and faculty alike.

JULIA WILSON
(Above)

The year 1890-1891 was a stellar time for women at NYU as it marked the admission of female students into the professional and graduate schools. In 1890 three women were also admitted to the University's School of Law. The School of Law was one of the first in the nation to admit women, and Rose Levere, Agnes Mulligan, and Julia Wilson were graduated in 1892. Also in 1892, Mary B. Dennis became New York University's first woman to receive a Ph.D. from the Graduate School of Arts and Science. Dennis's dissertation was entitled "Science Teaching in the Elementary Schools."

(Courtesy New York County Lawyers Association)

HELEN MILLER GOULD
(Above)

The creation of the new University Heights campus required money—a lot of money. Chancellor Henry Mitchell MacCracken, an ordained minister and professor of philosophy, was also an entrepreneur. In 1892, MacCracken approached railroad tycoon Jay Gould in the hopes of gaining financial support for his plan to build an uptown campus. Gould offered a modest $25,000 gift and then unexpectedly died, quashing MacCracken's dream of obtaining more Gould largess. All was not lost, however, when Gould's daughter, Helen Miller Gould, gave New York University $2 million in memory of her father. The money was largely used to help build the University Heights campus. The landmark gift by the Gould family represented the first immense philanthropy to New York University from one of America's barons of industry. Much later, in 1954, the Gould family would give another $2.5 million to New York University, this time to construct a student center at the University Heights campus.

THE UNIVERSITY HEIGHTS CAMPUS AT THE TURN OF THE CENTURY
(Below)

Chancellor Henry Mitchell MacCracken moved the undergraduate college to the pastoral University Heights campus in the Bronx. At the time, the Bronx was a rural suburb with ample space for residence halls, laboratories, libraries, recreation, and athletics.

WATCHING A FOOTBALL GAME, 1908
(Right)

Under the leadership of Henry Mitchell MacCracken, the University's chancellor from 1891 through 1910, NYU helped change the face of college athletics. After a tragic football accident in 1905, MacCracken declared the game needed regulation for the safety of the players. Heeding his call, the

Intercollegiate Athletic Association of the United States, consisting of 65 colleges, formed in December 1905 to regulate football. Five years later, the organization changed its name to the National Collegiate Athletic Association. Today, the NCAA governs the rules and regulations of almost all collegiate sports.

UNIVERSITY HEIGHTS CAMPUS, CA. 1918

(Above)
A group of students posed in front of the Hall of Fame, a colonnade of sculptures celebrating noted Americans.

GOVERNOR FRANKLIN DELANO ROOSEVELT SPEAKS

(Press release, right)
Governor Franklin Delano Roosevelt, at a ceremony marking the centennial of the University, said:

What impresses me most is that New York University is a positive and actual influence upon the lives of such a huge body of students. It has been and is a tremendous factor in educating not just the rich and leisure class but young people in practically every walk of life. In this it fits in with the true ideal of education in a democracy.

The final aim—the giving of honorable direction to the destinies of a great city—has been carried out as exemplified by the very large number of public-spirited citizens who, graduating from New York University, have taken a useful part in shaping the destinies and in aiding the public service of the City.

NEW YORK UNIVERSITY

Release Date

Bureau of Public Information
Alvin C. Busse, Director
Washington Square East, New York
Telephone § § Spring 9300

TUESDAY
APRIL 28, 1931.

31-4-165

For Radio Editors:-

    Governor Franklin D. Roosevelt, President James Rowland Angell of Yale University and Chancellor Elmer Ellsworth Brown of New York University are among the speakers on the program of the Charter Day Dinner of New York University to be broadcast this evening (Tuesday) from 9:45 to 10:45 over Station WOR.

    The dinner will commemorate the granting of a charter to the University one hundred years ago and will be the first of a series of educational and historical events which will extend over a year.

    Other speakers at the dinner will be Ogden L. Mills, under-secretary of the Treasury; Joseph M. Proskauer, former Justice of the Appellate Division of the Supreme Court of New York; and Dr. Frank P. Graves, president of the University of the State of New York and State Commissioner of Education.

    The New York University Glee Club, which recently won first place in the National Intercollegiate Glee Club Contest and the Beaux Arts stringed trio, will provide music for the dinner.

---0---

WASHINGTON SQUARE, CA. 1942

(Left)

During World War II, the University patriotically assisted the war effort, as it had in World War I. Indeed, military personnel—training and studying—were familiar sights on both the Bronx and Washington Square campuses.

Following World War II, yet one more wave of new students entered NYU. These were the returning veterans who were eager for education and advancement. By 1949, NYU, expanding at a heady pace, had more than 40,000 students, some 2,000 faculty, an array of flourishing programs, and a growing reputation.

Today, the expansion continues. Currently, the University has some 50,000 students (some 17,558 undergraduates, 19,051 graduate and professional students, and 13,804 students in noncredit programs), more than 3,000 faculty, and 14 schools and colleges occupying six major centers in Manhattan.

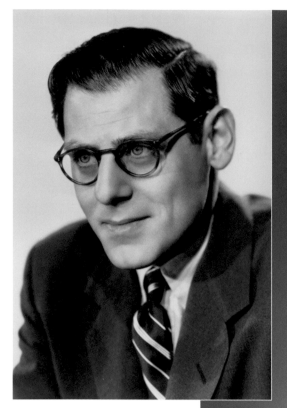

FLOYD ZULLI, JR.
(Above)

Sunrise Semester, the CBS-TV Emmy Award-winning television series produced in association with NYU, was first broadcast on September 23, 1957, from 6:30 to 7 a.m. Historians agree that *Sunrise Semester's* debut marked a milestone in higher education and television history. Dr. Floyd Zulli, Jr., an assistant professor of romance languages at the College of Arts and Science, taught the first course for academic credit. The 3-point course, Comparative Literature 10, studied the development of the novel from Stendhal's *The Red and the Black* to Hemingway's *The Sun Also Rises.* To get college credit, 177 students paid $25 a point. More than 700 students applied and some 120,000 others followed the course—without credit—on television. *Sunrise Semester* started as an experiment, but its immediate acceptance by the public prompted the University and CBS to extend this groundbreaking educational venture. The series ran for almost 25 years. It heralded the era of distance learning, solidified a creative partnership between CBS and NYU, and reinforced the power of television as a medium to educate.

JAMES M. HESTER
(Above)

James McNaughton Hester, a former Rhodes scholar, assumed the mantle of NYU's presidency in 1962 at the age of only 37. Although his tenure was marked by financial and social crises, he will be remembered for his prescient decision to sell the beloved University Heights campus in order to restore NYU's exhausted endowment. Hester understood that the future of NYU was at Washington Square. He believed that consolidation would strengthen the foundation of the University and thus prepare it for the coming task of building a great urban research university.

DR. SAUL J. FARBER

(Left)

Saul J. Farber, M.D., the Frederick H. King Professor of Internal Medicine and former dean of the NYU School of Medicine, embodies the University's highest traditions of medical research, education, and patient care. More than any other single individual, Dr. Farber forged the modern character of the NYU School of Medicine and helped build the Medical Center into a world-class institution.

Since 1948, Dr. Farber has been a distinguished member of the faculty in the Department of Medicine at NYU School of Medicine and has served as its chairman since 1966—the longest tenure of any chairman of medicine in the country. Dr. Farber has also served since 1966 as director of medicine at Bellevue and University (now Tisch) Hospitals. In 1987, Dr. Farber was named dean of the School of Medicine and provost of NYU Medical Center, posts from which he retired in 1997.

Dr. Farber's many accomplishments include creation of the integrated medical team concept and leadership in the building of the Skirball Institute of Biomolecular Medicine, thereby assuring the future of biomedical research at the School of Medicine. He also pioneered research on kidney and electrolyte metabolism and hypertension as well as studies that first demonstrated the link between changes in heart and kidney function in patients with congestive heart failure. In addition, a groundbreaking study—the first to use the balloon catheter he developed—paved the way for cardiac catheterization procedures that have saved and improved countless lives.

(Courtesy NYU Medical Center Archives)

THE ELMER HOLMES BOBST LIBRARY

(Below, left to right: NYU President James M. Hester; George Murphy, chairman of the NYU Board of Trustees; and Elmer H. Bobst, pharmaceutical pioneer) The Elmer Holmes Bobst Library and Study Center opened in September 1973. It assembled for the first time in one place the University's enormous library and research collections. Designed by architect Philip Johnson, Bobst Library lent a physical identity and locus to the Washington Square campus.

The Bobst Library was the major bricks-and-mortar achievement of my presidency. . . . It was the symbol and embodiment of the change in the academic experience at Washington Square that it was my task to bring about.

Adventure on Washington Square,
James McNaughton Hester

JOHN C. SAWHILL

(Above)

John C. Sawhill, a former head of the Federal Energy Administration, succeeded James M. Hester as president in 1975 and served until 1980. Sawhill is remembered as a cost-cutting leader who tirelessly worked to stabilize NYU's financial condition, thus positioning the University's development into one of the world's great urban research institutions.

JOHN BRADEMAS

(Left)

John Brademas, a Democratic congressman from Indiana for 22 years, served New York University as its 13th president.

During Dr. Brademas's service as president, more than $800 million was raised, with annual fund-raising soaring from $29 million in 1980-1981 to $123 million in 1989-1990. As a result, NYU built new facilities for student housing, research, teaching, and recreation. Of great importance, too, was a significant improvement during this period in the quality of NYU's student body as well as a rise in applications from across the nation and the world.

In becoming its 13th president in 1981, I committed myself to moving New York University into the front ranks of American research universities by building on our strengths in the visual and performing arts, the humanities, business and law, and bolstering our programs in the sciences, medicine and international studies. I believe that we have made great progress.

— "New York: University in the City," an address delivered by Dr. John Brademas to the New-York Historical Society on March 11, 1987.

C. F. MUELLER COMPANY

(Above)

1976—Financial difficulties, which coincided with the University's departure from the University Heights campus, were eased by the sale of the C. F. Mueller Company for $115 million. The Law Center Foundation had received ownership of the pasta company through a trust fund. The sale, for both the School of Law and the University at large, provided a life-saving transfusion of money. Though painful, the University's forced withdrawal from University Heights and the subsequent retrenchment that followed was necessary if the University was to fulfill its destiny as a major, modern, and progressive institution.

(Photo credit: Bob Handelman)

LAURENCE A. TISCH

Laurence A. Tisch was named chairman of New York University's Board of Trustees in 1978 and served with distinction for two decades. Tisch's years as chairman were marked by some of the most important changes in the University, most notably its metamorphosis from a regional university into a prestigious national research institution.

During his tenure, the University raised some $1.8 billion; saw the reconsolidation of the College of Arts and Science at Washington Square; endowed some 144 faculty chairs; saw freshman applications nearly quadruple; achieved records for average freshman SATs and acceptance rates; increased student housing nine-fold; renovated and constructed substantial new classroom, laboratory, residential, and other academic space; established the Center for Neural Science and the Skirball Institute of Biomolecular Medicine; relocated the Stern School of Business to Washington Square; constructed new quarters for the Tisch School of the Arts; founded the Bronfman Center for Jewish Student Life; and established Spanish, Irish, and Italian centers for international culture, among other undertakings.

"Laurence Tisch's time on the board, as member and chairman, encompasses what is probably the most profoundly important period for this University since its founding more than a century-and-a-half ago," said NYU president Dr. L. Jay Oliva at the time of Tisch's resignation. "The prestigious University we have now, this research institution that attracts scholars and students from throughout the world, is in large measure attributable to Larry Tisch's courage, steadfastness, foresight, dedication, and belief in his city and his alma mater."

Laurence A. Tisch, cochairman and CEO of the Loews Corporation and CEO of CAN Financial Corporation, graduated from New York University in 1942.

(Photo credit: Jon Roemer)

L. JAY OLIVA AT HIS 1991 INAUGURATION

New York University celebrated the inauguration of its 14th president, Dr. L. Jay Oliva, in 1991. Dr. Oliva, who has spent four decades at NYU, is the first president in the long history of the University to emerge from the faculty corps. In 1960, he joined NYU as an instructor in Russian history and attained the rank of full professor in 1969. He later served as dean, vice president, provost, and chancellor.

Dr. Oliva is largely credited with the transformation of the University in only a decade from what many regarded as a "safety school" into one of the world's premier research universities.

He also expanded the boundaries of the University. Believing that the University's future strength lay beyond its borders, he championed the notion of the global university in his 1991 inaugural address when he announced the formation of the League of World Universities. The League, which brings together the rectors and presidents of some 60 great urban universities from five continents, has matured into a major initiative. It has united the great universities of the world which, though separated by thousands of miles, are now bound by a common vision and purpose: the redefining of the role of a modern university in the life of a modern city.

In his inaugural address, Dr. Oliva shared personal thoughts of his professional life.

Thirty-two years is a long time in one place. Someone once told me that if you seek satisfaction in life, attach yourself to an institution which is noble in its essence, and live its life to the last. This University that I love—you all—have given me that chance—to share a lifetime with my faculty colleagues—turning my mind ever to the historical forces that fascinate me still—working to shape the institution with a staff of incredible virtues—and, in truth, most of all, teaching and learning with students who have defined my life—now some ten thousand in all over the years, and here gathered representatives of all those classes since 1960 to share this day with me.

(Photo credit: Ken Levinson)

SIR HAROLD ACTON AT VILLA LA PIETRA

(Left)

Villa La Pietra, a 57-acre Florentine estate with five villas, olive groves, and formal gardens, was bequeathed to New York University by Sir Harold Acton in 1994. His bequest also included his substantial art collection and an endowment.

NYU Villa La Pietra is the centerpiece of the University's study abroad program. A growing number of NYU students travel to La Pietra each year to study Italian language and culture and to take courses at the University of Florence. In addition, La Pietra is used by the academic departments of the University for a variety of scholarly conferences, colloquia, and symposia. At this juncture, the University is developing plans for the renovation of several of the villas and a master plan for the restoration of the formal gardens, considered among the finest English-Italian gardens in the world.

I did not have to look far to discover beauty, nor was there any need for me to rove beyond our garden gates

Memoirs of an Aesthete
by Harold Acton

BILLION DOLLAR CAMPAIGN GALA

(Left to right: President Emeritus John Brademas, Senior Vice President for External Affairs Naomi Levine and President Oliva at the Billion Dollar Campaign Gala)

In 1985, NYU announced a 15-year campaign to raise $1 billion by the year 2000. NYU, blessed with strong leaders who set specific goals and offered an outstanding product, formally marked the successful completion of its Billion Dollar Campaign (five years early) on March 15, 1995, at a gala celebration. Mrs. Levine led the campaign.

(Photo credit: Andrea Mohin/NYT Pictures)

IOANA DUMITRIU
(Above)

In 1997, Ioana Dumitriu, an NYU student from Romania, became the first woman ever to win the William Lowell Putnam Mathematical Prize, considered the Olympics of mathematics.

THE NCAA DIVISION III CHAMPIONS
(Right)

The NYU women's basketball team, led by Violet Marsha Harris, Number 21, wins its first NCAA Division III Championship on March 27, 1997.

(Photo credit: Steve Grieco)

(Photo credit: Bob Handelman)

CHAIRMAN OF THE BOARD OF TRUSTEES
MARTIN LIPTON

Martin Lipton, one of America's most distinguished attorneys, was elected chairman of the Board of Trustees of New York University in 1998. Lipton succeeded Laurence A. Tisch, who served as chairman of the board for 20 years. As a trustee, Lipton has been involved in some of the University's most important decisions, including the sale of the C. F.

Mueller Company and the clinical affiliation of the NYU Hospitals Center and Health System and Mt. Sinai Medical Center.

At the time of his appointment, Lipton stated:

Few things in my life have brought me as much pride or happiness as my long association with New York University. It is a great institution with an unwavering commitment to excellence in research and education, yet it continually strives to find new, better ways to advance human knowledge and

improve itself. I consider it a singular honor that my colleagues on the Board of Trustees have elected me chairman.

Lipton is an alumnus of the School of Law and a senior partner at Wachtell, Lipton, Rosen and Katz, which was established in 1965 by four graduates of the School of Law and has achieved a preeminent position among American law firms. He had been a trustee of the University for 22 years when he became chairman. He has also served as president of the School of Law Foundation

Board of Trustees. He is a recipient of the University's Gallatin Medal, its Vanderbilt Medal, and a Presidential Citation.

I know of no one better qualified to be chairman of the NYU Board of Trustees than Marty Lipton. His involvement in NYU has been long and distinguished, and his knowledge of the University and understanding of our goals is unmatched.

—Laurence A. Tisch

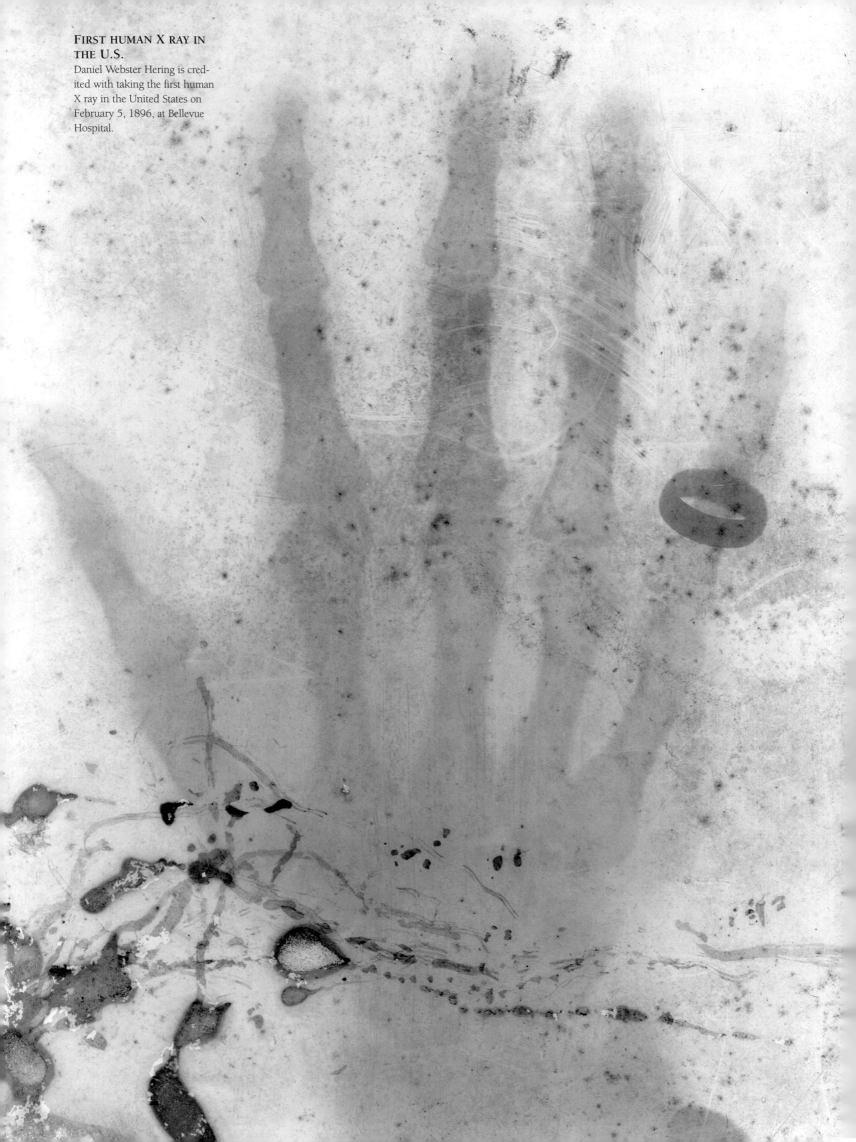

FIRST HUMAN X RAY IN THE U.S.
Daniel Webster Hering is credited with taking the first human X ray in the United States on February 5, 1896, at Bellevue Hospital.

Academic honors are one of the testaments to the greatness of an institution. Since 1964, NYU faculty members have received 124 Guggenheim Fellowships—53 in the last 15 years. NYU also claims nine winners of the Nobel Prize; winners include both faculty and alumni.

Additional honors to faculty include three Crafood Prizes, three Pulitzer Prizes, seven Lasker Awards, and seven Howard Hughes Medical Investigatorships. In addition, 22 faculty members have been elected to the National Academy of Sciences and 19, to the American Academy of Arts and Sciences. And every year, the number of awards bestowed grows.

"Our faculty—some 3,165 strong—leads our renaissance," says NYU president Dr. L. Jay Oliva. "They are pathfinders in the development of research and teaching programs. They are progressive in harnessing the newest technologies and immutable in their strengthening of the arts, sciences, and humanities."

VALENTINE MOTT, PROFESSOR OF SURGERY
In 1841, less than a decade after the founding of New York University, plans for a medical division were realized. Valentine Mott (1785-1865) was among the first doctors to teach at the new medical school; he was then considered the country's most famous surgeon. Mott was not a stranger to life in a burgeoning institution, having played a key role in the creation of Rutgers Medical College some years earlier. During Mott's tenure at NYU, medical classes were held at the Stuyvesant Institute, 659 Broadway, near Bond Street. In 1851, one year after Mott's retirement, the medical school moved to larger facilities on 14th Street between Third Avenue and Irving Place.

FIRST WOMEN'S LAW CLASS, 1890
(Above)

Emily Kempin, a graduate of the University of Zurich's law school, taught the first Women's Law Class on October 30, 1890. At that time, only a handful of law schools admitted women, and very few women practiced law. Kempin's course was intended for nondegree students and businesswomen. Within the year, NYU opened its two-year law degree program to female students. Kempin not only held the attention of NYU's legal-minded women; in 1890, she also taught a course on Roman law to male students. It's believed that this was the first modern instance of a woman lecturing on law to classes of young men.

DANIEL WEBSTER HERING, PROFESSOR OF PHYSICS
(Above)

Daniel Webster Hering was hired in 1885 as professor of physics. His first task was to install the department's laboratory. Under Hering's leadership, NYU became one of the first American universities to encourage classroom experimentation with active student experience of the scientific process. This approach replaced the old-fashioned and prevalent recitation of "natural philosophy."

NOBEL PRIZE-WINNING STUDENTS AND FACULTY

Awarded for excellence in such areas as science, letters, and peace initiatives, the Nobel Prize is the most widely recognized international symbol of achievement. NYU has both educated and been educated by recipients of the esteemed award. The following is a gallery of Nobel Prize winners associated with the University.

GERTRUDE ELION
(Above)
1983 Nobel Prize in Medicine. For Elion's work, with James Black and George Herbert Hitchings, on drug research. Scientific discoveries in 1984 by Elion and Hitchings helped lay the foundation for the development of the AIDS drug AZT. Elion received her Master of Science degree from NYU in 1942.

BARUJ BENACERRAF
(Above)
1980 Nobel Prize in Medicine. For Benacerraf's work on how cell structure relates to diseases and organ transplants. Benacerraf was a member of the Department of Pathology of NYU's School of Medicine from 1956 to 1968.

WASSILY LEONTIEF
(Opposite)
1973 Nobel Prize in Economic Science. Leontief was the founder and director of NYU's Institute of Economic Analysis at the Robert F. Wagner Graduate School of Public Service and professor of economics, Faculty of Arts and Science.

OTTO LOEWI

(Above)

1936 Nobel Prize in Medicine.
Cowinner. Loewi's research was on
the chemical transmissions of ner-
vous impulses. Loewi was a research
professor of pharmacology at NYU's
School of Medicine from 1940 until
his death in 1961 at the age of 88.

ELIHU ROOT

(Opposite)

1912 Nobel Peace Prize. Root graduated from NYU's School of Law in
1867. His illustrious career included
such positions as secretary of war
under President McKinley (1899-
1904); secretary of state under
President Theodore Roosevelt (1909-
1915); U.S. senator from New York
(1909-1915); and ambassador of a
special diplomatic mission to revolutionary Russia (1917). NYU's Root-
Tilden Scholarships, awarded by the
School of Law, are named in his
honor and that of Samuel J. Tilden,
class of 1841. In 1999, the scholarships were renamed Root-Tilden-
Kern in honor of Jerome H. Kern,
Class of 1960.

SEVERO OCHOA

(Above)

1959 Nobel Prize in Medicine.
Cowinner. Ochoa was a professor of
biochemistry at NYU's School of
Medicine from 1942 to 1977. His
work on the chemical nature of
heredity and genetics attracted international attention.

(Courtesy University of California, Irvine)

CLIFFORD SHULL
(Above)
1993 Nobel Prize in Physics and Chemistry. Shull, along with Bertram Brockhouse and George Olah, was given the award for discovering innovative methods of breaking up and reconstructing compounds of carbon and hydrogen. Shull received his doctorate from NYU's Graduate School of Arts and Science in 1941.

GEORGE WALD
(Opposite)
1967 Nobel Prize in Physiology of Medicine. Wald received this prize for work on the functioning of the human eye. He received his Bachelor of Science degree in zoology from Washington Square College in 1927.

FREDERICK REINES
(Above)
1995 Nobel Prize in Physics with Martin Perl. Reines was awarded the prize for his 1950s discovery of the neutrino, a subatomic particle. Reines graduated from NYU with a Ph.D. degree in physics in 1944. His

thesis, "The Liquid Drop Model for Nuclear Fission," remained unpublished for security reasons until the end of World War II.

FACULTY MEMBERS OF THE COURANT INSTITUTE OF MATHEMATICAL SCIENCES NAMED TO THE NATIONAL ACADEMY OF SCIENCES

(Photo credit: Marc Bryan-Brown)

NYU's Courant Institute of Mathematical Sciences now has 12 faculty members who have been named to the prestigious National Academy of Sciences. Election to the NAS is considered one of the highest honors that can be accorded a scientist or engineer. Gathering for a photograph of Courant's NAS members are, *seated left to right:* **S. R. Srinivasa Varadhan, Louis Nirenberg,** and **Peter D. Lax.** *Standing left to right:* **Charles S. Peskin, Henry P. McKean, Paul R. Garabedian, Andrew J. Majda, Cathleen S. Morawetz,*** **Jacob T. Schwartz,** and **Jeffrey Cheeger.** *Not pictured:* **Mikhail Gromov; Louis A. Caffarelli,** formerly of Courant, is now at the University of Texas in Austin. **Roy Radner** of the Leonard N. Stern School of Business; **William J. Baumol** of the Faculty of Arts and Science Department of Economics; **Rodolfo R. Llinas, Lennart Philipson, H. Sherwood Lawrence,** and **David D. Sabatini** of the School of Medicine are NYU's other members of the Academy.

In a biography *(A Beautiful Mind,* Simon and Schuster, 1998*)* of the mathematician John Forbes Nash Jr., author Sylvia Nasar offers this description of the origins of Courant:

The institute was the creation of one of mathematics' great entrepreneurs, Richard Courant, a German Jewish professor of mathematics who had been driven out of Göttingen in the mid-1930s by the Nazis. Short, rotund, autocratic, and irrepressible, Courant was famous for his fascination with the rich and powerful, his penchant for falling in love with his female "assistants," and his unerring eye for young mathematical talent. When Courant arrived in 1937, New York University had no mathematics worth speaking of. Undaunted, Courant immediately set about raising funds. His own stellar reputation, the anti-Semitism of the American educational establishment, and New York's "deep reservoir of talent" enabled him to attract brilliant students, most of them New York City Jews who were shut out of the Harvards and Princetons. The advent of World War II brought more money and more students, and by the mid-1950s, when the institute was formally founded, it was already rivaling more established mathematical centers like Princeton and Cambridge. Its young stars included Peter Lax and his wife, Anneli, Cathleen Synge Morawetz, Jurgen Moser, and Louis Nirenberg, and among its stellar visitors were Lars Hormander, a future Fields medalist, and Shlomo Sternberg, who would soon move to Harvard.

*Morawetz is the first female to be named to the NAS.

THOMAS WOLFE
(Right)
Between 1924 and 1930, Thomas
Wolfe intermittently taught in the
English department at Washington
Square College. During these years,
Wolfe wrote his well-known novel,
Look Homeward, Angel (1929). In a
1935 letter to NYU chancellor Harry
Woodburn Chase, Wolfe remem-
bered the Washington Square cam-
pus as filled with "eager, swarming,
vigorous life."

RALPH ELLISON
(Left)

One of America's most influential modern authors, Ralph Ellison held the distinguished post of Albert Schweitzer Professor of Humanities at NYU from 1971 until 1979. Ellison is best known for his 1952 novel, *The Invisible Man,* for which he won the National Book Award. As the Schweitzer Professor, Ellison encouraged the public's involvement in University events. He arranged various lectures and symposiums that were open to the New York community. Through his affiliation with the Department of English, Ellison taught literature and creative writing to undergraduate and graduate students.

ALICE KELIHER, CHAMPION OF DAY CARE IN AMERICA
(Right)

Alice Keliher was a renowned expert in early childhood education whose career at NYU spanned more than two decades. From 1936 to 1960, Keliher taught at NYU's School of Education where she wrote extensively on children. In addition to her work at NYU she served as the director of child and youth services of the New York Office of Civil Defense and as secretary to Mayor Fiorello H. La Guardia's Wartime Care of Children Committee. Keliher's experiences at the posts made her a vocal champion of day care in America. While at NYU, Keliher lived near Washington Square Park, in the same apartment building as Eleanor Roosevelt. Neighborliness led to friendship as the two women shared a commitment to human rights.

(Photo credit: Alan Orling)

Perlin Noise

(Left)

NYU's Center for Advanced Technology (CAT), under the direction of Kenneth Perlin, is one of New York State's cutting-edge research laboratories and the incubator of a range of multimedia ventures. Perlin brings to NYU more than his innovative research; he also assists faculty by bringing state-of-the-art multimedia technologies to their teaching and scholarship. In 1997, Perlin received a Technical Achievement Award from the Academy of Motion Picture Arts and Sciences for his development of Perlin Noise, a technique used to produce natural-appearing textures on computer-generated surfaces for motion picture visual effects. Examples of Perlin Noise can be found in such feature films as *The Lion King, Batman Forever, Jurassic Park, The Abyss, True Lies, Terminator II, Independence Day,* and *Toy Story.*

(Photo credit: Peter Freed)

NYU MACARTHUR FELLOWSHIP RECIPIENTS
(Above)
Joan Connelly, associate professor of fine arts, became in 1996 the ninth NYU recipient of a MacArthur Fellowship from the John D. and Catherine T. MacArthur Foundation. Other NYU recipients are anthropologist Faye Ginsburg, poet Galway Kinnell, mathematician Charles Peskin, art historian Kirk Varnedoe, neural scientist Robert Shapley, anthropologist Rita Wright, legal scholars Sylvia Law and Anthony Amsterdam, and the late mathematician Fritz John.

JENNY ROSENTHAL BRAMLEY
(Right)
The life and work of the first woman to earn a Ph.D. degree in physics from NYU were recognized in 1997 with the dedication of the Jenny Rosenthal Bramley Laser Laboratory, devoted to research using lasers. In 1929 at age 19, Dr. Bramley graduated from NYU, and her distinguished career included many achievements in laser science and technology. She eventually became the first recipient of the National Science Foundation Lifetime Achievement Award for Women in Science.

ACADEMIC INNOVATIONS

Academic innovation flows from a faculty concerned with expanding knowledge and creating an intellectual environment abundant with opportunity and ideas. New York University's leaders have always sought the best and the brightest—the Samuel F. B. Morses of the world—who have pushed the frontiers of knowledge, challenged students, and created the most effective programs of learning.

(Photo credit: Ken Levinson)

(Photo credit: Jon Roemer)

THE GLOBAL LAW SCHOOL PROGRAM

(Above)

A growing number of those in the academy and at the bar view the School of Law as the nation's premier institution for legal education. Its boldest venture to date is its Global Law School Program. In proposing the initiative in 1993, John Sexton, dean of the School of Law, and Norman Dorsen, the faculty member Sexton calls the "father" of the venture, precipitated a revolution in legal education. A chief goal in developing this new curriculum was to provide every NYU law student with a deeper understanding of the global dimen- sions a modern lawyer must face. Its growing and distinguished faculty, its rising pool of superb applicants, and the success of its graduates measure the program's success. Indeed, today, the Global Law School Program is considered the most significant step in legal education since Langdell developed the case method. Pictured *(left to right)* at the 1999 *Annual Survey of American Law's* dedication ceremony are Archbishop Desmond Tutu, First Lady Hillary Rodham Clinton, and Professor Alex Boraine of the NYU School of Law. Professor Boraine is also vice president of South Africa's Truth and Reconciliation Commission.

FACULTY RESOURCE NETWORK

(Above)

In 1990, 10 historically black colleges joined the University's Faculty Resource Network, expanding the scope of FRN's engagement of impor- tant issues in American higher educa- tion. The growth of FRN, an initiative devoted to faculty development and undergraduate teaching, was made possible by a $1 million grant from the Pew Charitable Trusts. The Faculty Resource Network was created in 1985 with a grant from the Ford Foundation, largely through the efforts of President L. Jay Oliva during his tenure as chancellor of the University, to link NYU's resources with regional liberal arts colleges through seminars and scholars-in-resi- dence at NYU. *Seated left to right:* Arthur Bacon, Louis Delsarte, Emma Amos, and Charles D. Rogers.

SPEAKING FREELY
(Right)

A novel approach to learning foreign languages while gaining a deeper understanding of different cultures is available to every NYU student through the NYU Speaking Freely Program, which provides free, non-credit language coaching in residence halls and other on-campus sites. Each week, students discuss a different topic and enjoy a related activity—a movie, concert, or neighborhood visit—as part of a small, informal language group. Ten-week sessions are offered in Chinese, Japanese, Korean, Swahili, French, German, Italian, Spanish, and Hebrew. NYU Speaking Freely is also excellent preparation for students who wish to study and travel abroad.

(Photo credit: Bob Handelman)

(Photo credit: Bob Krist)

THE MORSE ACADEMIC PLAN
(Left)

The College of Arts and Science's core curriculum, the Morse Academic Plan (MAP), began its pilot phase in 1993. MAP is named for Samuel F. B. Morse, the eminent artist, inventor of the telegraph, and an early faculty member of University College. In 1995, with support from the National Science Foundation and the National Endowment for the Humanities, the Faculty of Arts and Science voted to approve the new undergraduate core curriculum. Today, MAP is the intellectual core of the NYU experience and forms the general education portion of undergraduate education at the University.

(Photo credit: Peter Freed)

GALLATIN INTERNSHIPS
(Left)

Two Gallatin students at their Sony internship. Gallatin students have traditionally enjoyed a variety of internship opportunities.

The Gallatin School, which was created in 1972 as the University Without Walls, is another locus within the University that has pushed the boundaries of academic change by offering students alternatives to a traditional liberal arts education. At the Gallatin School, students design their own programs and take courses throughout the University. The Gallatin School's keynotes have been flexibility, innovation, and an interdisciplinary approach. Not surprisingly, many of its some 1,100 students are adults who are returning to school and who have had significant life experience.

(Courtesy NYU Medical Center Archives)

MORE THAN A CENTURY OF MEDICAL AND DENTAL INNOVATIONS
(Above)

The academic innovations of the medical and dental schools could fill every page of this book. Just one recent example of a path-breaking advance has been the introduction of minimally invasive heart surgery, which uses the Port-Access system and eliminates open-chest surgery for a wide range of patients. Minimally invasive heart surgery also means reduced pain, accelerated recovery, shortened hospital stays, markedly decreased scarring, and a quicker return to work. The group that introduced and refined minimally invasive cardiac surgery at NYU is *(left to right)* Patricia Buttenheim, R.N.; Dr. Stephen Colvin, chief of cardiothoracic surgery; Dr. Aubrey Galloway, director of surgical research; Dr. Greg Ribakove; and Dr. Eugene Grossi.

(Photo credit: Ken Levinson)

FIGHTING ORAL CANCER
(Left)

Bill Evans, WABC-TV meteorologist, interviews Dean Michael C. Alfano during Oral Cancer Awareness Week at the NYU College of Dentistry. The NYU Bobcat looks on.

RED BURNS, TOKYO BROADCASTING CHAIR, INTERACTIVE TELECOMMUNICATIONS PROGRAM
(Left)

Several years ago, a student in the NYU Tisch School of Arts' Interactive Telecommunications Program (ITP) was asked by a *Crain's New York Business* reporter to describe the program's learning environment. "It is heaven," the student replied. Only 25 years ago, ITP was little more than an incomprehensible acronym as it struggled in uncharted territory to find students. But Red Burns, chair of ITP, was indefatigable in her passion for electronic media and in her desire to educate students about using technology to communicate. Today, Burns is credited with educating new generations of entrepreneurs, explorers, and risk-takers who were critical in building "Silicon Alley" —the first new industry in New York City in nearly half a century. Today, ITP stands as an international mecca for people who want to experiment with multimedia, a magnet for those who dare think "out of the box." From an educational viewpoint, Burns has actualized *the* most creative environment for developing new media in the world.

THE PHYSICAL COMPUTING SHOWS—PART CIRCUS, PART SCIENCE FAIR
(Below)

The Tisch School of the Arts Interactive Telecommunications Program (ITP) is a pioneering graduate center for the study and design of new communication media forms and applications. At the core of ITP's curriculum are its physical computing courses, which challenge students to create interactive computer projects that do not rely on the use of a mouse, keyboard, or computer screen. The results of this creative expression range from the whimsical to the serious in content and are exhibited at the end of each semester. The physical computing shows have an atmosphere that is part circus and part science fair and are always eagerly anticipated.

College Students Learn to Transform Daydreams Into Hands-On Reality

By LISA GUERNSEY

WHEN Mary Schmidt Campbell, the dean of the Tisch School of the Arts at New York University, walked onto the fourth floor of the school's main building on May 12, she thought she knew what to expect. It was the second day of the new-media art show, an annual event where frenetic crowds and crazy computing projects have become standard fare.

But she wasn't quite prepared for the first exhibit: a talking gumball machine.

The machine looked normal enough. It was made of cherry-red plastic and was full of white gumballs. But when she approached it, the gumballs started to jiggle nervously. Then they squeaked with fear, begging to be left alone. After a twist of the knob, one ball tumbled forward, asking for mercy. When she looked at the ball, it seemed to have a human face, twisted in anguish over its fate.

"I just thought it was delightful," Ms. Campbell said. "I found myself talking back."

The gumball machine was one of nearly 60 projects on display at "Outside the Box: Experiments With Interaction," this spring's show for graduate students in the school's interactive telecommunications program. The students, from all disciplines, experiment with computer technology as a medium for creative expression. Most of the exhibitors were in a course called physical computing. They were asked to create interactive computer projects that do not require the use of a mouse, keyboard or computer screen.

Melanie Oswald and Craig Spain dreamed up the gumball machine late one night a few months ago. They rigged the machine and objects around it with sensors wired to a hidden computer equipped with speakers. When unsuspecting people stepped on a floor mat in front of the exhibit or turned the machine's knob, they activated motors that shook the balls around. They also triggered switches that turned on recorded voices. When the candy dropped into its dish, other switches turned on a projector hidden in a nearby potted plant that beamed an image of a human face onto the gumball.

Ms. Oswald and Mr. Spain programmed each movement with Basic, a simple computer language, then downloaded the programs onto a tiny computer chip that is wired to the gumball machine. Before entering the interactive-telecommunications program and embarking on the gumball project, neither student had ever attempted

to learn computer code, let alone worked with electrical wiring. Mr. Spain majored in screenwriting as an undergraduate, and Ms. Oswald's background is in art history and studio art.

"I had no programming experience at all," Mr. Spain said.

Over the din of computerized music and the chatter of dozens of gawking guests, other exhibitors claimed the same electronic innocence. Their backgrounds included theater and nursing, graphic design and chemistry. No one mentioned electrical engineering or computer science. But in the physical computing course, each of them had a crash course in circuits, cables and chips. Their fourth-floor laboratory, which was finally empty after a week of frenzied

At New York University's new-media art show, students showed off creations like dancing toasters (above right), refrigerators that nag (right) and animated children's toys (above).

preparation for the show, was strewn with wire cutters, soldering irons and screwdrivers.

"The learning that comes through the hands is really important for some people," said Dan O'Sullivan, who teaches the course.

But Mr. Sullivan and other professors also stressed that the computer itself was not supposed to be the center of attention.

"The currency here is imagination, not technical prowess," said Red Burns, the program's chairwoman.

Most computers, in fact, were hidden from view throughout the show. Some were draped with sheets under tables. Others were stuck behind black curtains. Flashing lights and projection screens dominated the

floor instead. And projects made use of a hodgepodge of accessories: a seesaw, X-ray film, baby toys, pinwheels, balloons, mirrors, household appliances and an old wood-en door chopped into pieces.

Rania Ho, who majored in theater as an undergraduate, found her inspiration in toasters, but she made them dance, not fly. Her project, titled "Toaster Fandango," used two banged-up toasters fitted with sensors to detect infrared signals. By standing above the toasters with an infrared remote control she created, Ms. Ho spurred the toasters to dance to the rock-and-roll sounds of James Brown blaring nearby.

"I just thought appliances needed to be liberated from their mundane existence," Ms. Ho said.

A nearby installation took another dig at kitchen appliances: The project, called "Fridgeraider," showcased a refrigerator with a video of a mother's face projected on its back wall. When a visitor took a box of chocolates out of the refrigerator, the mother taunted: "Yeah, that's just what you need! More chocolate."

Some of the exhibits actually veered toward usefulness or even commercial viability. They were not disqualified. Jonah Brucker-Cohen and Shii Ann Huang created Netgym, connecting stationary bicycles to computers that showed a virtual bike trail. Connecting bikes to computers is nothing

Using computers to turn whimsy into interactive electronic projects.

new, but the students hoped to create something more: an Internet-based game, where people on exercise bikes anywhere in the world could race each other in a virtual world while pedaling in their own homes.

The project on display, however, didn't quite do everything that Ms. Huang and Mr. Brucker-Cohen imagined. The virtual bike trail was there, but they had not yet incorporated the Internet. "It's a kind of a cheat," Ms. Huang admitted.

As the show wore on, some of the hands-on installations began to show wear and tear. Wires snapped and sensors broke. After a few hours, one of the dancing toasters had creaked to a halt. Ms. Ho, the mastermind behind them, was soon kneeling on the floor with the wounded appliance, a screwdriver in hand.

Meanwhile, the gumball machine was still jiggling with energy. And the fourth floor of the Tisch School had become a circus, packed with people and reverberating with blaring music. The cries of agitated gumballs were lost in the din.

RAE ZIMMERMAN, DIRECTOR OF THE INSTITUTE FOR CIVIL INFRASTRUCTURE SYSTEMS

(Left)

The Institute for Civil Infrastructure Systems (ICIS) at the Robert F. Wagner Graduate School of Public Service was established in January 1998 with funding from the National Science Foundation. The institute's vision is to become a principal U.S. center for new information, ideas, and collaborations about civil infrastructure systems and their role in modern communities. Led by its director, Professor Rae Zimmerman, ICIS integrates the perspectives of social science and engineering to support transportation, water, energy, communication, and waste management systems consistent with the goals of the communities they serve. ICIS works with community representatives, political leaders, applied social scientists, engineers, and members of other disciplines and various interest groups to integrate their perspectives and skills into infrastructure planning. The institute's purpose is to improve the process of developing civil infrastructure through innovations in community programs, information exchange, public policy, applications of advanced technology, and education. Fundamental to the mission of ICIS is the creation of networks and partnerships to design and carry out new initiatives within these program areas. Institutions that partner with ICIS are Cornell University, Polytechnic University of New York, and the University of Southern California.

(Photo credit: Ken Levinson)

(Photo credit: Don Hamerman)

THE PROFESSIONAL DEVELOPMENT LABORATORY

(Above)

The Professional Development Laboratory (PDL) is devoted to teacher development at 52 sites in 17 public school districts throughout New York City. The program uses an active, school-based laboratory model to enable experienced teachers to help other educators grow professionally. It is one of the few teacher development programs that takes place during the school day in working classrooms.

THE NYU SUMMER

(Above)

NYU's summer program is the largest summer session in North America, larger than the combined summer programs at Columbia, Harvard, and the University of Chicago.

(Photo credit: Jon Roemer)

THE BRENNAN CENTER FOR JUSTICE

(Above)

Dean John Sexton, School of Law, greets the late U.S. Supreme Court Justice William J. Brennan, Jr., at the inaugural ceremony in 1995 of The William J. Brennan Jr. Center for Justice. The Brennan Center, a cooperative venture with the NYU School of Law, is a nonpartisan center for study, discourse, and action committed to developing and implementing solutions to intractable problems of social justice.

CREDENTIALED PROFESSIONALS FROM OTHER NATIONS TRANSFER EXPERTISE TO U.S.

(Right)

The Ehrenkranz School of Social Work provides innovative cross-cultural education to make it possible for credentialed professionals from other nations to transfer their expertise to the United States. Specially designed programs for these professionals help assure that non-English-speaking New Yorkers can receive needed social services from those who understand their unique needs.

(Courtesy Shirley M. Ehrenkranz School of Social Work, New York University)

SELECTED CENTERS AND INSTITUTES

New York University's centers and institutes sponsor programs and seminars featuring writers, artists, philosophers, social scientists, and business and government leaders. Opportunities for broadening one's intellectual horizons are virtually unlimited. In fact, no other campus in America offers such a plenitude of choices.

Asian/Pacific/American Studies Program and Institute
Brennan Center for Justice
Edgar M. Bronfman Center for Jewish Student Life
Center for Advanced Digital Applications (CADA)
Center for Advanced Technology
Center for Direct Marketing
Center for Health and Public Service Research
Center for Hospitality, Tourism, and Travel Administration
Center on International Cooperation
Center for Neural Science
Center for Philanthropy and Fundraising
Center for Publishing

Center for Research in the Middle Ages and the Renaissance
Courant Institute of Mathematical Sciences
Alfred B. Engelberg Center on Innovation Law and Policy
Information Technology Institute
International Trauma Studies Program at NYU
Institute for Civil Infrastructure Systems
Institute of Fine Arts
Helen and Martin Kimmel Center for University Life
Metropolitan Center for Urban Education
NYU Institute for Education and Social Policy
NYU International Center for Advanced Studies
NYU New Media Center
Paul McGhee Undergraduate Degree Program for Adults
Real Estate Institute
Remarque Institute
Taub Urban Research Center
Lillian Vernon Center for International Affairs

(Photo credit: Ken Levinson)

INSTITUTE OF FINE ARTS
(Below)
The James B. Duke House, home to NYU's prestigious Institute of Fine Arts, was a gift of the late Doris Duke. *Left:* John L. Loeb, Dr. L. Jay Oliva, Sheldon H. Solow, and Dr. James R. McCredie, the director of the Institute of Fine Arts. Mr. Loeb served as chairman of the board of the Institute of Fine Arts from 1973 to 1992, when he was succeeded by Mr. Solow, the current chair.

For New York University students, no boundaries exist to a complete artistic, sporting, and intellectual life. It is as though the University provides a palette of rich colors with each student free to create his or her own personal painting.

A panoply of resources and pleasures affecting every aspect of campus life includes, to name but a few, internships that reach from Harlem to Wall Street and beyond; hundreds of chances to perform community service; and national houses and international centers and institutes that offer an unending cycle of intellectual stimulation.

There is also Bobst Library, one of the University's jewels; new and proliferating "smart" classrooms; the Iris and B. Gerald Cantor Film Center; new dormitory spaces that stretch from South Street Seaport to 14th Street; and a continual parade of dignitaries, scholars, and artists who eagerly engage students.

Plus, there is the fun of the annual Strawberry Festival; the NYU trolley; the Speaking Freely Program that makes learning a foreign language enjoyable and easy; the thrill of winning an NCAA basketball tournament and being feted by the mayor; "NYU Night" on the *David Letterman Show;* the sheer joy of a Greenwich Village bistro; an art gallery in SoHo; a Broadway or off-Broadway show; and finally, the triumphal moment of Commencement in Washington Square Park. Life simply does not get much richer in higher education . . . anywhere.

Indeed, so renowned is the quality of New York University campus life that it has on occasion entered the mythology of film and television. For example, Theo on *The Cosby Show* attended NYU, as did aspiring filmmaker Paul Reiser in *Mad About You. NYPD Blue* frequently incorporates the NYU Medical Center and its doctors into their storylines. A hilarious episode of *Seinfeld* featured an NYU

intern who was hired by Kramer to manage his affairs. Woody Allen wittily groused about life at NYU in *Annie Hall.* And the producers of the television drama *Felicity*—prior to production—requested that the title character be an NYU student. University officials, however, denied their request because they felt that Felicity did not properly represent the values of an NYU student. It's not so easy to be an NYU student!

But, after all is said and done, most aficionados seem to agree that the most charming and satiric slice of NYU life was depicted in the film *The Freshman,* when Marlon Brando unexpectedly visited Matthew Broderick, portraying an NYU student, in his dormitory room. In a send-up of his *Godfather* character, Brando darkly scanned the spartan room and then muttered the following immortal lines: "So this is college! I didn't miss nuttin'."

CLINTON HALL

(Below)

The University's first location, when it opened in October 1832, was in rented quarters in Clinton Hall, on the corner of Beekman and Nassau Streets. Clinton Hall, a four-story building constructed in 1830 to house the Mercantile Library Association, was at the bustling center of the city, a stone's throw from what is today City Hall.

TICKET TO AN 1845 READING

(Left)

While Samuel F. B. Morse, John William Draper, and Daniel Webster Hering extended scientific boundaries at New York University, a young woman named Anna Charlotte Lynch Botta, whose husband, Vincent, was an NYU faculty member, helped foster Washington Square's literary and artistic reputation. The Vermont native moved to New York in 1845, opening one of America's first literary salons, after the French fashion, at 116 Waverly Place. Her gathering proved an instant success, drawing artists such as Ralph Waldo Emerson and Edgar Allan Poe.

COMMENCEMENT: A SHORT HISTORY OF TIME AND PLACE

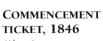

COMMENCEMENT TICKET, 1846
(Above)

NYU's first public graduation ceremony took place on July 17, 1834, just two years after the University opened. At this time NYU was called the University of the City of New-York, its classrooms were in Clinton Hall located at the corner of Beekman and Nassau Streets, and Commencement was held in nearby churches. In 1835, when NYU had completed its own University Building on Washington Square East (the present site of Main Building), Commencement was moved to the square.

From the mid to late 1800s, Commencement was held off campus at such places as the Astor Opera House, near the University; Niblo's Garden at Broadway and Prince Street; the Metropolitan Opera House; and Carnegie Hall.

Between 1900 and 1969, Commencement took place at NYU's University Heights campus in the Bronx. At first, exercises were held inside the auditorium of the Gould Memorial Library. Graduation ceremonies moved outdoors in the 1920s, when they were held near the Hall of Fame, adjacent to the Gould Library. From 1932 until the late 1960s, Commencement took place on Ohio Field. In 1969 Commencement was held in Madison Square Garden, and two years later, in Radio City Music Hall.

In 1976, Commencement returned to the site of its early days at the Square, this time for an outdoor ceremony in the park—a tradition that continues today.

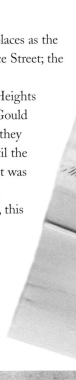

COMMENCEMENT ARMBAND, 1863
(Right)
Commencement was held at Niblo's Garden, an entertainment center located at Broadway and Prince Street and a frequent site of this event during the early history of the University.

NIBLO'S GARDEN
(Below)

CLASS OF 1854
(Left)

**COMMENCEMENT
PROCESSION, 1922**
(Below)
Some 1,200 students graduated.

COMMENCEMENT AT
UNIVERSITY HEIGHTS, 1936

NURSING GRADUATES AT COMMENCEMENT, 1947

A "PEACEFUL" COMMENCEMENT AT MADISON SQUARE GARDEN, 1971

(Photo credit: Don Hamerman)

GRAD ALLEY
(Left)

The first "Welcome to Grad Alley," also billed as a "blast from the past," was held on Wednesday, May 14, 1997, at West Fourth Street between Washington Square East and Mercer Street. A unique going-away party for newly minted graduates and their parents, Grad Alley included salsa, swing, disco, and rock and roll at Gould Plaza; Dixieland at Schwartz Plaza; readings and musical performances in the Violet Café; an NYU Musical Theatre Ensemble in the Frederick Loewe Theatre; and future Adam Sandlers and Molly Shannons performing in a cabaret. Fireworks by Grucci signaled the end of a glorious evening. At 8 p.m. the party was over. The only thing left to do was attend Commencement the following day and find a job.

(Photo credit: Harry Heliotis)

A RECORD OF DIVERSITY
(Left)

In 1997, *Black Issues in Higher Education* published results from a survey, using data compiled by the U.S. Department of Education, that ranked NYU first in the nation in total master's degrees conferred in all disciplines for students of color.

CLASS SPIRIT

The Class of 1894 held annual dinners without a break, beginning with its freshman year in 1891 and ending on the 50th anniversary of its Commencement in 1944. The University moved the College of Arts and Science to University Heights in 1894; thus the Class of 1894 became known as the "Last of the Washington Squarers." Class secretary John V. Irvin's notations in the Class Book conjure the youthful pleasures of student life and the abundant affection for alma mater. Irvin wrote:

Lest we forget the triumphs of undergraduate days and the picturesque life on Washington Square, where we acquired "all we've forgot, and all we know," reference is made to:

The risky feat of Church [Edward Francis Church, Jr.] climbing the weak flagstaff on the tower of the old building and nailing '94's flag to its top.

'Bones' [Prof. Addison Ballard] and the pill box in which he kept minute slips inscribed with our names—some never being called because lost.

The reception to the Class of February 12, 1892, by Chancellor and Mrs. MacCracken at their home No. 84 Irving Place, where we spent the entire evening giving college and fraternity cheers to the neglect and deafening of the ladies.

Old Matthews, the college janitor, and perhaps the treasurer as well, and his huge brass gong on which he beat the hours for class.

The gloomy and dark interior of Carnegie Hall, where the commencement speakers practiced afternoons for the benefit of Prof. Shaw, of School of Pedagogy fame, who was supposed to coach them; and the final glory of graduation in the brilliantly lighted Hall on the evening of May 31, 1894, observed by our particular friends and all the world, followed by the cheer-fraternity groups in the vestibule.

CLASS OF '94

(Above)
As freshmen in 1891.

(Opposite, top)
At graduation.

(Opposite, bottom)
At their 20th Anniversary Reunion, 1914. On the right is John Henry MacCracken, eldest son of Chancellor Henry Mitchell MacCracken. John Henry went on to become president of Lafayette College from 1915 to 1926.

PROGRAM OF FOUNDERS' DAY.

Wednesday, April 18, 1894.
Under the Auspices of the Class of 1894.

11 A. M. In the University Chapel:
Founders' Day Oration by John V. Irwin, '94.
Founders' Day Poem by W. F. Johnson, '79.

12 M. At the Main door of the University:
Removal of carved stones from the building, to be
sent to University Heights.
Oration by Theodore A. Gessler, '94.

2 P. M. Laying of Cornerstone of Gymnasium at University
Heights, and planting of Violets by the Class of '94.

[77]

**STUDENT DINNER,
CA. 1900**
(Above)

OLD MATTHEWS
(Left)
Old Matthews, the janitor, sounding
the brass gong, which indicated
when classes began and ended.

**PROGRAM, 1894
FOUNDERS DAY**
(Far Left)

THE BUILDING OF THE UPTOWN CAMPUS

In likely his most audacious stroke, Chancellor Henry Mitchell MacCracken moved the undergraduate college to a spacious campus in Fordham Heights in the Bronx, which was on the east side of the Harlem River and then a desirable and burgeoning locale. University Heights provided what McCracken believed essential for a college education—space for residence halls, laboratories, libraries, recreation, and athletics. The Heights campus was a place where students could—in McCracken's words—"enjoy the country environment, yet be able to study close at hand the great city."

To create this new campus, MacCracken hired one of the most prolific and distinguished architects of the era, Stanford White, whose father, Richard Grant White, graduated from the University in 1839. The younger White's accomplishments include the Washington Arch and Tiffany's on Fifth Avenue and 57th Street.

Originally MacCracken hoped to move the old University Building on Washington Square up to the new campus. This plan was rejected when the lowest estimate offered for dismantling and hauling the building was the mighty sum of $257,000, the cost of erecting perhaps four or five new buildings at the time.

Once the decision was made not to move the University Building uptown, a prolonged discussion of the architectural shape of the uptown campus ensued. Finally, White proposed the notion of creating an academic quadrangle with a colonnaded library as its centerpiece. The magnificent library—to be named Gould Library—would be next to lecture halls and an athletic field. White's elegant classical design was in stark contrast to the dark neo-Gothic tradition of the University Building. The Temple of Fame (a.k.a. Hall of Fame) woven into White's library design was intended, according to Thomas J. Frusciano and Marilyn H. Pettit, as a "temple of American wisdom and valor." In addition to all this, other buildings served as dormitories, laboratories, lecture halls, and a gymnasium.

Largely due to MacCracken's leadership, enrollment soared and the tremendous debt load incurred by the building and maintenance of the University Heights campus was eased—but never satisfied—by the income from its modest tuition.

An undated photograph of Chancellor MacCracken reveals an elderly man with a full white beard; he is unsmiling and his eyes betray no indication of lightness. He has the serious gaze one expects from an ordained Presbyterian clergyman.

MacCracken was a discerning student of the changing nature of higher education, and his appointment to vice-chancellor constituted the turning point for the university's transformation into a modern university.

New York University and the City
by Thomas J. Frusciano and Marilyn H. Pettit

One unsettling note about MacCracken emerges in James McNaughton Hester's history entitled, *Adventure on Washington Square: Being President of New York University 1962-1975.* Hester was New York University's 12th president.

"MacCracken was a dynamic man," wrote Hester, "but his views contrast rather vividly with what was to follow."

In a 1904 address in Albany, MacCracken is reported to have said: "It is hardly to be expected that the intellectual activity of either the Catholic or Jewish population will ever find its expression in Columbia or in New York University." Hester reports that MacCracken "expected and hoped" that New York University would continue to be allied with the "Scotch, Dutch, independent, or puritan" elements. MacCracken's hopes were dashed, of course, by the changing tides of immigration, which were to bring to New York University's doorstep the very people he might deny—Catholics and Jews.

**GOULD LIBRARY,
UNIVERSITY HEIGHTS**
(Above)

**INTERIOR OF GOULD
LIBRARY**
(Left)

SUMMER SCHOOL
(Opposite, top)
Summer School music classes,
University Heights, 1917.

(Opposite, bottom)
NYU Summer School bus to
University Heights, 1925.

THE TRIP TO THE UNIVERSITY HEIGHTS CAMPUS FROM WASHINGTON SQUARE

April 18 was a bright spring day, the sky clear, the temperature mild, a gentle breeze blowing across Washington Square. Inside the stately Gothic building that faced the Square on the east, a structure so magnificent that it had been the highlight of the visit of the Prince of Wales to the United States in 1860, the graduating class of the University of the City of New-York was conducting Founders Day exercises. Speeches, poetry, songs, and a banjo duet were the order of the day. At noon, the doors opened and the audience gathered at the main entrance. There, in the presence of the venerable Charles Butler, president of the University Council, who had been present at the laying of the building's cornerstone 63 years before, and to the ringing words of the class orator ("Let them descend, these grand old stones! / Let them be razed, these historic walls! / Depart from this ancient abode, O Alma Mater! / These sculptured heads shall rise again"), a stone and several gargoyles from the old building, which was to be demolished, were taken down and placed on a horse-drawn wagon decorated with the University's colors. The members of the Class of '94 climbed on the coach, followed by the Class of '96 and members of the Zeta Psi fraternity, for the nine miles to the University's new campus in the Bronx.

The violet-clad procession rode up Fifth Avenue, the students no doubt expressing their exuberance with college songs and cheer. They passed near the building of their arch-rival, Columbia College, on Madison Avenue and 49th Street (it, too, would soon be moving to a new location), past the new homes of the wealthy merchants and other leading citizens whose departure from the increasingly commercialized neighborhoods surrounding Washington Square had played a major role in the University's decision to move. It is not known over what bridge they crossed the Harlem River into the Bronx. If they had gone by a route further west than that which they most likely took, they would have passed the Bloomingdale Insane Asylum, soon to be the campus of Columbia College. That might have been their final destination, if the merger talks of a few years before between the two institutions had not failed.

"The Role of the University Heights Campus of
New York University," an essay by
Barnett W. Hamberger

When the procession arrived at the University Heights campus more than two hours later, the participants were graciously served lunch by Catherine Hubbard MacCracken, the wife of Chancellor Henry Mitchell MacCracken. Then the stone was laid as the cornerstone of the new gymnasium.

(Photo credit: Dan Pollard)

FOUNDERS DAY

Created at the urging of Chancellor MacCracken in 1889, Founders Day was a yearly celebration of the establishment of the University. The first Founders Day was attended by faculty, students, and guests and was held at the Washington Square campus. In 1894, a spire from the old University Building on Washington Square was transported to the Heights and came to be known as the Founders Monument. The monument was rededicated at the Square in 1973. It is currently located in the center of Arnold and Marie Schwartz Plaza off Washington Square South. In the 1950s, Founders Day became an occasion for honoring outstanding undergraduate students and faculty. The tradition lives on today and is a special occasion in the University's calendar.

FOUNDERS DAY HONORS CONVOCATION, 1990S
(Top)

FOUNDERS DAY INVITATION, 1899
(Above)

NYU'S 90TH BIRTHDAY CELEBRATION
(Left)
Dr. George Brown, president of the Council, speaking at the foot of the Founders Day Monument in commemoration of the University's 90th birthday in 1921.

CLASS DAY

Sometime around 1885, the NYU tradition of Class Day began. This was an occasion for the senior class to celebrate its existence in the presence of students from other classes. At these jovial events, students read their class history, the Glee Club sang, and the soon-to-be graduates presented awards to the most spirited lower-classmen. During the 1887 Class Day, freshmen blew tin horns while the class history was being read, and someone threw a cabbage at the orator! Class Day continued at the Heights until the campus was sold in 1973. In later years, Class Day became a more subdued evening convocation for graduating students at the Heights and later at Washington Square.

CLASS DAY, 1924
(Top)
The "Gloria Trumpeters" leading a mock procession, University Heights.

CLASS DAY, 1937
(Bottom)
Academic Convocation in the Gould Memorial Library, University Heights.

CLASS DAY, 1938
(Right)
Sara Delano Roosevelt, mother of the president of the United States, receiving a scroll on behalf of her daughter-in-law, Eleanor Roosevelt, who was honored for distinguished public service, University Heights.

CLASS DAY PROGRAM, 1896
(Below)

DANCES, PROMS, AND EVENTS

When NYU students aren't buried in their books, they might be found having a good time on the dance floor. Though the Heights campus did not become co-ed until 1959, women were always welcome to come uptown for social occasions. Downtown at the Square, mingling required less travel time. From the late 19th century, the campus was home to both male and female students.

**DANCE CARD FOR CLASS DAY
AND PROMENADE, 1898**
(Above)

VARSITY DRAMATIC CLUB
(Below)
Sheet music cover for the Varsity
Dramatic Club's performance of
Cap'n Kidd & Co, ca. 1908.

JUNIOR PROM DANCE CARD, 1905

PALISADES PROMENADE
(Above)
Pictured in NYU's Violet Yearbook,
1932.

GLEE CLUB
(Left)
Caroling in Times Square, 1950s.

WINTER DANCE
(Left)
Loeb Student Center, early 1960s.

ANNUAL EVENTS
(Below)
Punctuated by humor and pure fun, annual events have always been a part of the University's campus life. They include the Strawberry Festival, the Pancake Breakfast, Founders Day, and the Grad Alley extravaganza. At a recent Pancake Breakfast, University administrators prepared the flapjacks.

(Photo credit: Arnold Adler)

(Photo credit: Janice Panaro)

STRAWBERRY FESTIVAL
(Left)
The Strawberry Festival is held each spring on a block of La Guardia Place next to Bobst Library that is closed to traffic.

GREY ART GALLERY
(Below)
The Grey Art Gallery and Study Center was created in 1975 with a gift from Abby Weed Grey. Located on historic Washington Square Park, the gallery is New York University's fine arts museum. Grey Art Gallery collects, preserves, studies, documents, interprets, and exhibits the evidence of human culture.

(Photo credit: Tim Healy)

CLUB FAIR

(Left)

Each year students can choose their extracurricular activities from a number of clubs on campus.

VIOLET BALL

(Left)

Held annually in the spring, the Violet Ball provides an opportunity for the NYU community to put on their dancing shoes and celebrate in style in the elegantly decorated atrium of Bobst Library.

THE WASHINGTON SQUARE CAMPUS—ON THE ROAD TO THE "GOLDEN AGE"

Even before the University Heights campus was opened, great changes were occurring at Washington Square, where plans were afoot to demolish the old University Building and replace it with the Main Building, which remains to this day. The new Main Building was the creation of Alfred Zucker, a German immigrant whose commercial buildings graced the Washington Square area. Zucker constructed the 10-story loft building between 1894 and 1895. The first seven floors were leased to the American Book Company. The remaining three floors were reserved for New York University's graduate and professional schools and later an undergraduate arts and science division for students unable to attend the residential Bronx campus. One notable critic of the new Main Building was writer Henry James, who was born in 1843 at 21 Washington Place, the site of the new building.

. . . the effect for me, in Washington Place, was of having been amputated of half my history. The grey and more or less "hallowed" University building—wasn't it somehow, with a desperate bravery, both castellated and gabled?—has vanished from the earth, and vanished with it two or three adjacent houses, of which the birthplace was one.

As quoted in the essay "The Jamesian House of Fiction," by Denis Donoghue, in *Around the Square 1830–1890*

Despite James's pique, New York University was experiencing a period of genuine growth and optimism.

THE NEW MAIN BUILDING (*Below*)

REGISTRATION LINE, 1964
(Right)

Before the age of TorchTone, the University's telephone voice-response system (ca. 1992), registering for classes at New York University was usually an all-day affair. Students scurried from department to department assembling their schedule. Files were kept on index cards. Lines were long, and patience and a comfortable pair of shoes were almost as important as a student's grade point average. By comparison, today's NYU students probably spend no more than a few minutes registering. Indeed, one phone call completes initial registration; students may also use TorchTone to make schedule adjustments. And at the end of each semester, TorchTone will even report student grades.

LOOKING INTELLECTUAL
(Right)

Inside the Weinstein Center for Student Living, Washington Square, 1967.

MAIN BUILDING, WASHINGTON SQUARE EAST, 1940
(Opposite)

**MODERN-DAY
COMMENCEMENT
IN WASHINGTON
SQUARE PARK**

OVERVIEW OF THE MODERN CAMPUS

Today's NYU campus reflects the culmination of a billion-dollar building and renovation program that began more than 25 years ago and includes one of the largest open-stack research libraries in the nation and centers and institutes renowned for their research in applied mathematics, physics, neural science, and fine arts. NYU's foreign language and cultural centers offer a wide variety of lectures, films, and concerts. The University's art galleries, film screening center, and exhibition spaces further enrich the campus's cultural offerings. In addition, students have access to an award-winning Office of Career Services and state-of-the-art computer and multimedia facilities.

(Photo credit: Ken Levinson)

(Photo credit: Steve Freidman)

to varsity and club teams as well as intramural and recreational activities, the center holds a three-lane running track and tennis courts on the roof, a natatorium with an NCAA-regulation swimming pool and diving tank, modern weight room, squash and racquetball courts, and other facilities. Pictured at dedication *(left to right)*: John Brademas, then NYU president, with Geraldine H. Coles and Dr. Jerome S. Coles.

JEROME S. COLES SPORTS AND RECREATION CENTER
(Left)
The Coles Sports Center is a state-of-the-art facility serving the recreational needs of the NYU community. Home

(Courtesy KRJDA)

HELEN AND MARTIN KIMMEL CENTER FOR UNIVERSITY LIFE, WHICH INCLUDES THE SKIRBALL CENTER FOR THE PERFORMING ARTS
(Above)
To meet the expanding needs of students, the University is replacing Loeb Student Center with a new and greatly expanded facility, the Helen and Martin Kimmel Center for University Life. The Kimmel Center

will include a dining area and space for student organizations. In addition, a commitment from the Skirball Foundation will create the Skirball Center for the Performing Arts, to be housed within the Kimmel Center, which will be the city's largest performing arts center south of Lincoln Center. Pictured at right are University life trustee Helen L. Kimmel and her husband, Martin Kimmel.

(Photo credit: Alan Orling)

THE WIRED CAMPUS

(Above)

The emergence of new technologies, which has altered campus life, constantly underscores the importance of computing and networking tools in the day-to-day work of the NYU community. Indeed, the University's commitment to use technology to build a strong support structure for teaching, research, and administration is easily read in the following statistics. In September 1995, only 21,000 computer accounts of all types existed within the University for students, faculty, and staff. By fall

1996, 50,000 accounts existed. Today, the number exceeds 80,000. During the same period, expansion of the residential network system in the University's housing facilities has been astonishing. For example, in fall 1995, fewer than 100 connections existed. By fall 1997, there were 1,347 connections. With the addition of network connectivity to Alumni Hall, University Hall, Seventh Street Residence, and Carlyle Court in fall 1998, the number skyrocketed to 7,450. And with the University's additional expansions, these numbers will continue to soar.

THE ELMER HOLMES BOBST LIBRARY

(Right)

One of NYU's most important facilities and a great boon to the campus's intellectual life is the Elmer Holmes Bobst Library and Study Center, the centerpiece of nine NYU libraries with total holdings of more than 4.2 million volumes. Bobst's collections include books, journals, electronic resources, multimedia, archives, and special collections. In a quiet, comfortable environment equipped with hundreds of study carrels and five

two-story reading rooms overlooking Washington Square Park, students pursue their research and study. Students also have access to many of New York City's extraordinary library holdings, thanks to Bobst's cooperative agreements and memberships with other libraries. The library is named for the late pharmaceutical pioneer and NYU donor Elmer Holmes Bobst; his legacy lives on with the continuing support of his widow, Mamdouha Bobst. Mrs. Bobst is pictured with literary critic and author Malcolm Cowley.

(Photo credit: Lou Manna)

STUDENTS IN A NEWLY REFURBISHED LABORATORY
(Right)
NYU has cutting-edge facilities and resources for its students, including this newly refurbished Undergraduate Organic Chemistry Laboratory.

(Photo credit: Bob Handelman)

AN UNMATCHED RECORD OF ACHIEVEMENT
(Below)
Since 1991, NYU has seen a dramatic increase in the number and qualifications of its applicants.

In 1991, there were 10,000 applications received for freshman admission. By 1997, that number had doubled. By 2000, that number had tripled to over 30,750. Not only was it the ninth year in a row of record-setting application levels, it also made NYU the recipient of more applications for admission than any other private college or university in the country.

During this period, the acceptance rate—a key measure of selectivity—fell from 65 percent to about 29 percent.

And the qualifications of entering freshmen increased substantially, with average freshman SAT scores (adjusted) climbing by some 100 points (unadjusted scores have increased by some 140 points). The University's emerging appeal has enabled it to draw students of talent from around the country and around the world, and this has led to substantially increased geographic diversity among students. Fifteen years ago, roughly half the freshman class was from New York City; today it is less than one-fifth. And NYU has more students from foreign lands—some 5,000—than any other U.S. college or university.

EDUCATION

Admission to N.Y.U.: More Than Just Scores

By KAREN W. ARENSON

The glittering silver shoe rimmed in purple feather boa arrived at 22 Washington Square North — the town house that serves as New York University's admissions war room — with a note from Jessica. Now that she had one shoe in the door, the note said, she hoped to get the other one in, too.

Richard Avitabile, director of admissions at N.Y.U. (whose school color is violet) pronounced the shoe "cute, but not too cute."

Mr. Avitabile has seen many gimmicks, from balloons to brownies with the applicant's name on them. Some work. Many do not. But this one provided a bit of sparkle last week during the marathon process that constitutes admissions. "No one gets in just because she sends us a fancy shoe," he said. But if the rest of Jessica's application reflected the same creativity, he noted, it would be a strong plus.

Reading applications is an annual winter ritual on campuses across the country, one that has ballooned in scope at selective colleges as the number of applicants has climbed. But few colleges face anything like the deluge at N.Y.U.

Aided by New York's soaring popularity as a college town and by the university's climb in college ratings, N.Y.U. received 30,750 freshmen applications this year — more than any other private university. That is 10,000 more than it received four years ago and triple the number in 1990. And that does not even count the 4,700 transfer applications. (Even among the public universities, only a few get more applications;

Photographs by Richard Perry/The New York Times

Richard Avitabile, director of admissions at New York University, has seen many gimmicks arrive with applications, like the silver shoe below, and does like creativity.

added, "just like a student who is a dancer or a scientist."

What makes an applicant stand out? Mr. Avitabile says he wants students who do well in the most challenging courses and whose activities suggest they will be "active participants here."

Some favorite examples: There is the

TISCH SCHOOL OF THE ARTS
(Left)
In its short 35-year history, the Tisch School of the Arts has emerged as a major center for the study of the performing and cinematic arts. It is committed to providing an intellectual home for students that gives them the freedom, artistic skills, and social awareness they need to develop as artists. Graduates include Martin Scorsese, Oliver Stone, Amy Heckerling, and Spike Lee.

THE SCHOOL OF LAW
(Opposite)
The School of Law, one of the leading centers in the world for teaching and thinking about law, is a pioneer in the creation of many new methods of instruction in the areas of law, philosophy, clinical education, advocacy training, and international programs. One of its most recent innovations, the Global Law School Program—the first and finest program of its kind in the nation—has led the way in globalizing law study and in preparing students for the increasingly international nature of their work. Among the School of Law's many distinguished graduates are New York City Mayors Fiorello La Guardia, Edward I. Koch, and Rudolph W. Giuliani.

HEALTH CENTER

(Right)

The mission of the New York University Health Center (UHC) is to provide high-quality, accessible, and cost-effective treatment, prevention, education, and health-promotion services for the University community.

STERN SCHOOL OF BUSINESS

(Opposite)

Constructed in 1992, Stern's state-of-the-art Henry Kaufman Management Center united the graduate and undergraduate divisions of the Stern School of Business on one campus for the first time. This union helped Stern further its goal of becoming a world-class center for business and management education. To that end, Stern has aimed to enhance business knowledge and teaching effectiveness, maximize students' career opportunities, and build recognition and support.

(Photo credit: Jennifer Altman)

EDGAR M. BRONFMAN CENTER FOR JEWISH STUDENT LIFE

(Above and right)

The Bronfman Center, opened in 1996, is the central location for Jewish students. The center, providing a wide range of social, cultural, spiritual, and educational programs to students, also serves as a critical point of convergence for Greenwich Village's Jewish community. Morris H. Bergreen, University life trustee, is president of the Skirball Foundation, which has contributed generously to the Bronfman Center.

(Illustration: Robert Gantt Steele)

(Photo credit: Bob Handelman)

IRIS AND B. GERALD CANTOR FILM CENTER

(Right)

Formerly a neighborhood movie theatre, the Cantor Film Center—made
possible by a gift from Mrs. B.
Gerald Cantor—is one of the most
technologically advanced lecture hall
and screening facilities in New York
City. The center's classrooms, theatres, and other accommodations
help NYU carry on its tradition of
cutting-edge filmmaking.

(Rendering courtesy Brody Davis Bond)

(Photo credit: Don Hamerman)

PAULETTE GODDARD HALL, WASHINGTON SQUARE EAST

(Above)

ROBERT F. WAGNER GRADUATE SCHOOL OF PUBLIC SERVICE

(Right)

Phyllis Cerf Wagner, NYU life trustee
and spirit behind the Robert F.
Wagner Graduate School of Public
Service, is pictured here at the
announcement of the naming of the
school. *Left to right:* Robert F.
Wagner, former mayor of New York
City; Marshall Manley, president and
CEO of AmBase Corporation; Mrs.
Wagner; and then NYU president
John Brademas.

(Photo credit: Ken Levinson)

COURANT INSTITUTE OF MATHEMATICAL SCIENCES
(Right)

The Courant Institute is recognized as a leading international center for research and graduate education in applied mathematics and computational science. In the past few years, the institute has increased its focus on interdisciplinary research and education, developing new programs in atmosphere/ocean science, financial mathematics, and computational neuroscience. Faculty at the institute are among the best worldwide, claiming several prestigious awards and greatly contributing to Courant's international reputation

UNIVERSITY HALL

(Above and right)

Applications for admission to NYU have increased by 75 percent since 1992. Students from across the United States and 124 foreign countries are attracted to NYU for its scholarly and cultural resources, and many want to live at the center of campus life. University Hall, which houses approximately 650 students and two faculty residents, is located on East 14th Street at Irving Place and was opened in March of 1999. Each suite offers two bedrooms, a kitchen, bath, and living room with University telephones and cable television; all units are wired for Internet access.

ARTIST'S RENDERING OF THE NEW RESIDENCE HALL, FORMER SITE OF THE PALLADIUM THEATRE
(Above)
Made possible by a billion-dollar building and renovation program, the University has been transformed from a "subway school" into one of the world's great urban university campuses. In the process, from Wall Street to Midtown, the NYU student experience has been energized and recreated. Although a variety of residence halls have been added, certainly one of the most anticipated and ambitious University projects, expected to open in September 2001, is being built on the site of the old Palladium Theatre on East 14th Street. A spectacular addition to NYU's campus life, the $115 million residence hall will house 973 students and encompass a 65,000-square-foot athletic and recreation facility that will include a pool for swimming, diving, and water polo; a basketball court; and exercise spaces for dance, aerobics, and weight training.

HEMMERDINGER HALL
(Above)
Hemmerdinger Hall in Main Building
serves as a student lounge and study
area for the College of Arts and
Science and a focal point for all-
University events. The spacious hall,
dedicated in 1997, was made possible through a donation from H. Dale
Hemmerdinger, NYU trustee and a
1967 graduate of the Washington
Square College of Arts and Science,
as CAS was then known.

MAIN BUILDING
LABORATORIES
(Left)
Recent renovations in Main Building
include several science laboratories
and study centers.

(Photo credit: Bill Miller)

(Photo credit: Bill Miller)

(Illustration: Margaret Kittinger/Beyer, Blinder, Bell)

THE NYU TORCH CLUB

In fall 1999, the NYU Torch Club, a multilevel facility featuring a dining room, a pub, and several meeting places, opened to all NYU faculty, staff, and alumni (artist's rendering, above). The NYU Torch Club began to take shape in fall 1998 when President L. Jay Oliva convened a committee of faculty and administrators, with the late Senior Vice President Debra James serving as chair. The group researched ideas and suggestions for the club's decor and menu as well as for a reservations policy for the dining room and meeting rooms. Among the concepts that emerged from the committee's work was to incorporate the torch, long a symbol of New York University, as the name of the new club. In addition, the committee recommended the display of historic University artifacts and memorabilia inside the club, including the sterling silver torch that is carried in official NYU processions. Designed by Tiffany & Co., the torch was presented to the University in 1911 by Helen Miller Gould.

PERPETUATING AND STRENGTHENING THE PERFORMING ARTS

The purpose of the New York University Musical Theatre Hall of Fame, along with NYU programs in music and musical theatre, is to help perpetuate and strengthen an original and important American cultural art form, musical theatre.

Since 1981, the Graduate Musical Theatre Writing Program in the Tisch School of the Arts has been the only one of its kind designed for the major collaborators—composers, lyricists, bookwriters, and directors—in the creation of new musical theatre and opera.

Its accomplishments include the development of over 100 original works, the formation of many lasting collaborative teams, and the establishment of master teacher and guest artist programs that have brought to the classroom major musical theatre figures such as Harold Prince, Arthur Laurents, and Sheldon Harnick.

In addition, NYU School of Education's Department of Music and Performing Arts Professions offers a full sequence in music theatre. The curriculum gives students professional training in voice, acting, and dance for the musical stage. Students perform in fully staged productions as well as revues and cabaret theatre. Both undergraduate and graduate students are introduced to the many facets of music theatre in Manhattan and learn from professional Broadway artists.

Broadway luminaries who are NYU graduates include (to name a few) Betty Comden; playwrights George C. Wolfe and Tony Kushner; and Gerald Schoenfeld, chairman of the board of the Shubert Organization, Inc.

Inductees into the NYU Musical Theatre Hall of Fame include Jerome Kern, George and Ira Gershwin, Richard Rodgers, Oscar Hammerstein II, Alan Jay Lerner, Frederick Loewe, Mary Martin, and Ethel Merman. Honorees include Carol Channing, Jule Styne, Gwen Verdon, Betty Comden, and Adolph Green.

(Courtesy KRJDA)

SKIRBALL CENTER FOR THE PERFORMING ARTS
(Above)
Touted as the largest theatre south of 42nd Street and the only performing arts center of its kind south of Lincoln Center, the Skirball Center for the Performing Arts was made possible by a $15 million donation from the Skirball Foundation. Housed in the Kimmel Center for University Life, the center will include a 1,022-seat state-of-the-art theatre; a black box theatre for smaller performances; and the Arthur T. Shorin Music Performance Center, which will provide space for rehearsals, workshops, and recitals. The center's projection booth and integrated audio equipment will enable it to hold film screenings and festivals, including the Tisch School of the Arts annual First-Run Film Festival and the biennial NYU International Student Film Festival.

GOTTA SING! GOTTA DANCE!
(Opposite)
A student production of *Brigadoon* featured *(center)* President L. Jay Oliva.

THE GRADUATE ACTING PROGRAM

(Opposite)

A workshop production of *Angels in America: A Gay Fantasia on National Themes— Part II: Perestroika* by Tisch School alumnus Tony Kushner featured graduate acting students Jenna Stern and Daniel Zelman. From this workshop, the play—which retained many of its NYU players—moved to Broadway. The Tisch School of the Arts Graduate Acting Program, a three-year training program, prepares students for the professional theatre.

DEPARTMENT OF DRAMA, UNDERGRADUATE

(Above)

Students performing in the 1997 production of Marc Blitzstein's *The Cradle Will Rock*. Each year, there are more than 90 productions mounted on which student actors from 12 acting and technical studios within the Department of Drama can work together.

HELLO, DOLLY!

(Right)

NYU Musical Theatre Hall of Fame honored actress Carol Channing in 1993.

(Photo credit: Merk Redis)

ORCHESTRA '99

(Above)

The NYU Center for Music Performance brings a diverse range of programming to NYU throughout the academic year. The center produces workshops, lectures, and concerts such as Orchestra '99.

WHIRLIGIG

(Left)

Members of Whirligig, the New York-based acoustic group and Celtic ensemble, were artists-in-residence at NYU's Center for Music Performance.

(Photo courtesy of Whirligig. Photo credit: Jimmy Johnson)

(Photo credits: Merk Redis)

NYU CELEBRATES BLACK HISTORY MONTH HONORING DUKE ELLINGTON

(Above)

In February 1999, the Gallatin School of Individualized Study and the Center for Music Performance, in association with the Actors Equity Association Committee for Racial Equality, honored the 100th birthday and lifetime achievements of musician and composer Edward Kennedy (Duke) Ellington. The celebration featured discussions, musical dance performances, film screenings, and a keynote address by the maestro's granddaughter, Mercedes Ellington. Andre De Shields (Gallatin '91), a Tony Award nominee and 1999 NYU artist-in-residence, also offered various tribute performances. The highlight event was a concert version of Ellington's *Play On* (an adaptation of Shakespeare's *Twelfth Night*), narrated and directed by Sheldon Epps, seen here front row center (with scarf). Mercedes Ellington is to Epps's right.

ALL-UNIVERSITY GOSPEL CHOIR

(Left and below)

Closing ceremony of African Heritage Month featuring the NYU All-University Gospel Choir and guest speaker Professor Robin D. G. Kelley from the Department of History and Program in Africana Studies.

(Courtesy Bob Butler)

LA HERENCIA LATINA

(Above)

Latin Heritage Month was organized in 1990 by La Herencia Latina, a group of students from different clubs and organizations who saw the need for celebrating and teaching people about Latino culture and experiences. The student-run committee coordinates and hosts several programs, events, panel discussions, lectures, concerts, and cultural activities each November—the official month in which New York University recognizes Latino heritage and its worldwide impact.

ALL-UNIVERSITY HOLIDAY SING, 1999

(Opposite, top and bottom)

Each December, members of the NYU and Greenwich Village communities join together to participate in the All-University Holiday Sing. The event features a variety of student vocal and instrumental groups. The grand finale includes a performance by President L. Jay Oliva.

(Photo credits: Meir Redis)

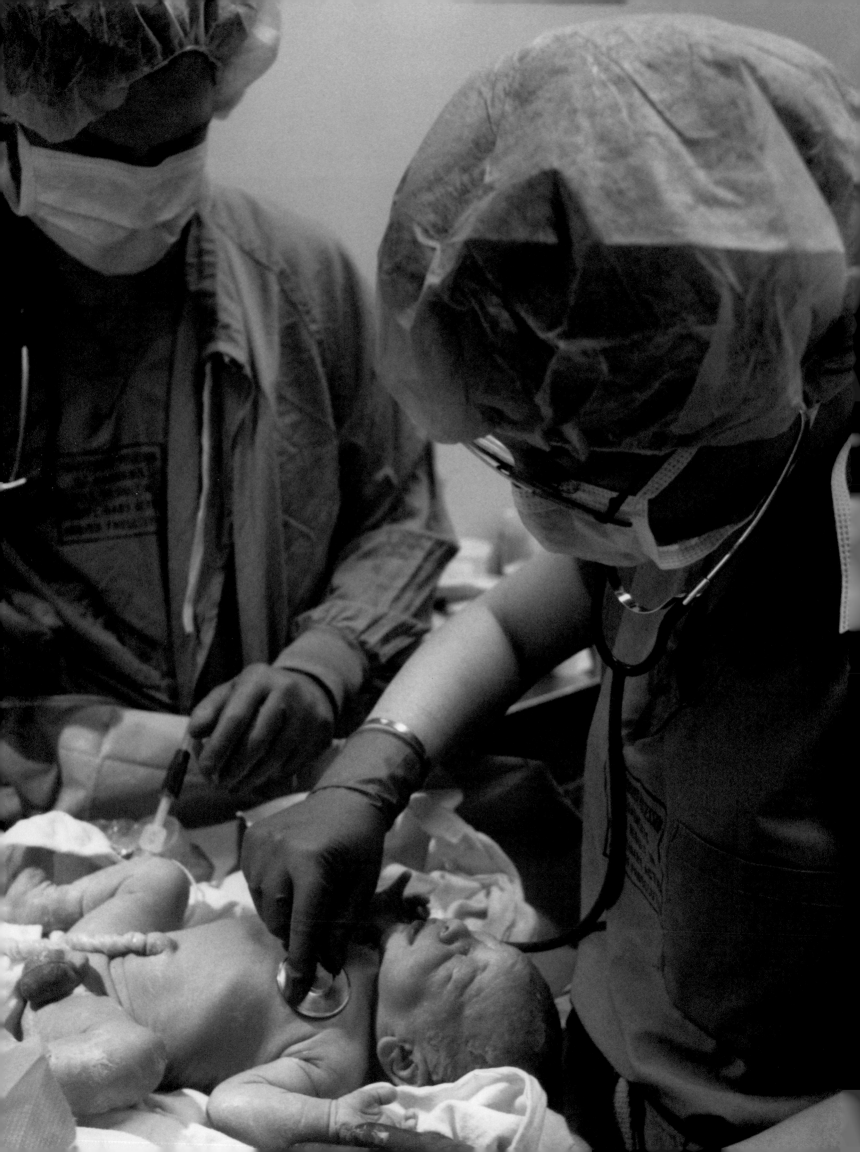

I n 1831, New York City was already a booming metropolis. Yet despite the city's growing reputation as a center for commerce and culture, it was often a hazardous place to be because there was no dependable water supply, no organized fire department, and no effective system of providing social and medical services.

The University's founders recognized that the city would benefit greatly from a community of scholars and students who would offer their services to those most in need. They also understood that community service should be an integral part of a well-balanced education, as enriching to the giver as to the receiver. Thus, this

MEDICAL STUDENTS LEARNING FROM SEASONED PRACTITIONERS (*Opposite*)

powerful commitment to serve flowed directly from the University's intellectual mission and from its determination to be a part of and a partner in the great city in which it dwelled.

An example of one of the University's earliest services to the city is found in an 1853 address to alumni by John William Draper, a revered professor of chemistry and natural history in the University's Medical Department. In this speech, Professor Draper talked passionately about the University's contributions to the city. In 12 years, Professor Draper noted, the Medical Department had trained some 1,200 physicians and treated some 2,000 destitute New Yorkers annually. Professor Draper asked:

> *Can you point out, in any part of the world, an Institution which has done more for the cause of learning and charity? Is not the City deeply indebted…for the charities so dispensed?*

As the years have passed, the University has continued to reach out in ever-widening circles in its efforts to serve the community. But in a city as large and diverse as New York, the number of compassionate and creative programs needed is infinite.

First Lady Hillary Rodham Clinton, appreciating the scale and commitment of the University's efforts, has made several visits to the University in which she shared her optimism about the future of national and community service at NYU. In a speech delivered at the University in 1997, the First Lady stated:

> *Citizen service is an essential part of every person's education.…Certainly one of the great leaders of our country, Dr. Martin Luther King, Jr., said it best when he said, "everyone can be great, because everyone can serve."*

SERVICE AND THE HEALING ARTS: NYU MEDICAL MILESTONES

1841

The New York University College of Medicine opens. Committed to strengthening the education of America's physicians, original faculty includes John Revere, son of patriot Paul Revere, and Valentine Mott, the foremost surgeon of his day.

1847

Clinical instruction begins at Bellevue Hospital.

1854

Human dissection in New York is legalized due to efforts of faculty at the NYU College of Medicine. Lewis A. Sayre, first professor of orthopedic surgery in the United States, performs the first successful resection of a hip joint.

1861

Bellevue Hospital Medical College is founded.

1861–1865

Faculty members of the NYU College of Medicine play a leading role in treating wounded Civil War soldiers, chiefly through their work with the United States Sanitary Commission.

1866

NYU professors of medicine produce a Report for the Council of Hygiene and Public Health. It leads to the establishment of New York City's Health Department.

HORSE-DRAWN AMBULANCES OUTSIDE BELLEVUE HOSPITAL
(Above)

FIRST STAFF OF INTERNS AT BELLEVUE HOSPITAL, 1856
(Left)

(Photos on pages 153-55 courtesy of the NYU Medical Center Archives)

1866

The first outpatient clinic in the United States opens at NYU.

1872

NYU's Stephen Smith, M.D., founds the American Public Health Association.

1884

The Carnegie Laboratory, the first facility in the United States devoted to teaching and research in bacteriology and pathology, is established at NYU.

1898

As the years pass, it becomes clear that University Medical College and Bellevue Hospital Medical College would benefit from consolidation. Thus, the medical school becomes an integral part of New York University in 1898 under the name of University and Bellevue Hospital Medical College.

1899

Dr. Walter Reed, an NYU graduate, discovers the transmission of yellow fever by mosquitoes.

1911

The first outpatient cardiac clinic in New York is established by NYU's Hubert V. Guile, M.D.

1931

Albert Sabin, who later developed a live-virus vaccine against polio, receives his M.D. degree at NYU.

1932

The first department of forensic medicine in the United States is established at NYU.

1932

NYU organizes one of the nation's first interdisciplinary research efforts, the Rheumatic Diseases Study Group, helping to usher in the era of modern rheumatology.

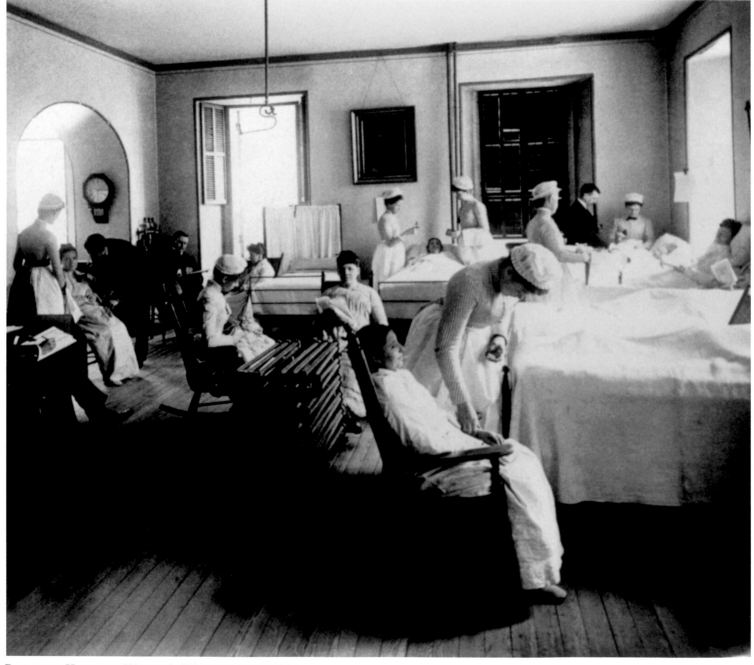

BELLEVUE HOSPITAL WOMEN'S WARD IN THE 1890S

1933

William S. Tillett, M.D., conducts groundbreaking studies of enzymes involved in blood clotting. His work leads to the development of streptokinase, used to combat heart attacks.

1935

University and Bellevue Hospital Medical College changes its name to New York University College of Medicine and, in 1960, to New York University School of Medicine.

1939

Jonas Salk, developer of the first vaccine against polio, receives his M.D. degree at NYU.

1941

NYU establishes the first department of physical medicine and rehabilitation in the United States.

1941-1945

During the war years, NYU-trained Julius Axelrod and faculty members work in the College of Medicine's malaria program. Dr. Axelrod is later awarded the Nobel Prize for medicine.

1947

A site for a new medical center, which would consist of the NYU College of Medicine, the Post-Graduate Medical School, University (now Tisch) Hospital, and the Rusk Institute of Rehabilitation Medicine, is selected.

1947

NYU establishes the Institute of Industrial Medicine.

1948

University Hospital is created through a merger of the New York Post-Graduate Hospital and New York Skin and Cancer Hospital.

1954

Lewis Thomas, M.D., assumes chairmanship of the Department of Pathology. He became chairman of the Department of Medicine in 1964 and dean of the school in 1966.

BELLEVUE HOSPITAL OPERATING ROOM IN THE LATE 19TH CENTURY

1955
The Medical Science Building and the Henry W. and Albert Berg Institute open at NYU.

1957
The Hall of Research and Alumni Hall are constructed.

1959
The Nobel Prize for Medicine is awarded to NYU faculty member Severo Ochoa, M.D., for his seminal study of biochemical genetics and nucleic acids.

1960
NYU establishes the Clinical Research Center, which is funded by the National Institutes of Health (NIH).

1960s
NYU pathologist Baruj Benacerraf, M.D., conducts pioneering research on genetic regulation of the immune system, for which he is later awarded the Nobel Prize in Medicine in 1980.

1962
NYU establishes one of the first M.D.-Ph.D. programs in the United States.

1963
The new University Hospital opens.

1964
The Institute and Department of Environmental Medicine are established.

ALEXANDRA JOYNER, SKIRBALL PROFESSOR OF GENETICS,
IS ONE OF THE UNIVERSITY'S THREE CURRENT HOWARD HUGHES MEDICAL INSTITUTE INVESTIGATORS

(Photo credit: Christopher Little)

1980

Saul Krugman, M.D., professor of pediatrics, develops the first vaccine against hepatitis B.

1981

NYU scientists present the first evidence linking a rare cancer, Kaposi's sarcoma, with immune deficiency in a distinct population of homosexual men, a key step in identifying AIDS.

1992

NYU Medical Center opens Women's Health Services under the auspices of the Departments of Obstetrics and Gynecology and Radiology.

1993

The School of Medicine's Skirball Institute of Biomolecular Medicine, the largest building project in NYU's history, opens. It is an uncompromising commitment to the advancement and understanding of molecular approaches for the treatment of disease.

1998

The Mount Sinai-NYU Medical Center/Health System is established.

1999

The academic affiliation between Mount Sinai School of Medicine and New York University becomes effective.

NEW YORK UNIVERSITY MEDICAL CENTER (CA. 1997)

(Photo credit: Lou Manna)

(Photo credit: Lou Manna)

SKIRBALL INSTITUTE OF BIOMOLECULAR MEDICINE
(Left)
Participants at the dedication of the Skirball Institute of Biomolecular Medicine included Adele Bergreen; Morris H. Bergreen, NYU life trustee and president of the Skirball Foundation; Thomas S. Murphy, then School of Medicine Foundation Board chairman; Charles Kenis; and Audrey Skirball-Kenis.

THE NYU DAVID B. KRISER DENTAL CENTER

In 1865, the New York College of Dentistry began modestly with 31 students and 10 faculty members. The teaching facility consisted of rented rooms on Fifth Avenue and 22nd Street, and the first class had nine graduates, four of whom were New Yorkers. In 1891, the New York College of Dentistry moved to its own building at 209 East 23rd Street where laboratories for practical work were installed.

The formal merger between the New York College of Dentistry and NYU occurred in 1925 and was based on the notion of uniting a high-quality professional education in conjunction with a fundamental awareness of people's needs. The College's founders felt strongly that dental students required the same rigorous training in the basic medical sciences as students training to become physicians. Soon after the merger with NYU, an affiliation, which remains strong to this day, was established with Bellevue Hospital.

With the dawning of NYU's clinical education in dentistry—which often reached out to those in dire circumstances—came the irrevocable link to community service that has remained unbroken for more than a century. The New York College of Dentistry's bulletin in 1875 reported some 8,000 surgeries had been performed in the College's clinic that year. Today, some 250,000 patient visits are made annually to the NYU Kriser Dental Center's clinics, where students and faculty provide a full range of oral health care. Most of the people who come to the clinics cannot afford private dental care. They are the indigent, the elderly, the homeless, and others in desperate need. One can only imagine the immense pride that the founders would feel if they could today behold the vast range of community service currently offered by its protean successor.

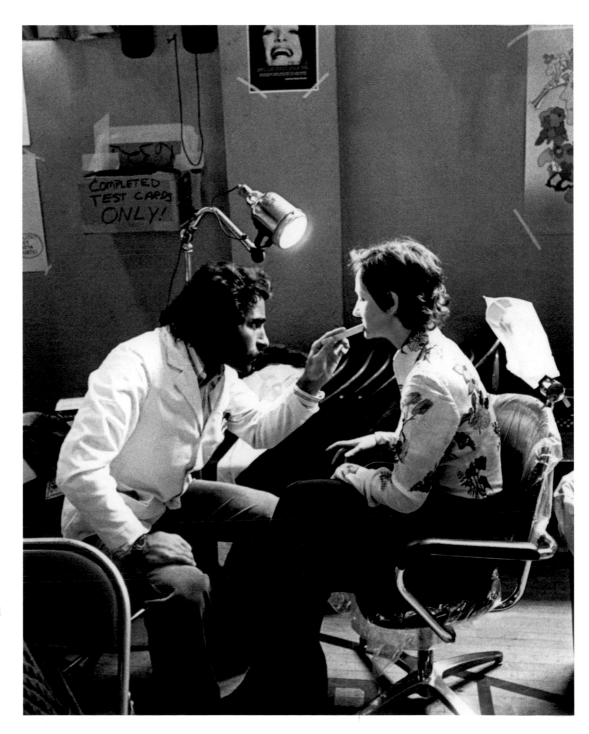

THE NEW YORK COLLEGE OF DENTISTRY, CA. 1930
(Opposite)

DENTAL CARE FOR EVERYONE
(Right)
The NYU Kriser Dental Center's annual free screening programs are the largest public health outreach activities in the nation. NYU's Dental Clinics annually provide more than 6,000 New York-area adults, children, and infants with free dental examinations, which include oral health-care instructions and screenings for dental health, oral cancer, and other cancers.

AN EXTRAORDINARY RANGE OF OUTREACH

Emergency dental services for more than 15,000 New Yorkers annually, including 5,000 emergency patients who are treated free of charge each year.

• Special treatment facilities for the physically and emotionally handicapped, the frail, the elderly, the medically compromised, and the neurologically impaired.

• Free oral health care provided directly to 5,000 children each year in their neighborhood schools and to 1,000 homeless children living in the city's shelters, in addition to free comprehensive care for homeless youngsters at the Kriser Center's clinics.

• Special infant dental education area for parents and caregivers.

• Free orthodontic care for poor and minority public schoolchildren.

• Nation's largest program of pediatric oral health services for children enrolled in the federally funded Head Start program.

• Free perinatal education and oral health care provided directly to homeless mothers and their infants in community shelters throughout the city.

• Low-cost, prepaid dental care programs for all New York City college students, their spouses, and dependents and for all city high school students.

• The only fully accredited, University-based Dental Hygiene Program in New York State, in addition to a certificate program for training dental assistants. Both programs broaden access to educational and career opportunities for nontraditional and minority students.

• An overseas dental outreach program to bring care to indigent populations in the Dominican Republic.

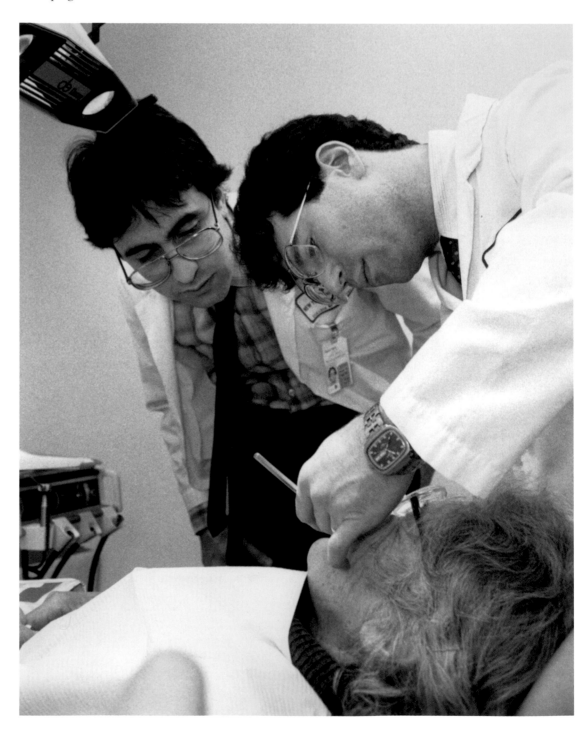

CARE FOR SENIORS
(Right)
NYU's "Golden Care" Program is the strongest and most extensive outreach program for the aging in the nation. Established in 1980, the program brings high-quality dental treatment directly to thousands of older New Yorkers in nursing homes and senior citizen facilities who would not otherwise have access to routine dental care.

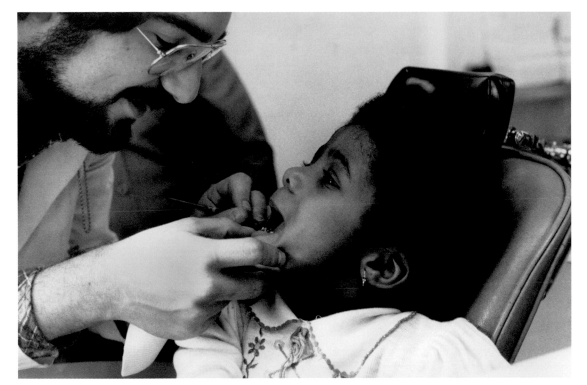

PEDIATRIC OUTREACH
(Left)
NYU's Pediatric Outreach Program provides more than 5,000 school-children each year with instruction in oral hygiene and nutrition at multiple off-site programs in different community settings. In addition, 3,000 physically and emotionally disabled youngsters receive free care annually in their neighborhood schools.

ARNOLD AND MARIE SCHWARTZ HALL OF DENTAL SCIENCES
(Left)
Marie Schwartz *(above)*, president, Arnold and Marie Schwartz Fund for Education and Health Research, and the late Arnold Schwartz *(above)* were major donors to New York University College of Dentistry's state-of-the-art facility located at East 24th Street and First Avenue.

(Photo credit: Phil Gallo)

NYU AND THE WAR EFFORTS

Military training was first introduced to NYU during World War I.

Following World War I, a wave of antiwar feeling swept the campus as NYU students took the Oxford Pledge, which opposed military training on campus. But Japan's surprising and devastating attack on Pearl Harbor in 1941 put to rest student antiwar activism, already curbed by the 1939 Hitler-Stalin Pact.

The world was at war. In this milieu, NYU would face one of its most dramatic challenges. Although the University would heroically support the war effort, an era of declining enrollment and severe budget deficits loomed. Despite a precarious future, it was apparent to anyone attending the Heights campus during World War II that the facilities of NYU to a large extent had been taken over by the army. Indeed, NYU was creatively engaged in fighting two wars: one, to save the world; the other, to save the University.

University administrators recognized NYU's potential for helping the government's defense activities. Through its War Placement Bureau, the University assigned many of its technically trained faculty and staff to military and civilian agency positions. Among these agencies were the Civil Service Commission, Office of Education, Office of Strategic Services, and War Production Board.

Another strategy, recalled Provost Rufus D. Smith in 1946, was the temporary transfer of faculty:

> . . .from subject to subject, from department to department, from school to school. . . .
>
> A teacher of philosophy with a latent background in mathematics and physics soon found himself teaching the latter subjects while a teacher of the classics, because of his knowledge in chemistry, secured a temporary divorce from Latin and Greek. . . .
>
> *New York University and the City*
> by Thomas J. Frusciano and Marilyn H. Pettit

NYU was among the first universities chosen by the army to train soldiers. It also was one of only three colleges in the country qualified to offer instruction in meteorology. A World War II issue of the *Violet* proudly brags about NYU's stalwart war efforts:

> Each man, after he receives his basic training, starts his study of wind changes, pressure areas, and barometer reading. Each man who finishes this nine- to ten-month course emerges as a well-trained weatherman ready for service at camps and airfields anywhere.

Monday, Aug. 3d. Today Germany declared war on France. Here, it is the last of the summer bank holidays, and it has been an eventful and a trying day for a good many Americans as well as English. The war situation is growing more acute for the English, while London is being filled with Americans who have rushed or have been rushed from the continent by the war, and in many instances are fairly stranded here.

THE GREAT WAR BEGINS
(Left)
An excerpt from "Tour of England, 1914," the travel journal kept by Dr. Daniel Webster Hering, professor of engineering and physics at University Heights.

NYU ANSWERS THE CALL
(Above)
When enrollment declined with the outbreak of World War I, NYU worked with the Department of War to provide military training. In 1918, NYU established units of the National Army Training Detachment and the Student Army Training Corps (SATC).

SOCKS FOR SOLDIERS
(Above)
Idle hands were nonexistent at NYU when it came to the war effort. In an NYU knitting group (ca. 1918), women knit socks for needy soldiers.

AMBULANCE VOLUNTEERS
(Left)
In 1917, NYU established units for service in the Red Cross ambulance companies. This company of 120 men was given a condensed course of instruction and was quickly called to France.

A LETTER DATED MAY 1, 1918,
THAT WAS SENT TO
CHANCELLOR ELMER BROWN
BY PRESIDENT TAFT

For the work this year the League must have more funds than it had last year. Issues are at stake that must be met. So we trust that you will be glad not only to renew the subscription you formerly made for the League's work, but, if possible, to increase it, and so increase our effectiveness. We are asking all of our subscribers to join with us in renewing their contributions before the coming Convention in Philadelphia May 16 and 17, so that the League may be assured of the support necessary to keep its great work going forward.

Heavy calls are being made upon all of us for Red Cross, Liberty Loans, and other war activities, but we make this call in full confidence because it is only through the creation of the League of Nations for which we are working that all of our sacrifices of men and money shall not have been in vain. We dare not shirk and pass on to other generations a task that is our own.

We are taking the liberty of enclosing a card so that you can indicate the amount of your subscription and the dates during the year when it will be most convenient to make payments.

Yours very truly,

W. H. Taft

W. H. Short

Herbert S. Houston

Edward A. Filene

"Our combined armies from now on will represent a league to enforce peace with justice." — SECRETARY-OF-WAR BAKER

League Formed in Independence Hall June 17, 1915

LEAGUE TO ENFORCE PEACE

WILLIAM HOWARD TAFT · · · President
ALTON B. PARKER · · · Vice-President

Chairman of Executive Committee:
A. LAWRENCE LOWELL

Vice-Chairmen of Executive Committee:
EDWARD A. FILENE   HAMILTON HOLT   THEODORE MARBURG

HERBERT S. HOUSTON, Treasurer   WILLIAM H. SHORT, Secretary

70 FIFTH AVENUE, NEW YORK

May 1, 1918.

EXECUTIVE COMMITTEE

LOUIS J. ALBER
C. B. AMES
CHARLES H. BROUGH
HUGH H. BROWN
ASA G. CANDLER
ARTHUR CAPPER
JOHN BATES CLARK
E. J. COUPER
OLIVER CROSBY
CHARLES STEWART DAVISON
HENRY S. DRINKER
JOHN H. FAHEY
JOHN B. FINLEY
GEORGE MUNRO FORREST
WILLIAM DUDLEY FOULKE
GLENN FRANK
EDWARD W. FROST
PHILIP H. GADSDEN
HARRY A. GARFIELD
JOHN HAYS HAMMOND
JAMES H. HAWLEY
JOHN GRIER HIBBEN
HERBERT S. HOUSTON
HAROLD J. HOWLAND
HENRY C. IDE
HOMER H. JOHNSON
FREDERICK N. JUDSON
W. T. KEMPER
CHARLES DEAN KIMBALL
DARWIN P. KINGSLEY
HENRY M. LELAND
HENRY D. LINDSLEY
FREDERICK LYNCH
VANCE C. McCORMICK
E. T. MEREDITH
MRS. PHILIP NORTH MOORE
ARTHUR E. MORGAN
LAVERNE W. NOYES
WILLIAM RUSSELL O'NEAL
BRUCE R. PAYNE
LEROY PERCY
MRS. THOMAS J. PRESTON, JR.
LEO S. ROWE
WILLIAM L. SAUNDERS
WM. JAY SCHIEFFELIN
ANNA HOWARD SHAW
FINLEY J. SHEPARD
WILLIAM H. SHORT
WILLIAM F. SLOCUM
BOLTON SMITH
OSCAR S. STRAUS
FRANK S. STREETER
HENRY SUZZALLO
M. CAREY THOMAS
RUFUS B. VON KLEINSMID
WILLIAM H. WADHAMS
CHARLES S. WARD
THOMAS RAEBURN WHITE
TALCOTT WILLIAMS

Dr. Elmer E. Brown,
32 Waverly Pl.,
New York City.

Dear Dr. Brown:

With the guns booming in France and our own men swinging into the tremendous contest, it is difficult, we confess, to plan for the great days of victorious peace. But, however difficult it may be, we must prepare for using victory even while we are fighting for it, or we shall fail to meet the test either of the present or the future.

In the letter we joined in sending you last week, we undertook to present a brief summary of the remarkable progress made in the past two and a half years by the League to Enforce Peace. That was a record of achievement made possible by the generous contributions which you and others placed behind the work.

The League, of course, places the supreme emphasis upon winning the war. Without that, all is lost. But the war is to be won. It must be and will be. Any other conclusion is unthinkable. And when the war is won, a League of Nations, standing for right and justice, must rise from the defeat of autocratic might.

It is clear, therefore, that during the remainder of the war, the League faces a double obligation -- to help keep the nation keyed up to fight for victory, and to plan to make the fruits of victory secure. The work before us is of the deepest import to the world. If it should fail, a generation or a century might pass before another opportunity to set up a League of Nations would be presented comparable to the present one.

STAYING PREPARED BETWEEN THE WARS
(Above)
ROTC field days were an annual event at University Heights. At the May 14, 1924, field day, Ohio Field was converted into a miniature battlefield, and each student was equipped with a blanket, helmet, and gas mask.

WORLD WAR II *VIOLET*
(Right)
Letter from NYU Chancellor Harry Woodburn Chase to the Class of 1944.

TO THE MEMBERS OF THE GRADUATING CLASS:

I AM happy to know that the edition of the annual VIOLET is not to be discontinued in spite of the war and the military occupation of University Heights. It is too good a publication to miss an issue.

It was only the other day when I read over a list of letters from this office that had been addressed to students and alumni that I realized how far New York University had gone since the days before Pearl Harbor.

Our total registration for this fall has dropped about twenty-seven percent under that of last fall, a heavy enough blow, but less than we had feared. It is no small matter that altogether by this time we have trained or have had in training at New York University over three thousand soldiers assigned to us for various types of programs. It is trying to carry on this effort for its soldier students and, at the same time, to be fair to the civilians who have enrolled. This is, I assure you, not an easy task in these days when teachers in certain specialized fields have become rarities and when faculty members are called away to take jobs in Government and industry.

We have our troubles but the heartening things about the University to me far outweigh the others. In the first place, the war has taught us how to work together in ways that we have never contemplated before. It has taught us how to do without many things for a while and yet we have made every effort to keep up the quality of our instruction. And it is a good quality. Reports of many sorts have come to me from many places speaking of the way in which the educational qualifications of New York University students stand up under competition with those from other places. This is a tribute both to the students and to the faculty and one of which we are proud, as we are proud of the records of advancement, promotion and bravery made by thousands of our former students in every branch of the armed forces.

University College, even amid war conditions is carrying on, and the College of Engineering is busy as never before. To both of them my best wishes and Godspeed.

Cordially yours,

Harry Woodburn Chase

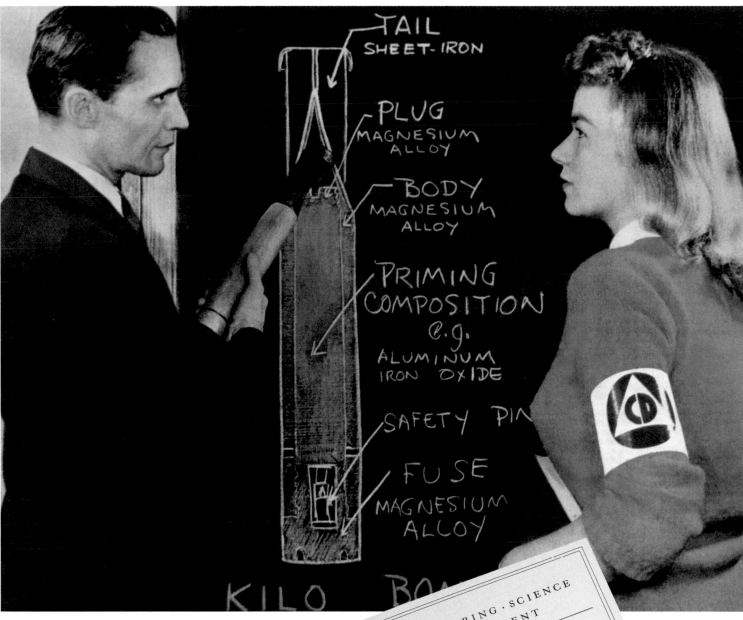

CIVIL DEFENSE
(Above)
In 1942, volunteers taught civil
defense courses for faculty and
students.

**SOLDIERS IN WASHINGTON
SQUARE**
(Opposite)
Soldiers were a familiar sight around
Washington Square during World
War II since NYU's military pro-
grams helped train students for the
army, navy, and air force.

LEARNING WAR SKILLS
(Right)
The Engineering, Science, and
Management War Training Division
of the College of Engineering offered
war-accelerated training courses at
the University Heights campus. The
efforts of the College of Engineering
now focused on the teaching of
meteorology and engineering to
cadets sent to NYU by military
authorities and government agencies.
By World War II's end, more than
18,000 students had been trained in
NYU's engineering courses.

WOMEN AND ENGINEERING
(Above)
Another World War II effort was the College of Engineering's eight-month program of basic training in aeronautical engineering for female graduates with majors in mathematics or physics. The Chance Vought Aviation Company provided full tuition scholarships and living accommodations.

DRILLING ON WASHINGTON PLACE
(Opposite)
During the war, soldiers in training at Washington Square were housed in converted classrooms and student lounges (July 1944).

NYU AND THE POSTWAR YEARS

Returning World War II veterans came home to a different America—a more optimistic, more modern America.

In Nassau County on Long Island, a private, low-cost housing development called Levittown was built especially for veterans and their families. Soon almost every American family would have a television, and Tuesday nights at 8 p.m. would be owned by comedian Milton Berle.

It was a new beginning for NYU, too. These returning veterans helped buoy NYU's student body. New faculty was added, and new programs created. As the University's reputation rose, more and more distinguished visitors such as Eleanor Roosevelt and Jackie Robinson came to share their wisdom.

The notion of service to New York City, always central to the philosophy of the medical and dental schools, grew in importance as each school within the University began to fully develop its special niche of services on a citywide, regional, state, national, and even international level.

A CHRISTMAS CELEBRATION
(Above)
The School of Education's annual Christmas concert enlivened the 1940 holiday season and was broadcast to New Yorkers over the Municipal Broadcasting System.

JACKIE ROBINSON
(Right)
Baseball great Jackie Robinson receives a plaque commemorating his participation in a public affairs and education lecture on December 12, 1957. The event was sponsored by the Graduate Students' Organization.

VISIT FROM THE FIRST LADY

(Left)

Many devotees of community service have visited NYU to share their wisdom and experiences with students and faculty. Former First Lady Eleanor Roosevelt discussed "Politics as It Affects Public Education" in NYU's Education Building on March 15, 1956.

THE NUTRITION LABORATORY (CA. 1950)

(Below)

Courses in nutrition were taught as early as 1927 in the School of Education's Department of Health Education and were later organized into a separate division in the Department of Home Economics. The courses prepared students for careers as dietitians, nutritionists, and research workers in food and nutrition.

AN EDUCATION REACHING FAR BEYOND THE CLASSROOM

The notion of service to the community is an underlying principle of education found in every school in the University.

At the School of Education, the Nordoff-Robbins Music Therapy Center provides clinical music therapy services for children with disabilities, offers advanced training to music therapists, conducts research, and regularly disseminates information to professional audiences and the general public. The Reading Recovery Program, an intervention program for first graders who exhibit early reading difficulties, serves as the primary teacher-leader training site for the Reading Recovery Program in New York and New Jersey. The Hartford Institute for Geriatric Nursing is shaping the quality of health care that elderly Americans receive by promoting the highest level of competency in the nurses who deliver that care.

(Photo credit: Phil Gallo)

ZZ TOP AT NORDOFF-ROBBINS MUSIC THERAPY CENTER
(Above)
Located at the School of Education, the Nordoff-Robbins Music Therapy Center sponsors events for special-needs children such as the session shown here with the musical group ZZ Top.

(Photo credit: Enrique Cubillo)

READING RECOVERY PROGRAM
(Above)
Approximately 2,500 children have been served by the 450 teachers trained through the program who now work in 300 schools.

DEVELOPING A NATIONAL AGENDA FOR IMPROVED GERIATRIC NURSING
(Right)
In 1996, the John A. Hartford Foundation of New York City continued its groundbreaking work in support of geriatrics by awarding NYU $5 million to establish the John A. Hartford Foundation Institute for Geriatric Nursing Practice. The institute was the first of its kind in the nation and is devoted to developing and implementing a comprehensive national agenda for improved geriatric nursing practice.

(Photo credit: Seligson)

At Tisch School of the Arts, the Department of Cinema Studies hosted a 1999 conference celebrating the work of legendary filmmaker Alfred Hitchcock. The five-day international gathering assembled well-known Hitchcock actors, writers, film professionals, historians, critics, and leading scholars to commemorate and explore the 50-year career of one of the most significant artists of the 20th century. The public came in droves. Tisch School's many student showcases, an

initiative of former dean David Oppenheim expanded by current dean Mary Schmidt Campbell, has brought student work to industry leaders for decades. This service to the nation's artistic community also proved a boon to the soaring careers of such alumni as Alec Baldwin, Tony Kushner, Spike Lee, Susan Seidelman, George C. Wolfe, and others.

(Photo credit: Enrique Cubillo)

TSOA HITCHCOCK CENTENNIAL
(Above)
In October 1999, the Tisch School of the Arts sponsored "Hitchcock: A Centennial Celebration," to commemorate the career of the influential artist Alfred Hitchcock. The event featured screenings of such famous works as *Psycho* and *North by*

Northwest. Present at the celebration were *(left to right)* actress Teresa Wright *(Shadow of a Doubt)*, actress Eva Marie Saint *(North by Northwest)*, daughter Pat Hitchcock, and actress Janet Leigh *(Psycho)*.

TISCH SCHOOL OF THE ARTS DEAN'S COUNCIL
(Opposite)
From left to right: Spike Lee, director; Iris Cantor, founder of the Iris and B. Gerald Cantor Film Center; Mary Schmidt Campbell, dean of Tisch; and actor Alec Baldwin at a 1997 Dean's Council meeting at the Tisch School of the Arts.

(Photo credit: Phil Gallo)

At the NYU School of Law, the Public Interest Law Center's Programs and Services are designed primarily to support public service commitment and increase public service career opportunities for NYU students. Its PSLawNet, a pro bono program founded at NYU Law in 1991, is now administered by the center for more than 95 schools nationwide. Through the PSLawNet database, students are placed throughout the country at more than 2,800 nonprofit organizations, public interest law firms, and government agencies to volunteer 5 to 10 hours per week during the school year or full time during the summer in law-related community service. In addition, the School

of Law 's Root-Tilden-Kern Scholarship remains the nation's foremost public service scholarship program.

In 1999, at the Shirley M. Ehrenkranz School of Social Work, a Sino-American cross-cultural training project brought 33 children's services workers to NYU from the Chinese Children's Fund of Taiwan. The project, under the direction of NYU professor Yuhwa Eva Lu, provided training in the general areas of child, youth, and family protection.

(Photo credit: Ken Levinson)

(Photo credit: Ken Levinson)

SEVENTH PUBLIC SERVICE FORUM

(Above)

Professor Alexander Boraine speaking at the Seventh Public Service Forum at the School of Law. Boraine is a professor at the NYU School of Law and the vice president of South Africa's Truth and Reconciliation Commission.

SINO-AMERICAN CROSS-CULTURAL TRAINING PROJECT

(Left)

The Shirley M. Ehrenkranz School of Social Work hosted this event for children's services workers from Taiwan.

At the Wagner Graduate School of Public Service, every student must complete a final project that encourages him or her to synthesize the knowledge that has been acquired. Almost all students take advantage of a Capstone course, which generally requires students to work together in teams to complete a project for an external client, often a government agency, nonprofit organization, or health care institution in New York City. These projects range dramatically from conducting a demographic analysis of downtown Manhattan for an urban planner, to researching and writing an economic development guidebook for a community advocacy group, to conducting a cost-benefit analysis of a proposed cardiac unit for a local hospital. By the time the project is completed, students have participated in an experience that helps them understand the rigors associated with examining and making recommendations on a real public service issue. By the time the project is completed, students

have also made a substantial contribution to the infrastructure and life of New York City.

In 1984, poet Sharon Olds began a special project within the Creative Writing Program in which NYU graduate students conduct classes for people with disabilities. Classes are held at the Coler-Goldwater Memorial Hospital, a municipal institution for the severely disabled located on Roosevelt Island. The program offers a unique opportunity to those imprisoned by illness and pain to express themselves. The program was begun with financing from Very Special Arts, a foundation created by Jean Kennedy Smith.

Just these few examples demonstrate the ability of the University to provide a variety of services and fill a mountain of needs while constantly enriching the student experience. This notion of service, woven within the fabric of the educational process, is so nuanced and natural that it sometimes goes unsung.

CREATIVE WRITING FOR THE DISABLED
(Left)

Through NYU's graduate Creative Writing Program, patients at the Coler-Goldwater Memorial Hospital for those with severe disabilities are able to take classes and learn to express themselves through the written word. Poet Sharon Olds created the program through funds from Jean Kennedy Smith's Very Special Arts foundation. Here, patient Vanessa Cole writes a poem with the help of student teacher Jennifer Keller.

THE CAT AUDIENCE
(Above)

The Creative Arts Team, or CAT, is the professional educational theatre company in residence at the Gallatin School. Founded in 1974, the company has pioneered the use of drama as an educational tool in public schools and community centers throughout New York City.

IN THE 1990S, THE NOBLE TRADITION CONTINUES

Senior Vice President Debra James

(Photo credit: Bard Martin)

In a career laced with accomplishment and spanning more than two decades, Senior Vice President Debra James's* contributions to the University's community service efforts are exemplary. Thanks to her dedication and hard work, thousands of NYU students, faculty, and staff are now engaged in over 130 community service projects.

James helped organize the President's C-Team in 1989. The initial group of 25 students performing at one local agency has grown to more than 250 working in eight settlement houses in Greenwich Village and on the Lower East Side of Manhattan. In 1990, James and Dr. Oliva founded the Annual C-Team Auction to raise funds for the agencies served by our C-Team volunteers, and to date the auction has raised $200,000. James is also responsible for NYU's America Reads program; last year that program placed 700 literacy tutors in 45 New York City public schools. Recently, community service initiatives have broadened to include a drive that to date has collected over 35 tons of clothing; Campus Harvest, which collects nonperishable food items from individuals, offices, and student organizations throughout the University; and a University-wide book drive. In 1996, a centralized Office of Community Service was created within the University to handle its ever-expanding initiatives.

The Office of Community Service also serves the University's schools by helping to facilitate the many ongoing activities they support. In addition, faculty, students, and staff are encouraged to apply for Community Service Project grants to initiate and expand service projects on the Lower East Side, in Greenwich Village, or in the neighborhood immediately adjacent to an applicant's school. In the schools' curricula, service-learning courses link structured academic course work with community service for academic credit.

"Since the University's founding," says James, "NYU has placed a high value on giving back to the city that surrounds and supports it. NYU students are known for their commitment to social activism, both at the national level and on their own city blocks. But NYU's commitment to service extends beyond its students. Faculty, staff, and administrators work alongside students in neighborhood settlement houses, soup kitchens, hospitals, and parks, creating an atmosphere of altruism that permeates all branches of the New York University community."

"A private University in the public service" is the University's motto and aptly embodies its paradigm of volunteerism and service.

*Debra James passed away July 19, 2000.

THE PRESIDENT'S C-TEAM

The President's C-Team volunteers have many different roles in youth programs. In preschools, they are teacher's assistants. In after-school programs, they serve primarily as tutors, assisting children with homework and remedial skills. C-Team volunteers lead recreational, artistic, and cultural activities and are encouraged to create classes and seminars for the programs. They also work in one-on-one capacities,

tutoring teens on the SAT and GED tests. A Place for Kids, Children's Aid Society, Educational Alliance, Grand Street Settlement, Greenwich House Preschool, Henry Street Settlement, Mentoring USA, and University Settlement also work in partnership with the C-Team.

(Photo credit: Elena Olivo)

(Photo credit: Douglas Levere)

AFTER-SCHOOL READING AND WRITING
(Left and above)
Members of the President's C-Team volunteer their services in after-school programs. Acting as mentors and tutors, they help youngsters develop their reading and writing skills.

GRAND STREET SETTLEMENT

(Right)

The Grand Street Settlement hosts several programs for young people at its Pitt Street headquarters in Manhattan. The settlement's Latchkey, Grand Academy, I Have a Dream, and LEAP programs aid children aged 6-18 with career exploration, tutoring, and academic success in general. The settlement is also the site for the Grand Street Junior High School, an after-school drop-in center with a full program of academic and recreational activities for younger adolescents.

A PLACE FOR KIDS

(Opposite, top)

A Place for Kids has been serving the Lower East Side's youth for nearly 30 years. Established in 1971, A Place for Kids has been a safe and fun after-school destination for thousands of children. Volunteers tutor and play with children in A Place for Kids' preschool and after-school programs.

UNIVERSITY SETTLEMENT

(Opposite, bottom)

Established in 1886, University Settlement was among the nation's earliest settlement houses. The settlement remains on Eldridge Street in Manhattan and has provided New Yorkers with a haven for advice, education, and leisure for over a century. At present, settlement volunteers tutor children aged 6-14 one-on-one in after-school programs.

(Photo credit: Phil Gallo)

(Photo credit: Joyce Culver)

GOD'S LOVE WE DELIVER

(Left)

Working with such organizations as City Harvest, Gay Men's Health Crisis, and God's Love We Deliver, NYU volunteers help feed the city's needy.

STUDENT WORKSHOPS

(Below)

During First Lady Hillary Rodham Clinton's first visit to New York University in 1994, she observed students involved in AmeriCorps/Project SafetyNet conducting peer mediation and conflict resolution workshops at Seward Park High School. "Education and service together are what make a difference as we build a better American ensemble," said Mrs. Clinton.

VILLAGE IMPROVEMENT DAY

(Opposite)

The University-wide "Day of Service" provides an opportunity for faculty, staff, administrators, and students to contribute valuable service to nonprofit organizations in the Lower East Side and Greenwich Village communities. An integral part of this day, also known as Village Improvement Day (VIP Day), is planting, painting, and beautifying historic Washington Square Park.

(Photo credit: Ken Levinson)

(Photo credit: Elena Olivo)

LETTER FROM LOUIS PASTEUR TO CHANCELLOR HENRY MITCHELL MACCRACKEN

Pasteur encouraged student exchange. A translation appears on page 186.

(Gift of Ada Ricci)

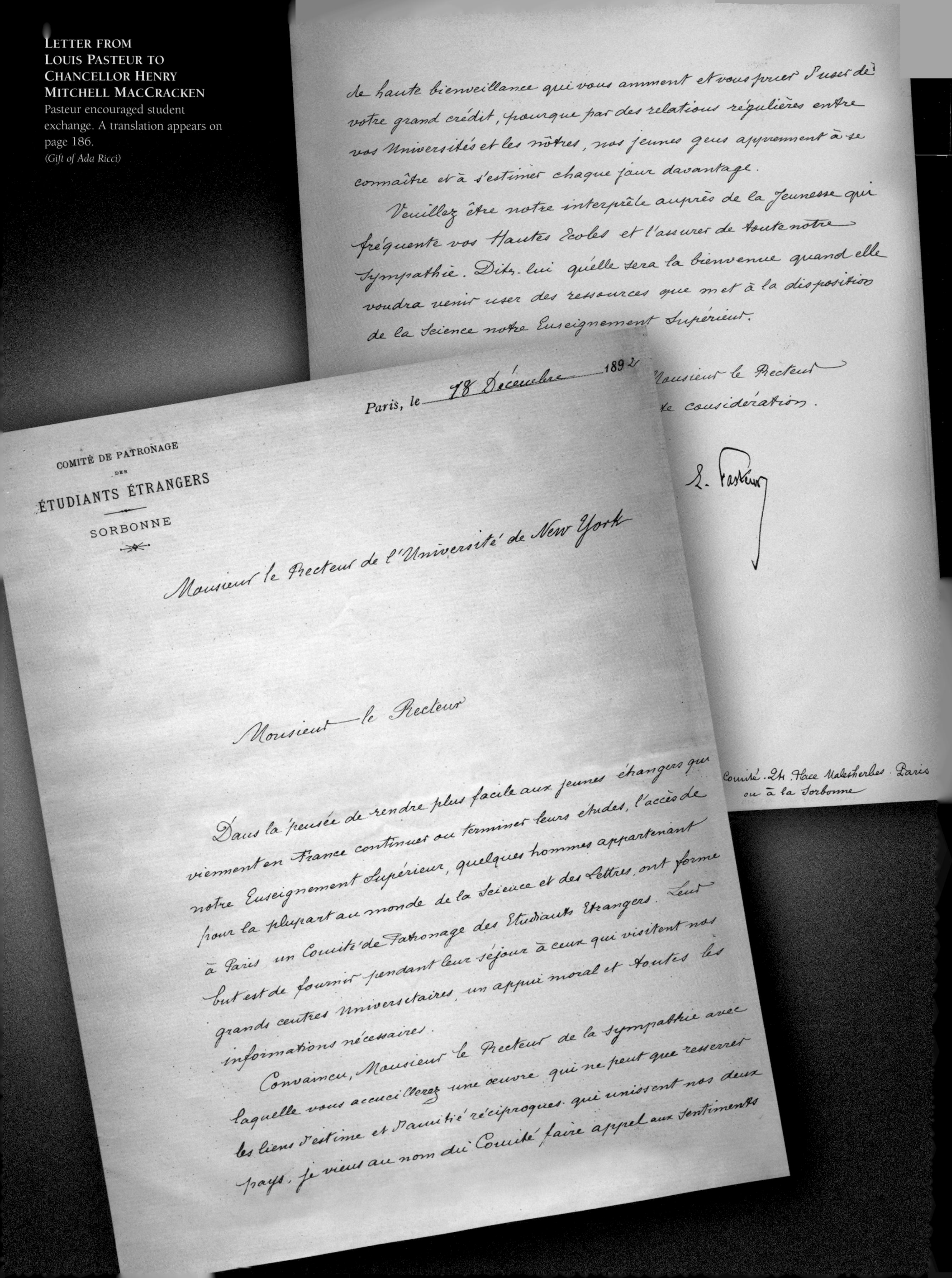

Paris, le 18 Décembre 1892

COMITÉ DE PATRONAGE
DES
ÉTUDIANTS ÉTRANGERS
SORBONNE

Monsieur le Recteur de l'Université de New York

Monsieur le Recteur

Dans la pensée de rendre plus facile aux jeunes étrangers qui viennent en France continuer ou terminer leurs études, l'accès de notre Enseignement Supérieur, quelques hommes appartenant pour la plupart au monde de la Science et des Lettres, ont formé à Paris un Comité de Patronage des Étudiants Étrangers. Leur but est de fournir pendant leur séjour à ceux qui visitent nos grands centres universitaires, un appui moral et toutes les informations nécessaires.

Convaincu, Monsieur le Recteur de la sympathie avec laquelle vous accueillerez une oeuvre qui ne peut que resserrer les liens d'estime et d'amitié réciproques qui unissent nos deux pays, je viens au nom du Comité faire appel aux sentiments

de haute bienveillance qui vous animent et vous prier d'user de votre grand crédit, pour que par des relations régulières entre vos Universités et les nôtres, nos jeunes gens apprennent à se connaître et à s'estimer chaque jour davantage.

Veuillez être notre interprète auprès de la Jeunesse qui fréquente vos Hautes Écoles et l'assurer de toute notre sympathie. Dites-lui qu'elle sera la bienvenue quand elle voudra venir user des ressources que met à la disposition de la Science notre Enseignement Supérieur.

Monsieur le Recteur

te considération.

L. Pasteur

Comité. 24. Place Malesherbes. Paris
ou à la Sorbonne

F*rom its inception the University has been infused and energized by the great eras of migration that have brought people to New York City from all over the world.*

Globalization has been further enhanced by an ever-increasing number of international students, by the University's commitment to international student and faculty exchange, by expansion on a school-by-school basis of international programs, by the proliferation of the University's national houses, and by the University's power to attract distinguished visitors from every corner of the world. Moreover, the faculty, transformed in recent years, represents the wider world in both background and scholarship. Members come here to teach, to conduct research, and to interact with other intellectuals, both inside and outside the academy.

At the start of his presidency, Dr. L. Jay Oliva quickly moved to solidify and strengthen the notion of New York University's internationalism. While most American universities chose to associate with a select group of their colleagues in this country, Dr. Oliva chose to identify New York University with a great league of international universities.

In his inaugural address, delivered November 21, 1991, he outlined a vision of major metropolitan universities from around the world collaborating to find solutions to the pressing social concerns of their cities. The immediate result was the formation of the Conference of World University Leaders, an alliance between New York University and 21 of the most renowned urban universities worldwide. Meeting together for the first time in 1991 during the days of Dr. Oliva's inaugural, this distinguished group of rectors, presidents, and chancellors participated in a landmark discussion in which they quickly discovered that they *all* shared a similar set of tensions and challenges. Subsequent meetings, covering an ever-expanding roster of subjects, have taken place at New York University and at other international sites during the last decade.

Another momentous initiative affecting the University's global ambitions was the gift in January 1994 of La Pietra, the spectacular Tuscan estate with its endowment and magnificent artworks, left to the University by Sir Harold Acton. Named after a Roman milestone at its gate, NYU Villa La Pietra also represents a milestone in the University's history. It stands as a center for global faculty inquiry and anchors the University's worldwide conferences of university leaders. It is a locus for the University as it continually broadens its commitment for study abroad.

```
Committee for Encouragement                    Paris, Dec. 18, 1892
            of
       Foreign Students
          Sorbonne
To the Chancellor of New York University
Dear Sir:

        With the thought of making access to our higher education
easier for young foreigners who come to France to continue or to
finish their studies, several men, belonging for the most part to
the world of science and letters, have formed in Paris a Committee
for Encouragement of Foreign Students.  Their purpose is to furnish
during their stay, to those who visit our great university centers,
moral support and all kinds of necessary information.

        Convinced, Mr. Chancellor, of the sympathy with which you
will welcome a project which can only reinforce the bonds of recipro-
cal esteem and friendship which unite our two countries, in the name
of the Committee, I hereby appeal to the sentiments of lofty benevolence
which move you, and beg you to make use of your great prestige, in order
that by systematic exchange between your universities and ours, our
young men may come to know and to esteem each other more and more every
day.

        Please be our interpreter to the youth of your colleges and
assure them of our entire sympathy.  Tell them how welcome they will
be if they wish to make use of the resources which our higher educat-
ion places at the disposal of science.

        Please accept, my dear Chancellor, the assurance of my high
regard.

                        (signed) L. Pasteur


Address correspondence to
Mr. Paul Nelson, General Secretary of the Committee,
21 Place Maleherbes, Paris,
    or to the Sorbonne
```

LETTER FROM LOUIS PASTEUR TO CHANCELLOR MACCRACKEN

(Original, page 184, and translation, opposite)

The letter from Louis Pasteur, famous inventor and scientist, to NYU Chancellor Henry Mitchell MacCracken, indicates the ongoing relationship NYU has always maintained with multinational scholars, statesmen, and artists.

LOUIS PASTEUR

(Left)

FOREIGN EDUCATIONAL MISSION

(Above)

In 1918 New York University was host to the Foreign Educational Mission, a group of European educators visiting the United States to study American teaching methods. Here, the group poses with Chancellor Elmer E. Brown *(center right, holding hat)* on the steps of the Gould Library on the University Heights campus.

CONFERENCE OF UNIVERSITIES
(Above)

In May 1932, President Elmer E. Brown invited educators worldwide to a Conference of Universities. The goal was to examine the changing role of universities in society, a question of significance because of the unrest in the world at that time. Administrators and educators from such renowned institutions as Yale University, the University of St. Andrews in Scotland, and the University of Minnesota joined NYU for the three-day conference at the Waldorf-Astoria.

PROGRAM

A CONFERENCE OF UNIVERSITIES

The obligation of universities to the social order

UNDER THE AUSPICES OF

NEW YORK UNIVERSITY
1831-1832
1931-1932

*At the Waldorf-Astoria
in New York
November 15-17, 1932*

(Photo credit: Bob Handelman)

VILLA ACTON AT
NYU VILLA LA PIETRA
(Above)

Sitting on a hilltop overlooking the city of Florence, NYU Villa La Pietra is a 57-acre estate of five villas, chief of which is Villa Acton, pictured above. Villa Acton has been described as the "epitome of elegance." The 17th-century baroque exterior conceals a much older building within a square structure around a central courtyard. The road leading up to the central courtyard is lined with cypress trees, and statues and pillars are found scattered amidst greenery in the formal gardens.

Sir Harold Acton, who bequeathed the estate to NYU, hosted many international literary figures at his home. Evelyn Waugh and Graham Greene, for example, were among those who lived and wrote at Villa La Pietra. The novelist and man of letters James Lord also resided there. He praised the setting, "save for the nightingales, which warbled so madly in the cypresses."

Since 1994, NYU has used Villa La Pietra as an academic center in Florence, as well as for meetings, conferences, and special events.

LEAGUE OF WORLD UNIVERSITIES

Launched in 1991, the League of World Universities is a group of major metropolitan universities from around the globe that meets regularly to address the pressing cultural, social, and political concerns of their cities as well as of urban centers in every corner of the world. In less than a decade, the League has grown from 21 members to include rectors and presidents representing 48 of the most renowned urban universities on six continents.

At five conferences held to date, the rectors and presidents have discussed a variety of issues that reflect the similar tensions, tasks, and missions of all of the member institutions. Building on the success of the inaugural meeting in 1991, the second conference, held in 1993, was entitled "Large City Universities and the Public School System," and the third, in 1995, "The Image of the University." In 1997, at the fourth conference of the League of World Universities, members agreed to experiment with multinational video teleconference courses,

which enable students from member institutions to access classes and faculty throughout the world. The fifth conference held in 1999 focused on corporate and foundation fund-raising. Heads of the Carnegie Corporation of New York, the Henry Luce Foundation, the Kresge Foundation, the Howard Hughes Medical Institute, the Texaco Foundation, and the Coca-Cola Foundation and NYU Board of Trustees chairman Martin Lipton offered presentations. In addition to these conferences, League members have held meetings and planning sessions at NYU Villa La Pietra, in Florence, Italy, and at the National Autonomous University of Mexico, in Mexico City.

The League has also helped New York University establish a system of student exchanges beyond the University's centers abroad. These networks will help NYU to realize even more fully its global vision and to make it possible for every NYU undergraduate to include a study abroad experience as part of his or her education.

(Photo credits: Jon Roemer)

THE LEAGUE OF WORLD UNIVERSITIES
(Above)
One of the central themes of Dr. L. Jay Oliva's presidency has been a persistent expansion of the University's internationalism. Dr. Oliva is pictured with members of the League of World Universities, an organization that he founded and chairs and that includes presidents, rectors, and chancellors of universities from South America, Europe, Africa, Asia, and Australia.

WHERE WORLD LEADERS ABOUND
(Right)
Boris Yeltsin, demonstrating his goodwill to the United States, visited the University soon after becoming president of Russia in 1991. In a classic photo opportunity, Yeltsin proudly displayed his new NYU sweatshirt—a gift from one president (L. Jay Oliva) to another. Yeltsin is but one of many world leaders to visit the University during its long history.

THE INESTIMABLE VALUE OF STUDYING ABROAD

The growth and development of study abroad programs form an integral part of NYU's global mission, and the University offers some of the most distinguished foreign study programs in the world. For example, the University operates more than 40 study abroad programs in 27 countries in Europe, Asia, Africa, and South America. These include NYU centers in Buenos Aires, London, Madrid, Paris, Florence, and Prague, where students may spend a summer, semester, or academic year taking courses toward their degrees and broadening their understanding of the world. Plans are under way to create new programs in Dublin, Istanbul, Cape Town, and various sites in Asia. In addition to attending one of the NYU centers, students may pursue their academic and professional interests

through NYU programs in Australia, Austria, Belgium, Brazil, England, Germany, Hong Kong, Israel, Japan, Korea, the Netherlands, Russia, Sweden, and Switzerland.

Another important global milestone for the University occurred when the Stern School of Business instituted the nation's first curriculum-based international study program. The result is that all entering Stern freshman now study abroad in their junior year on fully financed research projects. The first Stern student team, guided by Stern faculty, traveled to Japan in March 2000. Building on course work developed in the fall term of their junior year, students had the opportunity to collaborate with top Japanese business leaders.

AS SEEN IN

The New York Times

THE NEW YORK TIMES **EDUCATION** WEDNESDAY, MARCH 26, 1997

At N.Y.U., a Global Strategy to Encourage Foreign Study and Travel

By KAREN W. ARENSON

When L. Jay Oliva, the president of New York University, remembers his days at Manhattan College the memories are pleasant but unremarkable.

But graduate school, that was different. He studied in Paris for two years in the late 1950's. As he tells it, he came sharply alive, soaking up everything. He watched Charles de Gaulle be sworn in as President, met Ernest Hemingway in a bar in Majorca, ran with the bulls at Pamplona, watched the Nixon-Khrushchev kitchen debate in Moscow and hitchhiked through France.

Now, he wants N.Y.U. students to have similar experience, and the university hopes to encourage all students to go abroad, in part by not charging extra, as many universities do, but also by making registering for foreign study as easy as registering for a history or English course.

This year, the university is setting up new study centers overseas — in Prague in the fall, and Salamanca, Spain, next spring — and is working out student and faculty exchange agreements with urban universities from Accra, Ghana to Stockholm.

In turn, Dr. Oliva hopes to make the Washington Square campus more global in outlook, with students signing up for art and history classes conducted jointly with professors and students around the world and routinely attending classes taught by visiting foreign teachers. The univer-

In 1959, L. Jay Oliva hitchhiked through the Compiègne Forest on a wine truck while a student in France. Now president of New York University, Dr. Oliva said that in education, "a foreign experience is invaluable."

sity is importing professors from overseas by financing several programs, including special institutes and incentive payments to departments, and is building a center to house foreign guests.

"If education is about growing up, a foreign experience is invaluable," Dr. Oliva said. "It is about acquiring a language that belongs to someone else, about not being the center of everything, about living in a society that is not built around me or my expectations."

N.Y.U.'s international strategy is a broad embrace of a trend in which more and more American students seek internships and classes over-

seas, driven by the increasing globalization of business and the perception that employers favor students who have experience abroad.

"More and more universities are realizing that this is part of the curriculum," said Peggy Blumenthal, vice president for educational services at the Institute for International Education, which says a record 84,403 Americans studied abroad for credit in 1994-95, up 11 percent from the previous year. But the N.Y.U. program is unusual in its scale and aim, she said. "N.Y.U. is certainly being very vigorous and creative," she said.

Still, changing the culture will take

time. Of 12,000 undergraduates at N.Y.U., only 516 students went abroad for at least a semester at the university's own centers last year. An additional 1,155 went during the January intersession, and perhaps 50 to 100 made their own arrangements. Administrators say the most vital factor for students is to make it easy to take classes abroad, by offering things like registration by telephone, counseling abroad, even retention of seniority in the housing lottery, and they are working to make those arrangements possible.

To whet appetites for language study, the university has introduced free, not-for-credit language lessons

in the dormitories, with the focus on conversation and culture. On a recent evening, for example, 17 students in Paulette Goddard Hall listened with their instructor to Jacques Brel, Josephine Baker, Claude François and others croon French songs, then paired off discuss what they were hearing — in French, of course. This semester, nine languages are being offered, including Chinese, Hebrew and Swahili.

"The cool thing is that everyone wants to be here," said Alec Borisoff, a junior from New York who speaks French, Spanish and German and took the Japanese class last term. "Homework is voluntary," he added, "but everyone does it."

In an experiment last semester, N.Y.U. linked up with students and professors of the Free University of Brussels in the first transnational televideo class, a graduate course comparing the new European union and the 200-year-old American union. More international courses are planned, like European law, Celtic studies, Indian civilization and African music, dance, literature and art.

"The world today is not limited by national boundaries," said Robert Berne, vice president for academic development, one of the professors in the Brussels-New York class. "The question is how you provide opportunities for students and faculty to move out of their bounded notion of the academy."

Copyright © 1997 by The New York Times

ONE TRIP LEADS TO THOUSANDS OF TRIPS
(Above)

An article in the *New York Times* in 1997 talked about NYU's global strategy and its encouragement of foreign study and travel. The story also revealed how Dr. L. Jay Oliva, as a young graduate student, studied abroad. The experience, in addition to being great fun, helped shape his life and strengthen his resolve to cre-

ate a multitude of study abroad options for every NYU student. His adventures included seeing Charles de Gaulle sworn in as president, meeting Ernest Hemingway in a bar in Majorca, running with the bulls at Pamplona, and watching the Nixon-Khrushchev kitchen debate in Moscow. Here he is pictured on a wine truck while hitchhiking through France in 1959.

SUMMERTIME IN PARIS
(Right)
NYU in Paris includes a summer session that combines the study of language, literature, and the arts with activities designed to expose students to French daily life and culture.

(Photo credit: Bob Handelman)

(Photo credit: Bob Handelman)

THE EXPERIENCE OF A LIFETIME
(Left)
Making new friends is just one of the many benefits of international study.

THE GATEWAY TO CENTRAL EUROPE
(Right)
NYU in Prague offers students the opportunity to experience firsthand the historic changes happening in Central Europe as well as the region's rich heritage.

(Photo credit: Bob Handelman)

M.B.A. STUDENTS STUDY IN ST. PETERSBURG
(Left)
Stern School of Business students, as part of the Executive M.B.A. and International Residency Programs, visited St. Petersburg to study Russia's changing economy.

ACTING, DANCING, AND PERFORMING IN AMSTERDAM
(Right)
At the Tisch School of the Art's Experimental Theatre Wing in Amsterdam, students learn new dance, acting, and performance skills. Despite a rigorous schedule, students find plenty of time to enjoy the sights.

(Photo credit: Bob Handelman)

ANCIENT WONDERS
(Above)
NYU students visit the theatre at
Epidaurus, Greece.

NYU IS FIRST U.S. FILM SCHOOL TO SCREEN WORKS IN HAVANA
(Left)
Representing the Tisch School of the
Arts at the 21st Havana Film Festival
in December 1999 were *(left to right)*
Marcia Donalds, lecturer; David
Irving, chair of the Undergraduate
Division, Department of Film and
Television; Pari Shirazi, vice dean;
Sonia Arrubla, graduate student; Juan
C. Martinez-Zaldivar, alumnus; and
Arnie Baskin, associate professor of
film. NYU is the first American film
school to be invited to screen works at
the Festival Internacional del Nuevo
Cine Latinoamericano, a major show-
case for Latin American filmmakers
that draws an audience of 500,000.
Beginning in spring 2001, the Tisch
School will offer courses to its students in Cuba through a study abroad
program, as well as seminars taught
by NYU faculty to Cuban students.

A LOCUS OF INTERNATIONAL DISCUSSION AND DEBATE

NYU over the past decade has become one of the world's great centers of international intellectual discussion and debate. Critical to the University's success in motivating and stimulating this discussion and debate are the national houses of NYU, which offer an array of academic and cultural programs for the students, faculty, and staff as well as for the community beyond the University.

In recent years, the University has added the Lewis L. and Loretta Brennan Glucksman Ireland House and the King Juan Carlos I of Spain Center to an already impressive assemblage that, prior to 1991, consisted of La Maison Française, the Hagop Kevorkian Center, Deutsches Haus, and Casa Italiana Zerilli-Marimò. The international vision also finds expression in academic programs that address contemporary issues of policy and culture worldwide. The University's international programs and resource centers include the Asian/Pacific/American Studies Institute, the Global Law School Program, the Institute of French Studies, the Center for European Studies, the Skirball Department of Hebrew and Judaic Studies, the Center on International Cooperation, the International Center for Advanced Studies, the School of Law Center for International Studies, the Center for Japan-U.S. Business and Economic Studies, the Center for Latin American and Caribbean Studies, and the Remarque Institute. Each of these is interdisciplinary, drawing faculty members from a wide range of departments and linking them to create an international community of scholars to reflect on global concerns.

THE LILLIAN VERNON CENTER FOR INTERNATIONAL AFFAIRS

(Above)

The Lillian Vernon Center for International Affairs, a gift from NYU trustee Lillian Vernon, provides a home for global activities University-wide. Dedicated on February 11, 1999, the Vernon Center houses the Student Center for International Studies, the Center for European Studies, the European Union Center of New York, and the League of World Universities.

(Photo credit: Don Pollard)

LEWIS L. AND LORETTA BRENNAN GLUCKSMAN IRELAND HOUSE

(Right)

The Glucksman Ireland House was founded through the impetus of President L. Jay Oliva and the generosity of Lewis L. and Loretta Brennan Glucksman *(above)*. Ireland House established the Irish studies program at NYU and maintains a collaborative relationship with several Irish universities, promoting an exchange of faculty, students, and ideas to further the study of Ireland and the Irish in America.

(Illustration: Jane Ziegler)

(Illustration: Robert Gantt Steele)

KING JUAN CARLOS I OF SPAIN CENTER
(Left)

The King Juan Carlos I of Spain Center was founded, through the efforts of former President John Brademas, to promote a greater understanding of Spain and the Spanish-speaking world. The center offers programs in politics, business, economics, law, and the arts, as well as a community outreach program. Dr. Brademas is president of the King Juan Carlos I of Spain Center of New York University Foundation.

(Photo credit: Don Hamerman)

LA MAISON FRANÇAISE
(Left)

La Maison Française provides a forum for the exchange and flow of ideas between France and the United States. The program offers lectures, films, and concerts by prominent French and other politicians, writers, artists, and musicians.

HAGOP KEVORKIAN CENTER

(Above)

Selected as a National Resource Center for Middle Eastern studies, the Kevorkian Center is one of the premier centers for the study of the history, society, and current problems of the Middle East. The center's Richard Ettinghausen Library holds a superb collection of rare books and manuscripts and a state-of-the-art language laboratory. The courtyard displays the original tilework and ornaments from an 18th-century Damascene house.

CASA ITALIANA ZERILLI-MARIMÒ

(Right)

Casa Italiana was made possible through a gift from Baroness Mariuccia Zerilli-Marimò *(above)*, trustee of NYU and well-known philanthropist. One of America's largest graduate institutes of Italian studies, Casa Italiana serves as a center for a variety of academic, cultural, and social activities and home to the Department of Italian.

(Photo credit: Don Hamerman)

DEUTSCHES HAUS

(Left)

Deutsches Haus, the center for the Department of Germanic Languages and Literatures, promotes not only the study of the German language, but also German business, history, sociology, and the arts. In addition to many course offerings of the German department, Deutsches Haus conducts conferences, seminars, film series, and special visits by politicians, intellectuals, and celebrities to further the field of German studies.

SKIRBALL DEPARTMENT OF HEBREW AND JUDAIC STUDIES

(Right)

The Skirball Department of Hebrew and Judaic Studies offers one of the most comprehensive Jewish studies progams in North America, encompassing Hebrew language and literature as well as all facets of Jewish history and culture, from the ancient through the medieval to the modern.

A life trustee of New York University, Morris H. Bergreen *(above)* is also the president of the Skirball Foundation. His many contributions have had a profound impact on the University.

LOVE, UNIVERSITY-STYLE

(Below)

Naomi Levine, senior vice president for external affairs, places an affectionate buss atop the head of George H. Heyman, Jr., Stern G '38, private investor, life trustee, and longtime chairman of the Board of Trustees Development Committee. Levine and Heyman successfully partnered over two decades to raise billions of dollars for the University. Heyman Hall, the home of the Skirball Department of Hebrew and Judaic Studies located at 51 Washington Square South, bears the name of its great friend and patron.

(Photo credit: Michael St. John)

INTERNATIONAL STUDENTS AND SCHOLARS

With 5,000 students representing nearly 120 countries, NYU now has more students from abroad than any other American university. The University offers foreign scholars the unique opportunity to pursue an education at one of the world's first-rate academic institutions in the global capital of the financial, cultural, and entertainment industries. In addition, the links that NYU has forged with the great city that is its home make the wonders and possibilities of New York accessible to international students and, through them, to the wider world. Beyond undergraduates and graduates, New York University has attracted a number of distinguished international scholars and researchers to its faculty. In addition, the wide array of services that NYU provides to its foreign-born population facilitates their stay in New York. The Office for International Students and Scholars (OISS) assists members of the NYU international community with employment, immigration, personal, cross-cultural, and financial matters. OISS advisers serve as representatives and advocates in dealings with U.S. and foreign government agencies and other campus offices and departments. Making itself even more accessible and attractive to international students and scholars is one of the top priorities of NYU. To do so, the University provides the professorships, scholarships, fellowships, and services that play an important role in enabling foreign-born men and women to pursue their academic and professional interests at Washington Square.

(Photo credit: Enrique Cubillo)

IN SEARCH OF THE NEXT SPIKE LEE
(Left)
Mary Schmidt Campbell, dean, Tisch School of the Arts, meets with budding filmmakers at NYU's International Student Film Festival. The event, one that attracts student filmmakers from around the globe, also draws numerous agents, producers, and studio executives who are all looking for the next Spike Lee, Amy Heckerling, or Oliver Stone.

(Photo credit: Jon Roemer)

THE INTERNATIONAL CONFERENCE ON PAN-AFRICAN FILMMAKING
(Left)
Left to right: Harry Belafonte, Dean Mary Schmidt Campbell, and Sidney Poitier served as panelists at the International Conference on Pan-African Filmmaking, the first international academic conference and film festival devoted to black cinema.

WOLE SOYINKA
At the International Conference on Pan-African Filmmaking, Nigerian playwright and 1986 Nobel laureate Wole Soyinka described the gift of black storytelling.

(Photo credit: Jon Roemer)

(*Photo credit: Phil Gallo*)

STUDYING PUBLIC SERVICE—GLOBALLY

(Left)

The Robert F. Wagner Graduate School of Public Service has launched an international initiative to attract foreign students and collaborate with schools abroad to establish a more international curriculum. Robert Berne, vice president for academic development (*second row, left*), and graduate student Lisa Utzschneider (*second row, right*) talk with visiting scholars from Central and Eastern Europe who are studying public administration at the Wagner School.

THE ASIAN CONNECTION

(Below)

The Department of Physical Therapy at the NYU School of Education established ties with the physical therapy program at the National Yang-Ming Medical College in Taiwan in 1993. The two departments collaborate with faculty exchanges, a computer network linkup, and curriculum development and research. To help get the program started, Jerrold Ross, then associate dean for academic affairs, visited with students in China.

GOING GLOBAL WITH THE PRESIDENT OF THE UNITED STATES

On Monday, September 21, 1998, a remarkable event in the life of New York University occurred that might well serve as a metaphor for the future of the University. On that memorable day, President Bill Clinton, Prime Minister Tony Blair, then Italian Prime Minister Romano Prodi, First Lady Hillary Rodham Clinton, and leaders from labor, academia, business, and government attended an opening dialogue entitled "Strengthening Democracy in the Global Economy."

The New York University School of Law initiated this event, which offered insights into the direction that the University will be taking in the new century. To begin, the dialogue dramatically blurred the boundaries between academia and the real world on a scale never before accomplished by any institution of higher education. It echoed the University's desire to be a place where diverse perspectives are welcomed and assimilated. It advanced the notion of the University as an intellectual sanctuary in which an ever-widening circle of students, faculty, experts, politicians, and the general public may challenge fundamental premises.

The dialogue also presented a multimedia challenge of staggering dimensions. Indeed, no institution of higher education has ever initiated such a high-level event and then used multimedia to disseminate information about it in such an ambitious way. One important early decision was to put a live feed-up on a satellite, which would then be available for television networks and stations to send to television sets across the world. A housewife in Peoria, a student in South Africa, a farmer in England, a baker in Milan—just about

(Photo credits: Lisa Berg)

GOING GLOBAL AGAIN—THIS TIME WITH SIX WORLD LEADERS IN FLORENCE, ITALY
(Left)
In 1999 the Global Law School Program of the NYU School of Law and the European University Institute of Florence cosponsored the conference "Progressive Governance in the 21st Century," which was held in Florence, Italy, and attended by six world leaders. Pictured at the World Leaders Dinner at NYU Villa La Pietra were *(left to right)* Italian Prime Minister Massimo D'Alema, President Bill Clinton, Secretary of State Madeline Albright, NYU School of Law's Dean John Sexton, the European University Institute's President Patrick Masterson, and First Lady Hillary Rodham Clinton. Other attendees included British Prime Minister Tony Blair (inset), Brazilian President Fernando Cardoso, French Prime Minister Lionel Jospin, and German Chancellor Gerhard Schroeder. A group of NYU School of Law students, chosen by lottery, traveled to Italy to witness the conversations and to participate in a question-and-answer session with the world leaders. They then returned to the School of Law and shared their experience with both faculty and students.

anybody who had access to television or the Internet was able to see this event. The School of Law also reached out to universities across the United States that had campuswide cable systems. Some 20 universities around the country relayed the dialogue through their internal cable systems to classrooms, public meeting spaces, and student residence halls. Students at Duke, Tuskegee, MIT, San Diego State, Rochester Institute of Technology, Purdue, and Louisiana State (to name a few) watched the event live or at some future time as the material was archived. Many of these institutions were also linked to community cable channels that ran the programming live or at a later

date. NYU School of Law, which has its own Web site, also established a Web site for the event. The site was yet another method of information dissemination that provided extraordinary outreach to constituencies critical to the University's mission—graduate students, policy experts, historians, and journalists.

What made all this important is not that the technology was new, but that NYU recognized the power of this new technology and used it generously and effectively to strengthen its educational mission in a truly global way.

A PRESIDENTIAL ACCOLADE
(Above)
President Bill Clinton, in remarks at a dinner in honor of participants at the conference on "Progressive Governance in the 21st Century," at NYU Villa La Pietra, praised NYU's leadership as part of this "new renaissance." The audience, which included five world leaders, actor/director Roberto Benigni, and singer Andrea Bocelli, responded approvingly. The dinner took place November 20, 1999.

STATELY TUSCANY
(Right)
"Dialogue II: Progressive Governance in the 21st Century" was held at the Palazzo Vecchio in Florence, Italy, on November 21, 1999.

(Photo credits: Lisa Berg)

I ntercollegiate athletic competition was introduced at the Washington Square campus in the 1870s. But it was the move in 1894 to University Heights, with its generous play-ing fields, that gave athletics at NYU its enormous impetus.

The first NYU baseball team was formed in the early 1870s, and the team regularly challenged Rutgers, Yale, Columbia, and Manhattan College. Also in the 1870s, the University's first football team, one of the first collegiate football teams in the United States, was formed. By 1907, the University had varsity teams in baseball, football, basketball, tennis, and track.

Intercollegiate football quickly became the University's and nation's favorite sport; it was, as played then, a violent and dangerous sport that would claim the lives of many athletes—20 in 1905 alone. Appalled by the carnage at NYU and other colleges and universities, Chancellor Henry Mitchell MacCracken played a leadership role in making football safe by forming the Intercollegiate Athletic Association of the United States. This organization would later be renamed the National Collegiate Athletic Association.

More than 80 years later, another chancellor, L. Jay Oliva, participated in the rebirth of sports at NYU by championing the transition from Division I to Division III athletics. NYU was also a founding member with eight other institutions of the University Athletic Association, which endorsed strong academic goals while offering student athletes the opportunity to compete.

1901 BASEBALL TEAM
(Above)
Baseball has been a popular sport at NYU since the early 1870s when the Base Ball Club was founded by the Student Athletic Association. Hampered by the lack of playing space at Washington Square, baseball thrived with the move to University Heights. The newly prepared Ohio Field provided the opportunity to launch a full-fledged varsity athletic baseball program.

1903 TRACK TEAM

(Left)

Track was one of four varsity sports at the turn of the century (football, baseball, and gymnastics were the others). In 1903, Captain Albert Wilcox '03 *(second row, fifth from left)* led the team in a stunning series of victories. The team competed in several events, including the 100-yard dash, the hurdles, the high jump, the pole vault, and the discus throw.

1924 SOCCER TEAM

(Below)

Soccer was introduced to NYU athletics in 1923 as "soccer football" and became a varsity sport a year later. NYU played soccer for the next two seasons, then dropped it for 32 years. In 1958, soccer made a comeback in a big way—sweeping the league with a 5-0 record—and has remained strong ever since.

CHANCELLOR MacCRACKEN "CLEANS UP" FOOTBALL

It is recognized . . . that fatal accidents may come in any form of athletics, but in no game, in even the German student duels, has homicide become a characteristic, except in American football.

With these indicting words, New York University's Chancellor Henry Mitchell MacCracken declared war on the brutality of college football. Two days earlier, on November 25, 1905, at an NYU-Union College game at Ohio Field on the University Heights campus, Union halfback Harold R. Moore collapsed after being tackled in an otherwise "clean game." The unconscious player was placed in a "45 h.p. automobile" that rushed him to Fordham Hospital in less than 10 minutes. The game continued until NYU Violets won an 11-0 victory. Later that evening, the University and nation learned that Moore had died from a cerebral hemorrhage.

Chancellor MacCracken, within an hour of Moore's death, sent a wire to President Charles Eliot of Harvard, asking his influential colleague to "invite a meeting of university and college presidents to undertake the reform or abolition of football." Eliot refused, and MacCracken, impatient of politics, assumed the responsibility of establishing a national organization to control the excesses of collegiate sports.

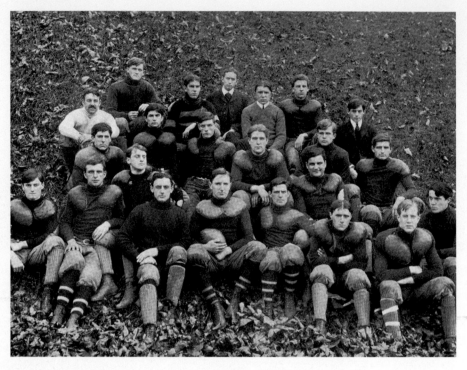

1902 FOOTBALL TEAM
Players did not wear helmets, and unsafe football plays such as the "the flying wedge" or the "hurdle play" were legal. However, several deaths in college football instigated a movement for change.

The "flying wedge" and the "hurdle play" (in which a player, carrying the ball, was thrown over the defensive line) were tactics designed with no consideration for safety. Neither helmets nor a "sense of sportsmanship" was mandatory. As a result, nationally, 19 other "footballers" died in October and November of the 1905 season. Moore was the first player from a well-known institution to die. This tragedy also disproved the theory that fatalities could not strike a well-trained, healthy player.

As NYU flags flew at half-mast, MacCracken instructed the University faculty to call for a conference to be held on December 9, 1905, with 19 "colleges against whom NYU has played since 1885." Despite headlines such as "Football Doomed" and "Football Must Go," the conference only sought to abolish football "as it is now played." Later that month, the conference reconvened under the title of the Intercollegiate Athletic Association of the United States; 65 colleges were represented. Five years later, the organization was renamed the National Collegiate Athletic Association.

Today, the National Collegiate Athletic Association—a voluntary association of more than 1,200 institutions, conferences, organizations, and individuals—stands as the organization through which the nation's colleges and universities speak and act on athletic matters.

1930 FOOTBALL PROGRAM
(Left)

The 1930 NYU football team participated in a postseason game against Colgate University, with proceeds to benefit New York City's unemployed. Although the Violets narrowly lost the game with a score of 7-6, some 20,000 fans filled Yankee stadium to see the game and to support a city charity.

MEN'S FOOTBALL ON THE BEACH
(Above)

Instead of canceling practice on a sweltering September day in 1931, Coach John "Chick" Meehan took his team to Lido Beach, Long Island. From 1925 to 1931, Meehan brought the little-known NYU football team to national attention. His charm and NYU's growing reputation helped recruit key players such as Ken Strong, Al Lassman, Len Grant, Jack Connor, Frank Briante, Dave Meyers, and Cowboy Hill.

NYU AND THE OLYMPICS

The year 1896 marked the birth of the modern Olympic Games.

Since 1904 a generous number of men and women from the NYU community have participated in the Olympic Games. Most participants were Olympians as NYU undergraduates; some were graduate students; others came to NYU after their Olympic experience; still others were staff members.

The following is a partial listing of those participants and their grand exploits:

1904—Sam Jones, an engineering student from 1898 to 1902, won the gold medal at the high jump, clearing the bar at 5 feet, 11 inches.

1912—Dr. Graeme Hammond was team physician. Over the years, Dr. Hammond served in a number of capacities, including a term as president of the United States Olympic Association.

1920—Brothers Howard and Ted Cann were the first members of the same family ever chosen for the Olympics. At the Olympics, Howard scored eighth in the shot put. Ted, a World War I Medal of Honor winner, was in a serious automobile accident prior to the Olympics and had to resign from the U.S. swimming team.

1928—NYU's first women athletes to participate in the Olympics competed at the Amsterdam Games. Ethel McGary Englesen represented the U.S. in the 400-meter freestyle. Lisa Lindstrom Olson tied for fifth place in the 100-meter backstroke. Mary Washburn Conklin was a member of the 400-meter relay team, which, despite breaking the world's record, won only the silver medal. Conklin also ran the 100-meter dash, the first women's track and field event ever held at the Olympics.

On the men's front: Phil Edwards, representing Canada, competed in his first of three Olympics in track and field. George Baird was a member of the gold medal-winning U.S. 4 x 400-meter relay, which won in a world record time of 3:14.2. Norman Armitage participated in the first of six Olympics on the fencing team. And Herman Witzig served as a member of the U.S. gymnastics team.

WOMEN'S VARSITY SWIMMING
(Below)

A varsity sport at NYU since the 1920s, women's swimming has produced a number of outstanding performers over the years. Champions include Esther Foley ('28), recipient of the New York Swimming Award and NYU coach for 42 years; Ethel McGary Englesen ('28), member of the 1928 Olympic team and coach at Hunter College for over 30 years; and Lisa Lindstrom Olson ('34), also a member of the 1928 Olympic team and inductee into the national Swimming Hall of Fame.

MARY WASHBURN CONKLIN
(Left)
Mary Washburn Conklin ('28) competed in the 1928 Olympics 100-meter dash event, the first women's track and field event ever held in the Olympics. She was a member of the 400-meter relay team that, despite breaking the world's record, only won the silver medal. Here, Washburn *(right)* runs the hurdles. While pursuing her track career, Washburn majored in French and competed on the NYU basketball and field hockey teams.

1932—Phil Edwards, again representing Canada and earning three bronze medals, competed against University of Kansas star Glenn Cunningham in the 1500-meter. Cunningham would later earn his Ph.D. in physical education at NYU. Sol Furth, an outstanding hurdler and sprinter, set the world's record in the half-mile relay.

All-American George Spitz, plagued by a bad ankle, finished ninth in the high jump. Peter Zaremba placed third in the hammer throw. Norman Armitage was once again a member of the fencing team, which finished fourth. The first undergraduate to make the Olympics in fencing was Miguel de Capriles, who would go on to compete in seven Olympics.

In gymnastics, Frank Cumiskey finished fourth in the side horse and 11th in the individual all-around. He also won a silver medal since the U.S. team was second in the team combined exercises.

Although the 1932 Games were the first at which there was an Olympic Village, women were not permitted to reside there and instead stayed at a Los Angeles hotel. The sole female Olympian from NYU was Joan McSheehy, a former School of Commerce student, who left school to train. She finished fifth in the 100-meter backstroke.

PHIL EDWARDS
(Right)
Phil Edwards *(far right)*, pictured here with NYU teammates, was a five-time Olympic bronze medal-winner for Canada. Edwards is considered the athlete most responsible for NYU's emergence as a national track presence in the 1920s. Prior to the 1928 Olympics, Edwards had won several national intercollegiate track titles both in individual events and as a member of NYU relay teams. Captain of the NYU track team, he was one of the first four inductees into the NYU Sports Hall of Fame.

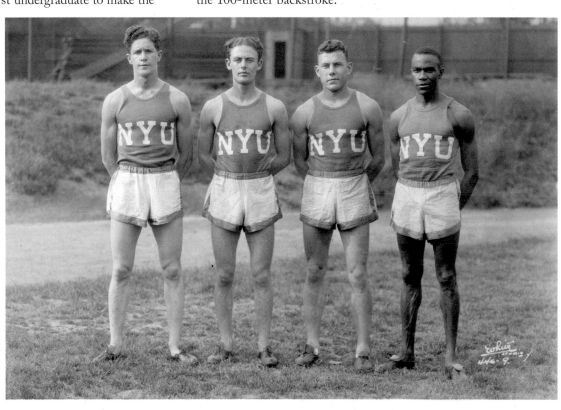

1936—The largest contingent of athletes since the Games began some 40 years earlier traveled to Berlin for the 1936 Olympics. In the 800-meter, Phil Edwards, still representing Canada and now a doctor, faced several opponents, including John Woodruff, who would later earn his M.A. at NYU. In the 800-meter, Woodruff won the gold and Edwards, the bronze medal.

Norman Armitage and Miguel de Capriles returned as members of the American fencing team. Armitage was on the sabre team that finished in a four-way tie for fifth place. De Capriles was also on the

sabre team. He was joined by his brother, José de Capriles, a five-time Olympian who fenced épée. José de Capriles also served as captain of NYU's fencing team. Miguel de Capriles later served as dean of the NYU School of Law (1964-1967) and vice president and general counsel of the University (1967-1974).

In gymnastics, Frank Cumiskey again competed. The only female Violet was Bernice Lapp, a School of Commerce student, who was a member of the bronze medal–winning 4 x 100-meter freestyle relay swimming team.

JULIA JONES PUGLIESE
(Left)
Women's fencing has always had a strong hold at NYU and has produced many college and Olympic champions. One of the founders of NYU women's fencing was Julia Jones Pugliese, who became the first U.S. Collegiate Fencing Champion. While at NYU, she cofounded the National Intercollegiate Women's Fencing Association and became its first champion. After graduation, Jones Pugliese coached the NYU team throughout the 1930s, winning several national championships. In 1976, she was inducted into the NYU Sports Hall of Fame.

EN GARDE!
(Above)
A varsity sport since 1923, NYU fencing soon obtained national and international recognition. The program has won numerous championships and produced several Olympic athletes. The 1929 fencing team, for example, pictured here practicing on the roof of the Main Building, included Miguel and José de Capriles, Olympic athletes and two of the top stars in the sport.

1948—The games were canceled during World War II, and 12 years elapsed before the next Olympics. The 1948 Games in London included 12 athletes with NYU affiliations, the largest number of Violets ever to compete.

Throughout NYU's rich basketball history, only one Violet hoopster has ever been on a gold medal-winning Olympic team. Ray Lumpp earned that distinction when the 1948 U.S. team took first place.

NYU's distinguished coach Emil Von Elling was the U.S. Olympic track team's assistant coach in 1948. Competing in track and field was Irving "Moon" Mondshein. He was captain of the 1948 U.S. decathlon team and finished eighth. Edward Conwell, known as "Bullet Ed," a School of Education student, was named to the 4 x 100-meter relay team as an alternate. An asthma attack prevented him from competing. Also competing in track and field, as a member of the Puerto Rican team, was Francisco (Frank) Castro.

In 1948 Norman Armitage and the de Capriles brothers were back on the Olympic fencing team and were joined by three addi-tional Violet swordsmen, Norman Lewis, Silvio Giolito, and Austin Prokop.

Also in 1948, Frank Cumiskey returned as a member of the gymnastics team. He was joined by Edward Scrobe. Allen Walz, a former NYU football captain, was the sweeps coach for the U.S. row-ing team, which won two gold medals and one silver medal.

JOSÉ DE CAPRILES, NORMAN LEWIS, AND MIGUEL DE CAPRILES
(Below, left to right)

These NYU fencers competed in a total of seven Olympics and won a combined total of over 20 national championships. José de Capriles was a five-time Olympian and captain of the NYU fencing team. Norman Lewis was cocaptain of the NYU fencing team (1936–1937); an IFA foil champion (1935–1937) and épée champion (1937); and the AFLA champion in foil (1939) and épée (1948, 1949, 1950). Miguel de Capriles, in addition to competing in the Olympics, won six national championships and served in later Olympics as an official.

1952—In this memorable Olympics, the Soviet Union competed for the first time. Ted Corbitt, who earned his graduate degree at NYU and was a veteran of almost 200 marathons, finished the Olympic marathon in 44th place. Martin Engel, a hammer throw contestant, was first at the U.S. trials. Frank Castro returned as a member of the Puerto Rican team in the long jump and triple jump.

In fencing, Norman Armitage, the de Capriles brothers, and Silvio Giolito all returned. Stanley Sieja, who at 17 was named coach of the NYU's freshman fencing team, served as the manager of the U.S. Olympic fencing team.

Frank Cumiskey returned as manager of the U.S. gymnastics team. Edward Scrobe returned as the gymnastics team's leading scorer as the U.S. placed eighth in the team combined exercises.

TED CORBITT
(Right)
Ted Corbitt, '50, ran almost 200 marathons in a career that spanned 27 years. He competed in the 1952 Olympics, finishing 44th. Corbitt, who earned his graduate degree in education at NYU, was the 1954 U.S. marathon champion and American record holder at 50 miles. A founder of the New York Road Runners Club and former president of the Road Runners Club of America, he is considered by many to be the "father" of long-distance running.

1956—The first NYU athlete to compete in the Winter Olympics made her appearance at Cortina D'Ampezzo, Italy. She was 16-year-old Carol Heiss, and she won the silver medal in figure skating. Heiss, an NYU undergraduate from 1957 to 1960, became the first student ever to receive an NYU Presidential Citation for outstanding accomplishments meriting special recognition.

The 1956 Summer Games featured four Violet track and field competitors on the U.S. team. Elliott Denman finished 11th in the 50,000-meter walk. Bruce MacDonald placed 16th in the 20,000-meter walk. Gordon McKenzie was the first American across the finish line in the 10,000-meter run and finished in eighth place. Aldo Scandurra served as an alternate on the U.S. marathon team. Irving Schoolman, a sprinter and quarter-miler while an NYU undergraduate, was assistant manager of the U.S. track and field team.

In fencing, Norman Armitage returned for the last time.

1960—Undergraduate Carol Heiss became NYU's first Olympic gold medal winner in 12 years. Eleven additional Violets followed the road to Rome and the 1960 Summer Games. They were Gordon McKenzie, Bruce MacDonald, Gordon Dickson, Cliff Bertrand, Jimmy Weddeburn. Mike D'Asaro, Gene Glazer, Wladimiro Calarese, Hugo M. Castello, Lou Rossini, and Benjamin Becker.

CAROL HEISS
(Left)

At age 16, Carol Heiss won the silver medal at the 1956 Olympics, going on to win the gold in 1960. The sophomore English major was greeted with a ticker tape parade up Broadway upon her return to New York. Heiss won a total of four U.S. titles and two North American championships and was inducted into the U.S. Figure Skating Association Hall of Fame in 1976.

1964—Tokyo, the original host of the canceled 1940 Olympics, finally received its chance in 1964, when the Games were held in Asia for the first time. Gary Gubner finished fourth as weight lifter in the heavy-weight division.

Two Violets competed in track and field. Cliff Bertrand wore the colors of the newly independent Trinidad and Tobago, but lost in the 200-meter quarter finals. Bruce MacDonald finished 26th in the 50,000-meter walk, and Jack Griffin, a former javelin thrower for NYU, served as assistant coach of the women's track team.

In fencing, Herb Cohen competed in the foil, as did Gene Glazer. Joe Byrnes, a professor of English at NYU, was the U.S. fencing teams' armorer. Wladimiro Calarese competed again for Italy.

Lou Rossini again coached the Puerto Rican basketball team, which finished fourth.

Largely due to Japanese enthusiasm for the game, baseball was an exhibition sport at the 1964 Olympics. Don Novick, NYU's Athlete of the Year in 1964, was on the U.S. all-star team. He later coached NYU's soccer team in 1982.

1968—NYU was represented in five different sports at the Summer Games in Mexico City.

In basketball, Lou Rossini returned as coach of the Puerto Rican team, which included one of the Violet players, Dolph Porrata. On the American side of the court, Ben Carnevale served as a member of the U.S. men's Olympic basketball committee and team manager.

In track, Aldo Scandurra served as a member of the U.S. Olympic track and field committee.

Five fencers competed at the 1968 Olympics: Jeffrey Checkes,

Herb Cohen, Jack Keane, Norman Lewis, and Wladimiro Calarese.

The first female Violet fencer in the Olympics was Sally Pechinsky Ballinger, an 18-year-old School of Education freshman. Ballinger's team lost in the early rounds.

Stuart Walker was a member of the eighth-place crew in 5.5-meter yachting. Edith Master was on the U.S dressage team, which finished eighth in the equestrian competition.

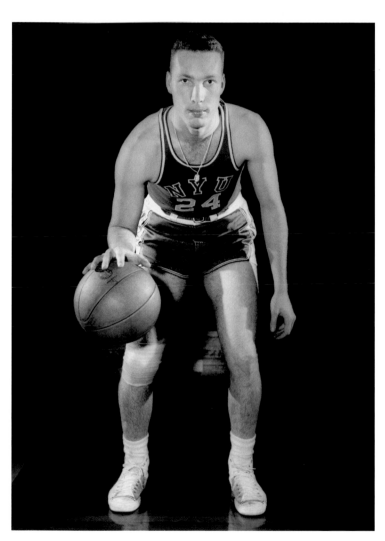

JIM FRONTERA, 1964 PUERTO RICAN BASKETBALL TEAM
(Above)
Jim Frontera, a 1963 graduate of the School of Commerce, competed in the 1964 Olympics on the Puerto Rican basketball team, under Coach Lou Rossini, his coach from the NYU team. The Puerto Rican team had their best showing ever, finishing fourth in competition.

DON NOVICK, 1964 U.S. OLYMPIC BASEBALL TEAM
(Opposite)
Baseball was an exhibition sport at the Tokyo Summer Games but was still very popular. Don Novick ('66), NYU's Athlete of the Year, competed on the U.S. team. Novick was also named to the U.S. all star team.

BYRON DYCE
(Right)
Byron Dyce is considered one of the most successful middle-distance running stars at NYU. He won four straight Metropolitan Amateur Athletic Union competitions in the 1,000-yard run and set several NYU school records. The mathematics major competed on the Jamaican track team during the 1968 Olympics in Mexico City.

1972—Sapporo, Japan, hosted the Winter Olympics.

Gilbert Jones served as head of the U.S. bobsled team.

At the Summer Games in Munich, Violet athletes represented four different countries and included Byron Dyce, Cheryl Toussaint Eason, Bruce MacDonald, Edith Master, Paul Apostol, Robert Dow, Martin Davis, George Masin, Jack Keane, Stanley Sieja, Ruth White Borock, Hans Wieselgren, and Risto Hurme.

1976—Eight NYU athletes and five officials journeyed to Montreal.

NYU athletes on the fencing team were Mike D'Asaro, Jack Keane, George Masin, Edward Ballinger, Martin Lang, Paul Apostol, Steve Kaplan, and Peter Westbrook.

Risto Hurme fenced for Finland.

Edith Master once again returned to the equestrian event, as the U.S. won a bronze medal in team dressage.

In track and field, Leroy Walker served as the head coach for the U.S. team; Jack Griffin, as assistant coach; and Bruce MacDonald, as assistant coach and manager.

1980—The United States boycotted the Olympic Games held in Moscow.

PETER WESTBROOK, U.S. FENCING TEAM
(Above)
This 1975 graduate of the School of Commerce competed in the 1976, 1984, 1988, 1992, and 1996 Olympics. Peter Westbrook, winner of 11 U.S. fencing titles and 10 world titles, won the only individual sabre medal for the U.S. since 1904 and the first U.S. fencing medal since 1960 (he won a bronze).

MICHAEL LOFTON, U.S. FENCING TEAM
(Left)
Continuing the tradition of NYU Olympic fencing excellence, Michael Lofton ('88) *(right)* participated in the 1984 and 1988 Olympics. Lofton is the only competitor ever to win four consecutive NCAA fencing championships (1984-1987) and the only male collegian on the 1984 fencing team. He had a NCAA career record of 72 wins and 1 loss.

1984—At the Los Angeles Olympics, Peter Westbrook, who did not get to compete in 1980 because of the boycott, made up for lost time when he earned the only individual sabre medal won by the U.S. since 1904 and the first U.S. fencing medal since 1960. Michael Lofton finished 17th. Steve Mormando finished 12th. Jack Keane performed double duty as manager and noncompeting team captain. Semyon Pinkhaso was the alternate team coach. Michael Watt swam in the 200-meter breaststroke and the 400-meter medley relay for his native Hong Kong.

1988—At the 1988 games in Seoul, Korea, sabre fencers Michael Lofton, Steve Mormando, and Peter Westbrook competed.

John Guira served as alternate to the U.S. wrestling team, and Dong Keun Park, a recreation instructor at NYU, was head coach of the U.S. Tae Kwon Do team, which competed in the demonstration sport.

1992—NYU had two athletes compete in Barcelona, Spain, at the Summer Olympics. Mika 'il Prasad Sankofa ('88) competed in fencing in the individual and team sabre competitions. Peter Westbrook competed in the team sabre competition.

1996—Peter Westbrook returned to the Summer Olympics held in Atlanta to participate on the U.S. fencing team. He competed both in individual and team sabre competition.

(Courtesy Steve Mormando)

STEVE MORMANDO, U.S. FENCING TEAM
(Left)
Steve Mormando participated in the 1984 and 1988 Olympics for sabre competition. Mormando received his master's degree from NYU and is now the coach of the NYU fencing team. The entire sabre team finished sixth at the 1984 Olympics, its best finish since 1968.

1936 FOOTBALL TEAM

(Left)

On Thanksgiving Day 1936 in Yankee Stadium, NYU's football team performed a miraculous upset against the highly favored Fordham University Rams. With Fordham leading the game 0-6, the Violets scored a touchdown in the second half and successfully completed the free kick for the extra point. By winning the game with a score of 7-6, the Violets broke the Rams' undefeated season and eliminated any Rose Bowl hopes for their city rivals.

1940S BASEBALL TEAM

(Below)

Despite persistent rumors that baseball at NYU would be discontinued for the duration of World War II, the 1940s were the "glory days" for Violet baseball. NYU took the Metropolitan Conference Championship 1943-1948, winning the coveted Ed Barrow Trophy six years running. William McCarthy, coach for almost 40 years, sent numerous players to the major leagues. Some stars include Eddie Yost (Washington Senators), Sam Mele (Boston Red Sox), and Ralph Branca (Brooklyn Dodgers).

THE BASKETBALL LEGACY

Although basketball was invented in Springfield, Massachusetts, in 1891, the game's spiritual home is widely considered to be New York City. The sport has been played throughout the metropolitan area in YMCAs, settlement houses, school gymnasiums, lofts, armories, and even dance halls.

At NYU, basketball began to take hold just after the turn of the century and has been a unifying theme and focal point for the University community and beyond for almost 100 years.

Basketball's debut at NYU in the 1906-1907 season occurred with one critical participant missing—a coach! Despite this handicap, NYU finished the season with a 6-2 record. When NYU retained coaches, however, they were legendary. Perhaps the most famous was Howard Cann, who led the team for 35 remarkable years. His record of 409-232 stands as a testament to his leadership and dedication.

In 1920, Cann played on the National Championship Tournament winning squad. His play in that tournament was so inspirational, the *Atlanta Constitution* crowned him "the greatest basketball player in the world." Not being content as a basketball giant, Cann went on to qualify for the U.S. Olympic team for the shot put later that year.

In his early coaching years, Cann's basketball teams enjoyed a rustic home setting. They played in a gym on the University Heights campus, which was created when two barns were joined together and dubbed "Cann's Barn." In the 1930s, the team would later play in a more hallowed hall—Madison Square Garden. In fact, in 1932, NYU's team had the distinction of playing the first basketball game there.

1907 BASKETBALL TEAM
(Below)

In 1907, basketball was introduced as a varsity sport at the Heights campus. Despite its lack of a coach, the first team had a winning record of 6-2. These early victories foreshadowed NYU's later success as a basketball powerhouse.

Cann once drolly remarked about winning, "Well, it's better than losing." He also could be philosophical. On the subject of coaching, something that came naturally to him, he said, "If you want the satisfaction of watching young men—unpolished diamonds—come to you as freshman and leave four years later, poised and capable, be a coach. If you want the thrill of having your athletes return years later and tell you of their successes in the civilian world, then turn to the coaching profession."

Lou Rossini, who would prove a highly capable replacement, leading the team to still more victorious seasons, succeeded Howard Cann.

1919-1920 MEN'S BASKETBALL
(Above)
The 1919-1920 men's basketball team became one of the few collegiate basketball teams ever to win the Amateur Athletic Union Championship. Led by Coach Ed Thorpe and the legendary Howard Cann (later a longtime coach of the NYU team), the Violets had an almost perfect season, suffering only one defeat at the hands of West Point. Although men's basketball has yet to capture a national championship, it continues to grow in popularity and success at NYU.

Among the stars were All-Americans Hagan Anderson, Milt Schulman, Jerry Fleishman, Sid Tanenbaum, Don Forman, Dolph Schayes, Cal ("the Hawk") Ramsey (top rebounder), Tom (Satch) Sanders, Mal Graham (number one leading scorer), Barry Kramer (number two leading scorer), and Boris Nachmankin (the first Violet to score 1,000 career points). These giants of the sport propelled NYU into the NCAA Division I Championships in the 1919-1920, 1942-1943, 1944-1945, 1945-1946, and 1959-1960 seasons. Violet games were a focal point for a university without many unifying themes, and the games at Madison Square Garden were always well attended, frequently selling out.

CAL RAMSEY
(Left)
As an undergraduate at NYU in the late 1950s, Cal Ramsey was a star forward and an All-American player in basketball. He went on to play in the NBA for the St. Louis Hawks, the Syracuse Nationals, and the New York Knickerbockers. He has served as chairman of the New York City Sports Commission and commissioner of Big Apple Games and has worked as an assistant principal and teacher in New York City junior high schools. Ramsey is currently NYU's assistant basketball coach and assistant director of alumni relations.

1959-1960 MEN'S BASKET-BALL
(Above)
The 1959-1960 basketball team, led by All-American Tom Sanders, captured the NCAA Eastern Regional title and finished fourth in the National Finals. The team carried out a winning streak that led them into the NCAA tournament for the first time in 14 years and ranked them as the 12th team in the country—NYU's highest ranking since the 1940s.

HOWARD CANN
(Left)
Howard Cann is recognized as one of the best all-around athletes in NYU's history. As a student, he set numerous records for track and field events and competed in the shot put at the 1920 Olympics. He was captain of the 1919 football team, as well as the 1920 basketball team, which won the national Amateur Athletic Union (AAU) Championship. His success in the AAU Championship won him acclaim as "the greatest basketball player in the world." After his graduation from the College of Engineering, Cann was NYU's varsity basketball coach from 1923 to 1958. Under his leadership, the team won 409 victories against only 232 losses. Cann was inducted into the NBA Hall of Fame in 1967 and NYU's Sports Hall of Fame in 1971.

MEN'S BASKETBALL PROGRAM FROM 1934
(Opposite)
Suffering only one defeat, the 1934-1935 season was one of the best for the NYU basketball team. The sport achieved a major following in a series of eight doubleheaders played at Madison Square Garden, which provided ample accommodation for the crowds. The Notre Dame game, the first that NYU played at the Garden, gave the Violets nationwide recognition.

COLLEGE BASKETBALL
Saturday December 29th, 1934

OFFICIAL PROGRAM

10 CENTS

Notre Dame
vs.
New York Univ.

St. John's College
vs.
Westminster

MADISON SQUARE GARDEN

College basketball reached a new level of popularity in 1934, when both City College of New York and New York University finished their seasons undefeated and played against each other in March for the unofficial championship of the city. The game was staged at the 168th Street Armory by Ned Irish (1905-1982), a sportwriter who had arranged games to benefit the city relief fund at the behest of Mayor James J. Walker, and drew a crowd of sixteen thousand.

The city and metropolitan area were the site during these years of the best collegiate basketball in the country. City College and New York University were always competitive....

The Encyclopedia of New York City
by Kenneth T. Jackson

Despite basketball's great popularity, the sport was almost shattered in 1951 when Manhattan district attorney Frank Hogan's investigation led to charges of "point shaving" (deliberately reducing the margin of victory in a game to serve bettors). More than 30 players were indicted from local schools, including players from New York University. College basketball games no longer were played at Madison Square Garden, and the game lost much of its luster. However, this period of turmoil led to a reevaluation of how collegiate sports might better be played and the eventual creation of the Division III status.

WOMEN'S BASKETBALL
(Below)
Basketball is not just a men's sport at NYU. No other sport at the University has come as far as women's basketball in terms of accomplishment and recognition.

Created in 1923, the program was considered a "co-ed activity" and did not become a varsity sport until the 1930s. Today, however, with the 1997 NCAA Championship, women's basketball is one of the top teams at NYU.

SPORTS PLAYED THE RIGHT WAY

For NYU, the dream became a reality on March 27, 1997, when the women's basketball team, the Violets, won their first NCAA Division III Championship at NYU's Coles Sports Center. It was a heart-stopping moment as NYU made a ferocious comeback from a 13-point half-time deficit. And it was the stupendous layup of Marsha Harris who, with only 1.5 seconds left in the game, gave NYU its 72-70 win over Wisconsin-Eau Claire.

The victory gave New York City its first NCAA Championship in nearly a half century. The last win in 1950 was the men's basketball team from City College, which won both the NCAA title and the National Invitation Tournament. This win, however, disintegrated into scandal the following year when major players were arrested for point shaving.

Said Marsha Harris to a *New York Times* reporter following the Violets' win, "We play because we want to, not because someone is paying us to play."

Harris's comment reflects NYU's critical transition from Division I to Division III athletics. This transition changed the life of NYU's athletics by protecting the University's athletes from the dark side of sports—payoffs, grade fixing, and relaxed eligibility practices. Given this context, it is not an exaggeration to say that the seeds of the Violets' 1997 victory were planted more than a decade earlier by then chancellor L. Jay Oliva, who pushed for and won Division III status for NYU.

In a 1986 essay in the *Washington Post*, Dr. Oliva discussed the problems of athletics and academics.

My own institution, New York University, is arguably...the largest private university in the world, and we've had athletics in every stage and condition. We've seen big-time football with crowds of 80,000 at Yankee Stadium; big-time basketball that made NCAA and NIT legends; track and field titles of every description; College World Series baseball appearances and 16 NCAA championships.

And I've also personally seen trouble up close: the dropping of football when competition could not be sustained; the basketball scandals of the 1950s and 60s; the financial struggles of the early '70s that caused the cutback of major sports, and a thousand smaller traumas.

But I've also participated in the regeneration of sports: the building of our magnificent Coles Sports and Recreation Center (1981); the restoration of basketball and other sports at the Division III level, which commits us in

(Photo credit: Ken Levinson)

1997: AT CITY HALL, THE MAYOR HONORS NYU'S BASKETBALL CHAMPS

The women's basketball team had a banner year in 1997 as they became the NCAA Division III champions. Led by Coach Janice Quinn and such stars as Jen Krolikowski and Marsha Harris, the team set many records on their way to the top. The women made headlines as the first New York women's college basketball team to win a national championship and the first college basketball team to win in the city in almost 50 years.

recruitment, finances and academics to treat all students alike; the excitement of strong competition; and the creation with eight other institutions similarly dedicated to equal treatment of students [of the University Athletic Association]....

In 1986, to seal this commitment, NYU helped found the University Athletic Association, a group that joined it with eight other urban universities in endorsing strong academic goals while still offering the chance to compete against the nation's leading universities. Members include Brandeis University, Carnegie Mellon University, Case Western Reserve University, Emory University, Johns Hopkins University, New York University, University of Chicago, University of Rochester, and Washington University in St. Louis.

Thus, at NYU a set of rules has existed for more than a decade for every student athlete. Regular admissions procedures without athletic scholarships are the dictum. Priorities have shifted from the need to have a winning sports team to the need to build a superb student body and faculty, a strong research environment, a meaningful student life, and excellent facilities for living, teaching, and learning. Into this milieu, student athletics have been incorporated (as the Violets' 1997 win proved), but always in proper relationship to the University's academic goals.

SPORTS AT NYU TODAY

NYU has always been proud of its strong athletic traditions. The basketball and fencing programs, NYU's most successful teams for both men and women, are joined by powerhouses in eight other sports, including men's and women's soccer, track, tennis, volleyball, and swimming. However, NYU's athletic excellence is matched by its commitment to academic scholarship, as shown by its membership in the University Athletic Association. The primary principle of the UAA is that athletics are essential to the educational experience and should be conducted in a manner consistent with the school's academic mission.

Illustrating NYU's success in keeping this commitment, NYU teams have won 14 team championships, and 34 athletes were named Most Outstanding Individual Performers in the last eight years of UAA competition. Also, in addition to the women's basketball team's 1997 NCAA championship win, 42 NYU students were named

Division III All-Americans, and 31 were Academic All-Americans—two of the highest honors bestowed by the NCAA.

In keeping with the belief that athletics are an important part of a balanced education, NYU urges all students—not just varsity athletes—to take advantage of its comprehensive recreational sports program. The hub of this program is the Jerome S. Coles Sports and Recreation Center. Home of the University's varsity teams, the center also offers classes, club sports, and intramural activities for students, faculty, and alumni.

Coles will soon be joined by a new athletic complex in the Palladium residence hall. The Palladium will feature an eight-lane swimming pool, basketball courts, a climbing wall, a weight room, and an aerobic fitness room. These expanded facilities will help NYU continue its commitment to athletic excellence for years to come.

(Courtesy NYU Sports Information Office)

THE NYU BOBCAT
(Opposite)
Representing the link between NYU's academic and athletic commitments, the NYU Bobcat (named for the *Bob*st Library *Cat*alog character) is the beloved mascot of NYU athletes.

JEROME S. COLES SPORTS AND RECREATION CENTER
(Above)
Home to NYU's 18-sport intercollegiate program, the Coles Sports Center offers advantages for the casual athlete as well. Pictured are just a few of the center's facilities: basketball courts, indoor tennis courts, and squash and raquetball courts.

FENCING
(Above)

Since the days of the de Capriles brothers and Julia Jones Pugliese, the NYU fencing program has produced championship teams. Coach Steve Mormando also continues another tradition of a long stewardship of the program. Currently in his 19th year at NYU, Mormando is a world champion who has guided the men toward 10 straight UAA titles and the women toward five.

SOCCER
(Left)

Led by new coach Jon Clement, the women's soccer team had its best winning percentage ever in 1999. The men, guided by Coach Joe Behan, '95, posted an 11-6-2 record in the same season—their first winning season in four years.

MEN'S BASKETBALL
(Opposite)

True to its strong tradition as a basketball powerhouse, the Violets have emerged as a strong contender once more in the NCAA. In the 1990s, the team had several postseason appearances, seven NCAA Tournament bids, and one trip to the NCAA Division III National Championship Game.

SWIMMING AND DIVING

(Opposite, top, left)

Strong contenders in the UAA Conference and the NCAA Division III, the NYU swimming and diving teams rank high honors in individual and team events. In 1999, the men's team enjoyed their best season in recent years, finishing with an 8-3 record. The women were successful as well, finishing 8-2, and were also honored by the College Swimming Coaches Association of America for earning the 10th highest grade point average of all Division III programs.

VOLLEYBALL

(Opposite, top, right)

The 1999 seasons proved to be the most successful in team history for both the men and the women. The men, led by former NYU record-setter José Piña, posted a school record 20-8 and qualified for the Eastern Intercollegiate Volleyball Association Division III Championship for the first time in school history. Kelly Stosik, 1998 Coach of the Year, guided the women to their second NCAA appearance in the team's history.

COLES SPORTS CENTER ROOF

(Opposite, bottom)

The Coles Sports Center's roof was designed with a state-of-the-art rooftop track and tennis courts.

TRACK AND CROSS-COUNTRY

(Right)

The NYU track teams share a commitment to personal best. This goal is evidenced by a number of records set in recent years by both the men and the women. One of the biggest honors was that of Melissa Wiltzius, who became NYU's first women's track-and-field All-American during the 1994 indoor and outdoor seasons. Pictured here is Joanne Moreau, '99.

(Courtesy NYU Sports Information Office)

(Photo credit: Don Pollard)

N*ew York University has some 350,000 alumni throughout the United States and abroad. In fact, it is now virtually impossible to go through life on planet Earth without coming into contact with an NYU alumna or alumnus.*

While the numbers are impressive, the quality of people who have, as author Thomas Wolfe has observed, roamed the "corridors and classrooms of Washington Square" is even more impressive. Indeed, included among NYU's alumni are some of the country's and the world's top leaders in business, government and public service, education, the arts and sciences, and the health and caring professions.

As a group, NYU alumni have consistently demonstrated their loyalty and generosity. The results have been a plethora of endowed professorships and named student scholarships. In addition, alumni giving has helped transform the University's campus from a "subway school" into one of America's great urban campuses. One has only to walk the campus to discover a multitude of buildings, classrooms, conference rooms, departments, centers, institutes, and residence halls and residence hall suites that bear the names of alumni benefactors.

That NYU appreciates its alumni is a given. That NYU alumni appreciate their alma mater is also a given. Clearly, this volume's Alumni chapter has been the most difficult to prepare of all the chapters in this book. The challenge: How to honor 350,000 living alumni? How to honor the hundreds of thousands who preceded them?

To meet this challenge, the University's Office for University Development and Alumni Relations has painstakingly chosen from its rosters less than 1 percent of its total contemporary alumni list. The resultant roll includes those who have returned to New York University since 1995 to accept an honor or award for professional achievement or service to the University or to share their experiences with faculty and students. They are recipients of honorary degrees, the Presidential Medal, and school and University-wide Distinguished Alumni and Meritorious Service Awards. They are also presenters of master classes and speakers at University and school commencement exercises, deans' days, celebratory events, and alumni panel discussions.

The listing of these alumni—most if not all will be instantly recognized—is offered only as emblematic of the larger and even more distinguished number. Omissions will abound, of course. And for this, apologies in advance are offered.

KEY TO ABBREVIATIONS

ARTS	University College of Arts and Science (Heights)	ESSW	Shirley M. Ehrenkranz School of Social Work	IFA	Institute of Fine Arts	STERN U	Leonard N. Stern School of Business Undergraduate College
CAS	College of Arts and Science	GAL	Gallatin School of Individualized Study	LAW	School of Law		
				MED	School of Medicine	TSOA	Tisch School of the Arts
CIMS	Courant Institute of Mathematical Sciences	GSAS	Graduate School of Arts and Science	SCPS	School of Continuing and Professional Studies	WAG	Robert F. Wagner Graduate School of Public Service
DEN	College of Dentistry	HON	Honorary degree	STERN G	Leonard N. Stern School of Business Graduate Division		
ED	School of Education						

(Photo credit: Phil Gallo)

ALUMNI LIST

RUTH J. ABRAM
(GSAS '84), *founding president, Lower East Side Tenement Museum*

MILDRED ALLEN
(ESSW '67, WAG '77, GSAS '83), *executive director, Fordham-Tremont Community Mental Health Center*

THERESA A. AMATO
(LAW '89), *attorney, Citizens Advocacy Center*

EDWARD L. AMOROSI
(MED '59), *associate professor of clinical medicine, New York University School of Medicine*

MICHAEL T. ANDREEN
(TSOA '88), *film production executive*

SHERIL D. ANTONIO
(TSOA '99), *associate dean for film, television, and new media, Tisch School of the Arts, New York University*

PETER S. ARONSON
(MED '70), *chief, section of nephrology, Yale University School of Medicine*

FELICIA B. AXELROD
(MED '66), *Carl Seaman Family Professor of Dysautonomia Treatment and Research and professor of neurology, New York University School of Medicine*

JULIUS AXELROD
(GSAS '41), *Nobel laureate in physiology or medicine*

ALEJANDRO BADIA
(MED '89), *physician, Miami Hand Center*

ALEC BALDWIN
(TSOA '94), *actor*

LAWRENCE J. BANKS
(STERN U '55), *retired private investor*

EDWARD E. BARR
(STERN U '57), *chairman and CEO, Sun Chemical Corporation*

(Above)
At the first Graduate School of Arts and Science Dean's Day in 1999, Dean Catharine R. Stimpson presented the GSAS Alumni Achievement Award to Nobel laureate **Dr. Julius Axelrod** (GSAS '41).

(Right)
Sheril D. Antonio (TSOA '99) is representative of the scholars who have graduated from the Tisch School of the Arts with a passion for the arts. As a student, she made the most of the school's opportunities, receiving in 1981 a B.F.A. in film and television and in 1999, a Ph.D. from the Department of Cinema Studies in contemporary African American cinema. Along the way, she also picked up an M.A. in liberal studies from the Graduate School of Arts and Science in 1986. Currently, she serves as associate dean for film, television, and new media at TSOA. Dynamic, funny, and beloved by students, she frequently teaches and lectures.

(Right)
Edward E. Barr (STERN U '57), chairman of the board of Sun Chemical Group, serves on the Board of Overseers of the Stern School of Business and has established the Nancy and Edward Barr International Scholars Program at Stern.

MARIA BARTIROMO

(CAS '89), *anchor, CNBC's* Business News

WILLOW BAY

(STERN U '91), *cohost, CNN's* The Moneyline News Hour

VICKI L. BEEN

(LAW '83), *professor, New York University School of Law*

BRUCE BERGER

(STERN U '66), *president, Sutton Group Services, Inc.*

WILLIAM R. BERKLEY

(STERN U '66), *chairman and CEO, W. R. Berkley Corp.*

RICHARD A. BERNSTEIN

(ARTS '68), *chairman and CEO, R. A. B. Holdings, Inc.*

(Photo credit: Elena Olivo)

(Photo credit: Elena Olivo)

(Photo credit: Don Pollard)

(Above)
Maria Bartiromo (CAS '89), CNBC's *Business News* anchor, addressed faculty and alumni at the 1999 College of Arts and Science Dean's Day.

(Left)
Willow Bay (STERN U '91) *(left)*, cohost of CNN's *The Moneyline News Hour,* is pictured with Professor Carol Noll Hoskins (ED '73) of the School of Education's Division of Nursing. Bay was the narrator for Hoskins's new videotape, *Journey to Recovery: For Women with Breast Cancer and Their Partners,* which was designed to help couples cope with the severe stress of breast cancer.

(Left, bottom)
A private investor, **Richard A. Bernstein** (ARTS '68) has shared with NYU a wealth of experience as a business and community leader. In addition to serving as a University trustee and on the Stern School of Business Board of Overseers, Bernstein served as cochairman of the Stern Campaign for Excellence, which helped to fund the Kaufman Management Education Center.

(Right, bottom)
William R. Berkley (STERN U '66), chairman of W. R. Berkley Corporation, is a member of the NYU Board of Trustees and chairs its Business Initiatives Committee. He is also chair of the Stern Board of Overseers.

(Photo credit: Don Pollard)

(Photo credit: Phil Gallo)

(Above)
In 1996, President L. Jay Oliva presented the President's Alumni Achievement Award to **Robert R. Bishop** (GSAS/CIMS '68), an alumnus of the Graduate School of Arts and Science and chairman of Silicon Graphics, a company that specializes in the design and manufacture of advanced computing equipment.

(Right)
School of Education dean Ann Marcus *(left)* congratulates renowned author **Judy Blume** (ED '61), who received the 1997 NYU Alumni Association Distinguished Alumna Award.

GARY BETTMAN
(LAW '77), *commissioner, National Hockey League*

ROBERT R. BISHOP
(GSAS/CIMS '68), *chairman, Silicon Graphics, Inc.*

MARC R. BLACKMAN
(MED '72), *chief, division of endocrinology and metabolism, Johns Hopkins Bayview Medical Center*

MARTIN J. BLASER
(MED '73), *chairman, department of medicine, New York University School of Medicine*

LOUIS BLATTERFEIN
(DEN '33), *internationally acclaimed prosthodontist*

RONALD BLAYLOCK
(STERN G '89), *chairman and CEO, Blaylock & Partners*

OSCAR BLOUSTEIN
(CAS '39, LAW '42), *attorney*

MANFRED BLUM
(ARTS '53, MED '57), *professor of clinical medicine and radiology, New York University School of Medicine*

JUDY BLUME
(ED '61), *author*

ROBYN BLUMNER
(LAW '85), *past executive director, American Civil Liberties Union of Florida; columnist, St. Petersburg Times*

LEONARD BOXER
(STERN U '60, LAW '63), *senior partner, Stroock & Stroock & Lavan*

PATRICK A. BRADFORD
(LAW '89), *partner, Davis, Polk & Wardwell*

JANE EISNER BRAM
(CAS '58, ESSW '79, '00), *psychotherapist*

CATHERINE C. BRAWER
(GSAS/IFA '66), *president, Ida and William Rosenthal Foundation*

MARTIN BREST
(TSOA '73), *film director*

BERNIE BRILLSTEIN
(STERN U '53), *award-winning film and television producer*

KEVIN R. BRINE
(STERN G '81), *senior vice president and member of the Board of Directors, Sanford C. Bernstein and Company*

LONNIE R. BRISTOW
(MED '57), *first African American to be named president of the American Medical Association*

THOMAS R. BROME
(LAW '67), *partner, Cravath, Swaine & Moore*

IONE CAREY
(ED), *public health nursing professor*

CALEB CARR
(CAS '77), *best-selling author*

SUSAN CARTSONIS
(TSOA '84), *senior vice president, 20th Century Fox*

ROBERT J. CELOTTA
(GSAS '69), *physicist, National Institute of Standards and Technology*

BETTY WEI CHUNG CHANG
(MED '78), *chief of allergy, Kaiser Permanente Medical Center; one of eight physicians named to "Top Doctors" list by* Washingtonian *magazine*

ENRIQUE CHEDIAK
(TSOA '97), *filmmaker, recipient of Sundance Film Festival Award for Best Cinematography*

DEBRA CHRAPATY
(STERN G '92), *president and COO, E*Trade Technologies*

NOEL L. COHEN
(ARTS '51), *Mendik Foundation Professor, chairman of the Department of Otolaryngology, director of the Cochlear Implantation Program, and vice dean for clinical affairs, New York University School of Medicine*

JERRY L. COHEN
(STERN U '53, STERN G '59), *vice chairman, Tishman Speyer Properties*

WILLIAM B. COHEN
(MED '63), *physician, Cedars-Sinai Medical Center*

GERALDINE H. COLES
(CAS '38), *philanthropist*

CHRIS COLUMBUS
(TSOA '80), *film director*

BETTY COMDEN
(ED '37, HON '99), *composer, lyricist, writer*

JOEL CONARROE
(GSAS '66), *president, John Simon Guggenheim Foundation*

WILLIAM A. COOK
(ESSW '71), *oncologist, St. Vincent's Hospital, New York*

FRANK CORACI
(TSOA '88), *film director*

LORRAINE CORTÉS-VÁZQUEZ
(WAG '83), *president, The Hispanic Federation*

JIM COX
(TSOA '98), *filmmaker, recipient of Sundance Film Festival Award for* Atomic Tabasco

JOHN J. CREEDON
(STERN U '52, LAW '55, '62), *former president and CEO, Metropolitan Life Insurance Co.*

BILLY CRUDUP
(TSOA '94), *actor*

BILLY CRYSTAL
(TSOA '70), *actor, comedian, entertainer*

CLIVE DAVIS
(CAS '53), *founder and president, Arista Records*

CHARLES H. DEBROVNER
(MED '60), *clinical associate professor of obstetrics and gynecology, New York University School of Medicine*

MARISA J. DEMEO
(LAW '93), *regional counsel, Mexican American Legal Defense and Educational Fund*

(Photo credit: Enrique Cubillo)

(*Left*)
New York University presented honorary degrees to musical theatre legends **Betty Comden** (ED '37) and her collaborator Adolph Green at the 1999 NYU Commencement ceremony.

(*Opposite*)
After receiving an honorary degree from New York University in 1995, **Neil Diamond** (STERN U) entertained the Commencement audience in Washington Square Park with a rousing rendition of "Louie, Louie."

DOMINICK P. DePAOLA

(DEN '69), *president, Forsyth Institute in Boston; past president, American Association of Dental Schools*

E. JON DE REVERE

(ARTS '60), *choral conductor*

ANDRE DE SHIELDS

(GAL '91), *actor, director, entertainer*

NEIL DIAMOND

(STERN U, HON '95), *singer, songwriter*

MORTIMER L. DOWNEY, III

(WAG '66), *deputy secretary, U.S. Department of Transportation*

DANIEL B. DRACHMAN

(MED '56), *professor of neurology and neurosciences, Johns Hopkins University School of Medicine*

ARTHUR DRICKMAN

(ARTS '51, MED '55), *clinical professor of pathology, University of Southern Florida Medical College*

SARA DRIVER

(TSOA '82), *director; instructor, Department of Film and Television, Graduate Division, Tisch School of the Arts, New York University*

DEBORAH DUNCAN

(STERN G '84), *executive vice president, Chase Manhattan Corporation, Chase Manhattan Bank*

HARRY W. EICHENBAUM

(CAS '57, MED '61), *physician, St. Petersburg General Hospital*

JOEL S. EHRENKRANZ

(LAW '61, '64), *senior partner, Ehrenkranz & Ehrenkranz, LLP*

BETTY WEINBERG ELLERIN

(CAS '50, LAW '52), *justice, Appellate Division, First Department, Supreme Court of the State of New York*

SCOTT ELLIOTT

(GAL '93), *theatre and film producer*

(Photo credit: Lou Manna)

(Photo credit: Tim Healy)

(Photo credit: Phil Gallo)

(Above)
In 1997, **Dr. Saul J. Farber** (CAS '38, MED '42) completed 50 years of service to the New York University School of Medicine. An esteemed educator and exemplary leader, Farber held the posts of dean and provost for nearly 20 years.

(Left)
Mary C. Farrell (STERN G '76), an alumna of the Leonard N. Stern School of Business and an NYU alumni trustee, addressed fellow graduates at the 1997 NYU Alumni Day in Florida.

(Bottom, left)
Bronx Borough President **Fernando J. Ferrer** (ARTS '72) received the Eugene J. Keogh Award for Distinguished Public Service from the NYU Alumni Association in 1995.

KENNETH ENG
(MED '67), *Arthur Localio Professor of Surgery, New York University School of Medicine*

CLAIRE MINTZER FAGIN
(ED '64), *former interim president, University of Pennsylvania; pioneer in psychiatric nursing*

SAUL J. FARBER
(CAS '38, MED '42), *former dean and former chairman of the Department of Medicine, New York University School of Medicine*

MARY C. FARRELL
(STERN G '76), *managing partner and senior investment strategist, PaineWebber, Inc.*

BRUCE J. FERBER
(TSOA '75), *writer and director*

FERNANDO J. FERRER
(ARTS '72), *president, Borough of the Bronx, New York City*

MURRAY M. FIELDS
(LAW '34), *partner, Buchalter Nemer Fields & Younger Charitable Foundation*

WALTER L. FIELDS, JR.
(WAG '90), *owner, Fields Communication, Ltd.*

ROBERT L. FREEDMAN
(TSOA '83), *screenwriter*

LOUIS J. FREEH
(LAW '84), *director, Federal Bureau of Investigation*

THOMAS E. FRESTON
(STERN G '69), *chairman and CEO, MTV Networks, Inc.*

LESLEY M. FRIEDMAN
(LAW '85), *president, Special Counsel International Inc.*

ARTHUR FROMMER
(CAS '50), *originator and author, Frommer Travel Guides*

ANNE SUTHERLAND FUCHS
(CAS '69), *senior vice president and group publishing director, Hearst Magazines*

RICHARD S. FULD, JR.
(STERN G '72), *chairman, president, and CEO, Lehman Brothers Holdings, Inc.*

ELAINE FULTZ

(WAG '91), *senior policy analyst, United Nations International Labor Organization*

FRANCESCA GANY

(WAG '93), *director, New York Task Force on Immigrant Health*

DEBORAH GARRISON

(GSAS '91), *poet; senior editor,* The New Yorker

JOHN R. GARRISON

(WAG '64), *managing director, American Lung Association*

ARTHUR GELB

(CAS '46), *president, The New York Times Company Foundation, Inc.*

MARVIN C. GERSHENGORN

(MED '71), *Abby Rockefeller Mauze Distinguished Professor of Endocrinolgy in Medicine, Joan and Sanford I. Weill Medical College, Cornell University*

BERTIE GILMORE

(ED '57, '81), *professor and director, Practical Nursing Associate in Arts Degree and Bachelor of Science Programs, Department of Nursing, Medgar Evers College, City University of New York*

RUDOLPH W. GIULIANI

(LAW '68), *mayor, New York City*

LEWIS L. GLUCKSMAN

(STERN U '51), *senior adviser, Salomon Smith Barney*

JON D. GOLD

(SCPS '91), *vice president of real estate, Chase Manhattan Bank*

STEPHEN GOLDEN

(GAL '90), *former president, Forest Products Group, The New York Times Company*

HARVEY GOLUB

(STERN U '61), *chairman of the board, American Express*

NORMAN GOODMAN

(ARTS '47, LAW '50), *county clerk, New York County*

JOHN M. GREANEY

(LAW '63), *associate judge, Massachusetts Supreme Judicial Court*

(Right)
New York City mayor **Rudolph W. Giuliani** (LAW '68), received the Eugene G. Keogh Award for Distinguished Public Service from the NYU Alumni Association in 1998.

(Below)
For his outstanding commitment and loyalty to the NYU School of Continuing and Professional Studies, **Jon D. Gold** (SCPS '91) received the Dean's Alumni Service Award. Pictured left to right are Gold, SCPS director of development and alumni relations Leslie Smith, and Arthur Margon, director of graduate studies and academic affairs at the SCPS Real Estate Institute.

(Photo credit: Ken Levinson)

(Photo credit: Harry Heliotis)

HOWARD GREENBERGER

(LAW '54), *professor, New York University School of Law*

ALAN GREENSPAN

(STERN U '48, GSAS '50, STERN G '77), *chairman, The Federal Reserve*

HOWARD M. GREY

(MED '57), *president and scientific director, La Jolla Institute for Allergy and Immunology*

MARTIN GROVE

(TSOA '68), *columnist,* Hollywood Reporter; *film critic,* In Flight *magazine*

HENRY A. GRUNWALD

(CAS '44), *publisher, editor, author, and diplomat*

ALDEN HAFFNER

(WAG '60, GSAS '64), *president, College of Optometry, State University of New York*

LISA GAY HAMILTON

(TSOA '85), *actress, cast of* WABC's The Practice

MARCIA GAY HARDEN

(TSOA '88), *actress*

LORENZO HARRISON

(WAG '93), *deputy executive director, Strive Employment Group*

JEROME M. HAUER

(GAL '75), *former director, New York City Mayor's Office of Emergency Management; international security expert*

RITA HAUSER

(LAW '59), *international attorney, peace advocate, and philanthropist*

JESSICA HECHT

(TSOA '87), *actress*

H. DALE HEMMERDINGER

(CAS '67), *president, The Hemmerdinger Corporation*

JONATHAN M. HERMAN

(ARTS '69, LAW '73), *partner, Dorsey & Whitney*

GEORGE H. HEYMAN, JR.

(STERN G '38), *private investor*

(Courtesy World Wide Photos)

(Photo credit: Don Pollard)

(Photo credit: Bob Handelman)

(Above)
Chairman of the Federal Reserve **Alan Greenspan** (STERN U '48, GSAS '50, STERN G '77), a graduate of the Stern School of Business and the Graduate School of Arts and Science, spoke about America's new economy at the Haskins Partners Dinner in May 1997. He received the Charles Waldo Emerson Haskins Award, which is given each year to recognize outstanding individuals whose careers have been characterized by the highest level of achievement in bridging the worlds of business and the public sector.

(Left)
NYU trustee and benefactor **H. Dale Hemmerdinger** (CAS '67) cut the ribbon at the dedication of Hemmerdinger Hall. Pictured from left are Laurence Tisch; Dean Matthew Santirocco, CAS; H. Dale Hemmerdinger; President Oliva; and Philip Furmanski, former FAS dean.

(Left, bottom)
As chair of the Trustee Development Committee for 21 years, **George H. Heyman, Jr.** (STERN G '38), led NYU through a period of remarkable financial growth, helping the University to raise over $2.3 billion during his tenure. A life trustee and generous benefactor himself, Heyman is a recipient of the Alumni Meritorious Service Award from the NYU Alumni Association and the Distinguished Service Award from the Stern School of Business.

(Photo credit: Elena Olivo)

(Left)
Internet entrepreneur **Murray Hidary** (CAS '93) discussed "Technology and Its Challenges" at the 1999 College of Arts and Science Dean's Day.

(Below)
A world-renowned cardiologist, **Martin L. Kahn** (MED '63) takes a break from making rounds at the Tisch Hospital. A 1963 graduate of the NYU School of Medicine, Dr. Kahn has spent his entire teaching career, which spans over 35 years, at his alma mater.

(Courtesy NYU Medical Center Archives)

MURRAY HIDARY
(CAS '93), *cofounder and executive vice president, EarthWeb, Inc.*

STUART M. HIRSCH
(DEN '71), *associate dean for clinical affairs, New York University College of Dentistry*

ROBERT E. HOLMES
(CAS '66, LAW '69), *executive vice president, Music Group, SONY Pictures Entertainment, Inc.*

RUSH HOLT
(GSAS '74, '81), *U.S. congressman from New Jersey*

WINIFRED J. HOLZMAN
(TSOA '83), *screenwriter*

JOEL HOPKINS
(TSOA '98), *filmmaker*

KEIKO IBI
(TSOA '98), *Oscar-winning filmmaker*

ALLEN JACOBSON
(ARTS '62), *partner and senior policy strategist, Washington Analysis Corporation*

BORIS A. JORDAN
(CAS '88), *CEO, Renaissance Capital Group*

WILLIAM H. JOYCE
(STERN G '71), *chairman, president, and CEO, Union Carbide Corporation*

MARTIN L. KAHN
(MED '63), *professor of clinical medicine, New York University School of Medicine*

YALE KAMISAR
(ARTS '50), *Clarence Darrow Distinguished University Professor of Law, University of Michigan Law School*

MAX M. KAMPELMAN
(ARTS '40, LAW '45), *lawyer, diplomat, educator; recipient of the Presidential Medal of Freedom*

EDWARD G. KAUFMAN
(DEN '43), *former dean, New York University College of Dentistry*

(Photo credit: Phil Gallo)

(Photo credit: Phil Gallo)

(Above)
On April 28, 1999, the Stern School of Business dedicated the Henry Kaufman Management Center. The center was named in honor of NYU trustee **Henry Kaufman** (ARTS '48, STERN G '58). Pictured at the ceremony, left to right: Henry Kaufman and Dean George Daly, Stern School.

(Left)
Judith Smith Kaye (LAW '62), chief judge of the New York State Court of Appeals, has received several awards from New York University including the NYU Alumni Association Eugene J. Keogh Award for Distinguished Public Service and the Law Alumni Association Achievement Award.

(Photo credit: Enrique Cubillo)

(Photo credit: Phil Gallo)

(Photo credit: Phil Gallo)

(Above)
On March 25, 1999, at the Robert F. Wagner Graduate School of Public Service, former New York City mayor **Ed Koch** (LAW '48) asked, "So You Want to Run for Office?" The lecture explored the challenges of running for office and how they have changed over the years. He is pictured with Dean Jo Ivey Boufford, Wagner School.

(Left)
In recognition for the support they received at the Courant Institute of Mathematical Sciences during the formative years of their careers, **Joseph B. Keller** (CAS '43, GSAS/CIMS '46, '48), at left, and **Herbert B. Keller** (CAS '48, GSAS/CIMS '54), at right, established the Keller Fellowship, a postdoctoral position in applied mathematics. The brothers returned to NYU in 1998 for a dinner in their honor.

RICHARD JAY KOGAN
(STERN G '68), *chairman of the board and CEO, Schering-Plough Corporation*

ABBY KOHNSTAMM
(ED '77, STERN G '79), *senior vice president, marketing, IBM*

LAWRENCE I. KONSTAN
(CAS '63, GSAS '70), *former director of food stamps and assistant commissioner of financial management, Human Resources Administration, New York City*

JEFFREY L. S. KOO
(STERN G '62), *chairman and CEO, Chinatrust Commercial Bank*

BORIS KOSTELANETZ
(STERN U '33), *of counsel, Kostelanetz & Fink, LLP*

TONY KUSHNER
(TSOA '84), *playwright*

GERALD LANDSBERG
(ESSW '67, WAG '79), *associate professor, Shirley M. Ehrenkranz School of Social Work; chair, Social Welfare Programs and Policies; director, Institute Against Violence, New York University*

KENNETH G. LANGONE
(STERN G '60), *chairman, president, and managing director, Invemed Associates, Inc.*

IRA J. LAUFER
(CAS '48, MED '53), *clinical associate professor, New York University School of Medicine*

ANDREW LAZAR
(TSOA '89), *president, Mad Chance Productions, Warner Brothers*

ROBERT LEDLEY
(DEN '48), *inventor of the ACTA Scanner (CAT Scan)*

ANG LEE
(TSOA '84), *film director*

SHELTON "SPIKE" LEE
(TSOA '82, HON '98), *producer, director, and writer*

MARVIN LEFFLER
(STERN U '42, STERN G '51), *president, Town Hall Foundation*

(Photo credit: Don Pollard)

(Photo credit: Hakan Moberg)

(Photo credit: Don Pollard)

(Left)
Shirley M. Ehrenkranz School of Social Work professor and alumnus **Gerald Landsberg** (ESSW '67, WAG '79).

(Right)
At the annual NYU Alumni Association awards dinner and presentation on June 3, 1999, President L. Jay Oliva presented the Distinguished Alumnus Award to medical pioneer and College of Dentistry alumnus **Dr. Robert Ledley** (DEN '48).

(Top)
Richard Jay Kogan (STERN G '68) was inaugurated as a new NYU trustee in 1999. He is the president and CEO of Schering-Plough Corp., a leading pharmaceutical company located in Madison, New Jersey.

(Photo credit: Brian Brown)

(Left)
Chairman, president, and managing director of Invemed Associates, Inc., NYU trustee **Kenneth G. Langone** (STERN G '60) has shared his business expertise at several University events. In the spring of 1998, he served as the keynote speaker at the first All-University Conference on Self-Employment, Business Ownership, and Entrepreneurship, and in November of that year, he spoke about "A Businessman's View of the Economy and Trends for Investments" at the NYU Alumni Association Finance Forum. He was also recently named chairman of the NYU School of Medicine Foundation Board.

(Below, left)
Celebrated filmmakers and alumni **Ang Lee** (TSOA '84) and **Spike Lee** (TSOA '82) shared insights about their craft at a reception in their honor at the Tisch School of the Arts.

(Photo credit: Phil Gallo)

(Photo credit: Phil Gallo)

(Left)
Martin Lipton (LAW '55) became chairman of the New York University Board of Trustees in 1999. He has been a trustee of the University for 23 years and was elected vice chairman in 1998. He has also served as president of the NYU School of Law Board of Trustees, and he is a recipient of many University honors, including the Gallatin Medal, Vanderbilt Medal, and a Presidential Citation.

(Below)
After being inaugurated as the president of the American Dental Association, **Dr. Richard Mascola** (DEN '68) was honored by the NYU College of Dentistry. He is pictured with Dean Michael C. Alfano, at right.

(Photo credit: Enrique Cubillo)

(Right)
Education alumnus **Frank McCourt** (ED '57, HON '00) signed copies of his best-selling memoir *Angela's Ashes* at NYU's Lewis L. and Loretta Brennan Glucksman Ireland House.

(Below)
Alumnus and eight-time Oscar-winning composer **Alan Menken** (ARTS '72, HON '00), in center, celebrated the announcement of a scholarship in his name with two students from the NYU School of Education's Department of Music and Performing Arts Professions. Menken established the Alan Menken Scholarship in Music Composition, awarded to promising music composition undergraduates.

(Photo credit: Ken Levinson)

(Photo credit: Don Pellard)

RAYMOND M. MACEDONIA
(WAG '69), *principal scientist, Textron Defense Systems*

CAMRYN MANHEIM
(TSOA '87), *Emmy and Golden Globe award–winning actress*

JILLIAN MANUS
(TSOA '84), *literary agent*

JOHN A. MARINO, JR.
(WAG '81), *managing partner, Dan Klores Associates, Inc.*

JORGE O. MARISCOL
(GSAS '86), *chief investment strategist for Latin America and director of the Latin America Equity Research Group, Goldman Sachs*

ELAINE MARKS
(GSAS '58), *past president, Modern Language Association*

RICHARD MASCOLA
(DEN '68), *president, American Dental Association*

LOWELL MATE
(TSOA '78), *senior vice president, creative affairs, Home Box Office Independent Productions, Time Warner, Inc.*

MARGARET MAXWELL
(GSAS '52), *professor of history and writer*

FRANK McCOURT
(ED '57, HON '00), *author and teacher*

KATHRYN BACH MEDINA
(GSAS '92), *executive editor and vice president, Random House*

ALAN MENKEN
(ARTS '72, HON '00), *Academy Award–winning composer*

PHILIP L. MILSTEIN
(STERN G '74), *president and CEO, Emigrant Savings Bank*

CATHY E. MINEHAN
(STERN G '77), *president, Federal Reserve Bank of Boston*

HAL J. MITNICK
(MED '72), *clinical professor of medicine, New York University School of Medicine*

(Photo credit: Ken Levinson)

(Photo credit: George Breithaupt)

(Above)
Philippe de Montebello (GSAS/IFA '76), director of the Metropolitan Museum of Art and IFA trustee, was congratulated by President L. Jay Oliva for receiving the Distinguished Alumnus Award from the NYU Alumni Association in 1998.

(Left)
Life trustee **George A. Murphy** (LAW '42) was chairman of the NYU Board of Trustees from 1963 to 1969.

(Photo credit: Ken Levinson)

(Above)
Acclaimed author **Cynthia Ozick** (CAS '49) received the NYU Alumni Association Distinguished Alumna Award in 1998.

(Right)
President of the University of the Sacred Heart **José Jaime Rivera Rodríguez** (ED '72) and Dean Ann Marcus, School of Education, display Rivera's School of Education 1996 Distinguished Alumni Achievement Award plaque.

(Photo credit: Phil Gallo)

LESTER POLLACK
(LAW '57), *managing director, Lazard Frères & Co., LLC*

IGNATIUS N. QUARTARARO
(DEN '52), *clinical professor of surgical sciences (endodontics), New York University College of Dentistry*

SALVATORE RANIERI
(CAS '70), *attorney and private investor*

BRETT RATNER
(TSOA '91), *film director*

SCOTT H. RECHLER
(SCPS '90), *prominent real estate developer*

JUDITH RESNIK
(LAW '75), *Arthur Liman Professor of Law, Yale Law School*

JOSÉ JAIME RIVERA RODRÍGUEZ
(ED '72), *president, University of the Sacred Heart, San Juan, Puerto Rico*

STEVEN ROACH
(GSAS '70, '73), *chief economist and director of global economic analysis, Morgan Stanley*

MIMSIE ROBINSON
(ED '93), *1997 New York State Teacher of the Year*

RACHEL ROBINSON
(ED '61, HON '96), *humanitarian, civil rights advocate, chairperson, Jackie Robinson Foundation*

MICHAEL J. ROSENBERG
(STERN G '55), *former executive vice president, Rosenthal and Rosenthal*

LAWRENCE "MUZZY" ROSENBLATT
(WAG '92), *acting commissioner, New York City Department of Homeless Services*

LARRY W. ROSENTHAL
(DEN '72), *founder, The Rosenthal Group for Esthetic Dentistry, New York*

TATIA ROSENTHAL
(TSOA '98), *filmmaker*

LANNY J. ROSENWASSER

(MED '72), *head, division of allergy and clinical immunology, National Jewish Medical and Research Center*

DANIEL F. ROSES

(MED '69), *New York State chair, American College of Surgeons Cancer Liaison Program; Jules Leonard Whitehill Professor of Surgery and director of the Comprehensive Breast Cancer Center at the Rita J. and Stanley H. Kaplan Comprehensive Cancer Center, New York University School of Medicine and Mount Sinai-NYU Medical Center and Health System*

ISABELLA ROSSELLINI

(GAL), *actress and model*

LEONA ROSTENBERG

(WSC '30), *author, rare book collector, and co-owner of Leona Rostenberg and Madeleine Stern Rare Books*

ELKE ROSTHAL

(TSOA '95), *filmmaker*

NAOMI F. ROTHFIELD

(MED '55), *chief, division of rheumatic diseases, University of Connecticut School of Medicine*

BARON EDOUARD DE ROTHSCHILD

(STERN G '85), *partner, Rothschild & Cie Banque*

LEWIS RUDIN

(STERN U '49), *cochairman, Rudin Management Co., Inc.*

LOUIS K. SALKIND

(GSAS/CIMS '90), *computer systems and financial software designer*

THOMAS "SATCH" SANDERS

(STERN U '60), *vice president and director, Player Programs, National Basketball Association*

BROTHER THOMAS J. SCANLAN

(GSAS '73), *president, Manhattan College*

ELLEN SCHALL

(LAW '72), *professor of health policy and management, Robert F. Wagner Graduate School of Public Service, New York University*

(Courtesy NYU Medical Center Archives)

(Left)
Dr. Daniel F. Roses (MED '69), Jules Leonard Whitehill Professor of Surgery at the NYU School of Medicine, was elected the New York State chair of the American College of Surgeons Cancer Liaison Program.

(Below)
President Oliva presents the 1997 NYU Alumni Association Distinguished Recent Alumnus Award to computer software entrepreneur **Louis K. Salkind** (GSAS '90).

(Photo credit: Ken Levinson)

(Photo credit: Ken Levinson)

(Photo credit: Phil Gallo)

(Above)
The first recipients of the Lewis Rudin New York City Scholarships are pictured here with President L. Jay Oliva, center, and trustee **Lewis Rudin** (STERN U '49), to President Oliva's left. The scholarship program was named for Mr. Rudin in recognition of his contributions to New York City and to NYU.

(Left)
An NYU basketball star, **Thomas "Satch" Sanders** (STERN U '60) is best remembered for his spectacular performance in the 1959-1960 season, scoring an average of 21.3 points per game and leading his team to the Final Four Championships. He is now vice president and director of Player Programs for the National Basketball Association.

(Photo credit: Harry Heliotis)

(Photo credit: Enrique Cubillo)

(Above)
A special screening of alumnus Martin Scorsese's *Casino* served as a fund-raising event for the Tisch School of the Arts. Pictured from left are Preston Robert Tisch, **Martin Scorsese** (CAS '64, ED '68), and President L. Jay Oliva.

(Left)
Connecticut congressman **Christopher Shays** (STERN G '74, WAG '78) discussed "The Future of Social Security" at a symposium held at the Robert F. Wagner Graduate School of Public Service on April 6, 1999. He is joined by Dean Jo Ivey Boufford, Wagner School.

(Photo credit: Ken Levinson)

(Above)
NYU trustee **Larry A. Silverstein** (ARTS '52) congratulates Patricia Kluge, president and CEO of Kluge Investments, on her inauguration into the Founders Society. Silverstein himself has received the Albert Gallatin Medal, awarded each year to a member of the University community who has made an outstanding contribution to society.

(Right)
Author **Alix Kates Shulman** (CAS '62, GAL '79) was presented the Distinguished Alumna Award by former Gallatin School dean Richard J. Koppenaal in 1996.

(Photo credit: Ken Levinson)

GERALD SCHOENFELD
(LAW '49), *chairman of the board, The Shubert Foundation*

FREDERICK C. SCHULT, JR.
(ARTS '50, GSAS '51, '62), *professor of history, New York University*

RICHARD SCHWARTZ
(WAG '89), *senior advisor, Office of the Mayor, New York City*

SEYMOUR I. SCHWARTZ
(MED '50), *Distinguished Alumni Professor and chief, department of surgery, University of Rochester School of Medicine and Dentistry*

MARTIN SCORSESE
(CAS '64, ED '68), *film director*

OSBORNE SCOTT
(TSOA '75), *television and film director*

JOHN P. SGANGA
(WAG '86), *president and CEO, Innovatix, Inc.*

MOLLY SHANNON
(TSOA '87), *performer, comedian, actress*

CHRISTOPHER SHAYS
(STERN G '74, WAG '78), *U.S. congressman from Connecticut*

CHARLES J. SHERR
(GSAS '72, MED '72), *investigator, Howard Hughes Medical Institute, St. Jude Children's Research Hospital*

CLIFFORD G. SHULL
(GSAS '41, HON '95), *physicist, Nobel laureate, emeritus professor, Massachusetts Institute of Technology*

ALIX KATES SHULMAN
(CAS '62, GAL '79), *author*

GEORGE N. SIDERIS
(GSAS '92), *science lecturer, School of Continuing and Professional Studies, New York University*

JULIUS SILVER
(ARTS '22, HON '77), *attorney*

HERBERT R. SILVERMAN
(STERN U '32), *senior advisor, Bank Julius Baer*

LARRY A. SILVERSTEIN
(ARTS '52), *president, Silverstein Properties*

(Photo credit: Ken Levinson)

(Photo credit: Ken Levinson)

(Top)
For her outstanding efforts on behalf
of Native Americans, **Harriett Skye**
(GAL '93) received a Distinguished
Alumna Award from the NYU Alumni
Association. She is pictured with
Gallatin professor Laurin Raiken, in
center, and fellow Gallatin alumnus
and awardee Yale Strom (GAL '84).

(Above)
On March 15, 1999, Mr. and Mrs.
Leonard N. Stern (STERN U '57,
STERN G '59) *(left)* and Mr. and
Mrs. Laurence A. Tisch (STERN U
'42) were awarded the Sir Harold
Acton Medal at the gala celebrating
the completion of the first Billion
Dollar Campaign. The Sir Harold

Acton Society recognizes the
University's foremost benefactors—
those who have made gifts of $1 mil-
lion or more to NYU to advance
teaching, research, and student life.
Both Leonard Stern and the Tisch
family have made gifts of $30 million.

(Photo credit: Jim Berry)

(Top)
Award-winning film director
Oliver Stone (TSOA '71) gives a
master class at the Tisch School of
the Arts. He has frequently returned
to the NYU campus to speak with
students and alumni about the art of
filmmaking.

(Above)
In 1972, University trustees Preston
Robert Tisch *(center)* and **Laurence
A. Tisch** *(right)* (STERN U '42) and
then-NYU President James Hester
broke ground at 44 West Fourth
Street, now the location of Tisch Hall

and the home of the Stern School of
Business. A generous gift from the
Tisch Family Foundation helped
to build the structure, named in
honor of Al Tisch, father of the Tisch
brothers.

(Photo credit: Don Pollard)

LILLIAN VERNON
(CAS), *founder and CEO, Lillian Vernon Corporation*

MICHAEL A. WALDMAN
(LAW '87), *former deputy assistant to the president of the United States and director of speechwriting at the White House*

LEONARD M. WEINTRAUB
(STERN U '42, LAW '45), *criminal attorney*

STANLEY WEISER
(TSOA '72), *screenwriter*

MELVYN I. WEISS
(LAW '59), *senior partner, Milberg Weiss Bershad Hynes & Lerach, LLP*

PETER WESTBROOK
(STERN U '75), *six-time U.S. Olympic fencing champion; chair, The Peter Westbrook Foundation*

ALLEN D. WHEAT
(STERN G '77), *CEO, Credit Suisse First Boston Corporation*

JULES L. WHITEHILL
(MED '35), *retired surgeon and philanthropist*

MICHAEL WILLIS
(ED '95, '99), *staff nurse, Emergency Ward/Critical Care Service at Bellevue Hospital Center*

GEORGE C. WOLFE
(TSOA '84), *Broadway director and producer*

NICHOLAS WOOTTON
(TSOA '94), *Emmy award-winning television writer; supervising producer, NYPD Blue*

ROBERT F. WRIGHT
(STERN G '51), *president, Robert F. Wright Associates, Inc.*

BENJAMIN WU
(CAS '85), *counsel to the Technology Subcommittee of the House Committee on Science, U.S. Congress*

MARTIN J. WYGOD
(STERN U '61), *chairman, Synetic, Inc.*

RAYMOND F. ZAMBITO
(DEN '53), *prominent dentist*

BARRY ZARET
(MED '66), *chief, section of cardiovascular medicine, Yale University School of Medicine*

MICHAEL A. ZASLOFF
(GSAS '73, MED '73), *vice chairman and executive vice president, Magainin Pharmaceuticals, Inc.*

SAMUEL ZELENSKY
(CAS '34, LAW '37), *attorney*

ARTHUR ZITRIN
(GSAS '41, MED '45), *professor emeritus and clinical professor of psychiatry, New York University School of Medicine*

(Above)
Lillian Vernon (CAS), an NYU trustee and CEO of the Lillian Vernon Corporation, generously endowed the Lillian Vernon Center for International Affairs, which opened on February 11, 1999. The center serves as the home for NYU's global activities and houses the Student Center for European Studies, the European Union Center of New York, and the League of World Universities.

(Photo credit: Phil Gallo)

(Photo credit: Ken Levinson)

(Above)
Theater director and producer
George C. Wolfe (TSOA '84), pictured here with TSOA dean Mary
Schmidt Campbell, shared the
secrets of making a Broadway hit at a
symposium at the Tisch School of
the Arts.

(Left)
Peter Westbrook (STERN U '75),
former United States Olympic fencer,
founder of the Peter Westbrook
Foundation for New York City
inner-city youth, accepts the 1998
NYU Alumni Association
Distinguished Alumni Award from
President L. Jay Oliva.

SELECTED BIBLIOGRAPHY

Baldridge, J. Victor. *Power and Conflict in the University: Research in the Sociology of Complex Organizations.* New York: J. Wiley & Sons, 1971.

Bender, Thomas. *New York Intellect.* Baltimore: The Johns Hopkins University Press, 1987.

Cantor, Mindy, ed. *Around the Square 1830-1890: Essays on Life, Letters and Architecture in Greenwich Village.* New York: New York University, 1982.

Davis, Kenneth C. *Don't Know Much About History.* New York: The Hearst Corporation, 1990.

Diamondstein, Barbaralee. *The Landmarks of New York III.* New York: Henry N. Abrams, 1998.

Dolkart, Andrew S. *Guide to New York City Landmarks.* New York: John Wiley & Sons, 1998.

Dorsen, Norman. "How NYU Became a Major Law School." *NYU: The Law School Magazine,* 1 (fall 1991): 42.

Frusciano, Thomas, and Marilyn Pettit. *New York University and the City.* New Brunswick: Rutgers University Press, 1997.

Gitlow, Abraham L. *New York University's Stern School of Business: A Centennial Retrospective.* New York: New York University Press, 1995.

Hamann, Horst. *New York Vertical.* New York: te Neues Publishing Co., 1997.

Hemley, Samuel, Ellison Hillyer, and Jacob Shapiro, eds. *A Historical Sketch of New York University College of Dentistry: Prepared in Connection with the Seventy-fifth Anniversary, 1866-1867 to 1941-1942.* New York: New York University, 1942.

Hester, James McNaughton. *Adventure on Washington Square: Being President of New York University, 1962-1975.* New York, 1996.

Homberger, Eric. *The Historical Atlas of New York City.* New York: Henry Holt and Co., 1994.

Jackson, Kenneth T. *The Encyclopedia of New York City.* New Haven: Yale University Press, 1995.

Jones, Theodore F. *New York University, 1832-1932.* New York: New York University Press, 1933.

Lankevich, George J. *American Metropolis: A History of New York City.* New York: New York University Press, 1998.

Lowe, David Garrard. *Stanford White's New York.* New York: Watson-Guptil Publications, 1999.

Simmons, Peter. *Gotham Comes of Age: New York Through the Lens of the Byron Company, 1892-1942.* Rohnert Park, CA: Pomegranate Communications, 1999.

Still, Bayrd. "A University for Its Time: The Formative Years, 1830-1870," first in a series of lectures on the history of New York University, March 1982. New York University Archives, Manuscript Collection 43.3.

_____. *Mirror for Gotham: New York as Seen by Contemporaries from Dutch Days to the Present.* New York: New York University Press, 1956.

Stoddard, George D. *The New York University Self-Study Final Report.* New York: New York University, 1956.

Wainwright, Jonathan M. "Considerations upon the Expediency and the Means of Establishing a University in the City of New-York." New York, 1830.

ACKNOWLEDGMENTS

Acknowledgments for *Miracle on Washington Square* must begin with Naomi Levine. She inspired and championed this project. Without her fire, guidance, and full support, this volume simply would not be. We also are indebted to those historians, writers, and educators who came before us. Their scholarship made our job possible. Respect, credit, and thanks are due to J. Victor Baldridge, Thomas Bender, John Brademas, Lynne Brown, Norman Dorsen, Diane Fairbank, Thomas J. Frusciano, Abraham Gitlow, Barnett Hamberger, James M. Hester, Theodore F. Jones, L. Jay Oliva, Marilyn H. Pettit, and Bayrd Still.

In addition, grateful appreciation is due our colleagues in the University's Office of Public Affairs, the Archives, the Photo Bureau, the Office for University Development and Alumni Relations, and the Office of Advertising and Publications.

The Public Affairs staff wrote the appendix of school histories. For this, we thank Patricia Allen, John Beckman, Helen Horowitz, Christopher James, Barbara Jester, Iva Kocijan, Richard Pierce, and Joshua Plaut. Helen and Josh also patiently read various drafts of the book and offered important editorial insights. Jeanne Huang, Joan's student assistant, was a marvel of orderliness in keeping voluminous files and photos straight.

The Archives' magnificent treasure of photographs, drawings, memorabilia, and editorial material was the major source for this volume. Graduate students Maurita Baldock, Jessica Cooperman, Elena de la Rosa, Meaghan Dwyer, Meave Hamill, Taja-Nia Henderson, Ariana Huberman, Tristan Kirvin, Daniel Link, Erin McMurray, Nezha Mezhoudi, and Amy Surak all approached the project with a sense of fun and genuine dedication. They proofread, assisted with research, scanned hundreds of photographs, and in general were invaluable to the project. Thanks also to Nancy Greenberg, special project archivist, for her input.

Designer Lenny Levitsky was with us from the start. His exceptional gifts of organization and design are evident in the finished product. He was indispensable.

Our thanks also go to Advertising and Publications editors Elizabeth O'Connell and Betsy Mickel. Their combined editorial skills immeasurably improved the book.

Others vital to the project were Laura Stiles, Elisa Guarino, and Dianne Bondareff, who helped compile the modern photo collection. Carol Leven, Susan Dietz, and Deborah Broderick shepherded the project through an arduous production schedule. David Koehler, Adrienne Rulnick, Cheryl Gravis, and Sara Thygeson contributed the alumni chapter list. David Finney and the late Debra James reviewed copy and offered important suggestions. John Sexton generously gave Joan a summer off to complete the project.

Finally, our family and friends enthusiastically read copy and offered wise counsel. Thanks to Carl Cricco, Stuart Dim, Abigail Johnston, Niko Pfund, Johanna Rosman, and Ken Weine.

JMD
NMC

New York University
Fall 2000

THE MIRACLE ON
WASHINGTON
SQUARE

NEW YORK
UNIVERSITY

APPENDIXES

THE COLLEGE OF ARTS AND SCIENCE

The history of the College of Arts and Science begins with the founding of the University in 1831 by a number of prominent New Yorkers. Unlike other institutions of the time, it was nonsectarian and provided, in addition to the standard classical curriculum, a practical and "utilitarian" education designed for the working-class sons of the metropolis. From its founding, it was a center of arts and science. Samuel F. B. Morse—one of the first faculty members—invented the telegraph. John William Draper, a pioneer in photography, produced the first photograph of the moon, which was taken from the top of the old University Building in 1840. In 1895, Chancellor Henry Mitchell MacCracken moved the College to the University Heights campus in the Bronx in an effort to attract the best students nationally. MacCracken believed that students of this era sought not only fine teaching, but also a rustic setting abundant with extracurricular activities, fraternities, and intercollegiate athletics. An undergraduate presence was restored downtown with the opening of the Collegiate Division in 1903, which became Washington Square College in 1914. This school had a more diverse student body, opening its doors to women, immigrants, commuters, and professional students. For more than 60 years, undergraduate liberal arts education at NYU took place in two locations—University College (and the College of Engineering) at the Heights and Washington Square College in Greenwich Village, both offering excellent, but different, educational and social experiences. In the 1970s yet another transformation took place when financial pressures forced the closing of the University Heights campus and the merging of University College with Washington Square College. The new institution, known as the Washington Square and University College of Arts and Science, retained the traditions of the residential and collegiate culture of the Heights and the Square's progressive, urban focus. In the 1970s, the decision was also made to recruit the very best faculty and students, to update and expand the physical plant, and to create distinguished programs both here and abroad. Today, the College of Arts and Science is a recognized national leader. With its reconceived liberal arts core, the Morse Academic Plan, at the center of its curriculum, the College emphasizes student inquiry and research, offers unique opportunities for international and preprofessional study, and uses the city as a site for learning and service.

THE SCHOOL OF LAW

The School of Law, founded in 1835, is the oldest professional school of New York University and one of the oldest law schools in the nation. Benjamin F. Butler, at the time attorney general in the cabinet of President Andrew Jackson, drew up the "Plan for the Organization of a Law Faculty," outlining a three-year curriculum. Butler's plan, the first designed to teach law by the course method, became the model for the structure of modern legal education. Today, the School of Law stands as a premier research and teaching institution and as a learning community—a place where students address the most fundamental concepts and questions facing societies. Students are instilled with an awareness of their responsibilities as citizens and professionals and the notion that the legal profession must serve all of society. The School of Law faculty, the largest and one of the most distinguished national and international faculties in the United States, displays strength across a broad range of fields, from the theoretical to the practical. This diversity is reflected in the curriculum, most particularly in the pioneering methods of instruction in the areas of interdisciplinary study and clinical education. In addition, NYU's Global Law School Program has led the way in "globalizing" law study and preparing students for the increasingly international nature of their work. From the admission of women in 1890 to the founding of the nation's first Black American Law Students Association in 1967, the School of Law has proudly achieved the vision of the University's founders, which is to provide access to the legal profession to everyone.

THE SCHOOL OF MEDICINE

The New York University School of Medicine was founded in 1841 as the University Medical College; its present form was the result of an 1898 merger with the Bellevue Hospital Medical College. From the outset, it has emphasized a threefold mission: the training of physicians, care for the sick, and the search for new knowledge. The School of Medicine can claim numerous "firsts" that helped shape the nature of American medical education and care: the first successful resection of a hip joint was performed in 1854 by NYU's Dr. Lewis Sayre, who was also the first professor of orthopedic surgery. In 1884, the Carnegie Laboratory was established as the first facility in the U.S. devoted to teaching and research in bacteriology and pathology. In 1911, NYU opened the nation's first outpatient clinic. In 1932, NYU established the first department of forensic pathology. In 1980, Dr. Saul Krugman developed the first vaccine for hepatitis B. In 1981, NYU scientists presented the first evidence linking Kaposi's sarcoma with immune deficiency in homosexual men. Its faculty and alumni are distinguished by their many critical and renowned contributions. These include Drs. Jonas Salk and Albert Sabin, who each developed polio vaccines; Dr. Walter Reed, who discovered the transmission mechanism for yellow fever; Dr. William Tillett, whose work on blood-clotting led to the development of strepto-kinase; Dr. Julius Axelrod, who conducted malaria research and was later awarded a Nobel Prize; Dr. Severo Ochoa, who received the Nobel Prize for his work on biochemical genetics; and Dr. Baruj Benacerraf, a former NYU pathologist who received the Nobel Prize for his work on genetic regulation of the immune system. Medical students and residents gain clinical experience through the NYU Hospitals Center, which includes the 704-bed Tisch Hospital and the 174-bed Rusk Institute of Rehabilitation Medicine, both of which are part of the Mount Sinai-NYU Medical Center/Health System.

THE COLLEGE OF DENTISTRY

New York University College of Dentistry was officially established in 1925, when an existing proprietary school, the New York College of Dentistry, merged with the University. The College had originally been founded in 1865. With 31 students under the direction of 10 faculty members in rented quarters at 22nd Street and Fifth Avenue, it became a leading source for dental care in the city in the late 19th and early 20th centuries. Following the merger with NYU, the College's educational programs expanded to include postdoctoral studies. Almost 135 years later, the New York University College of Dentistry has educated more dentists than any other dental school in the United States. The College annually provides state-of-the-art training to over 1,300 predoctoral and postdoctoral students, as well as to students in dental hygiene and dental assistant training programs. Its students come from all over the United States and from more than 60 foreign countries. Half of all practicing dentists in New York City and almost half the dentists in New York State graduated from NYU. In addition to its educational programs, the NYU College of Dentistry is committed to an active research program, to innovation in practice and the delivery of care, and to public health and community service. Through its clinics and through affiliations with many major hospitals and long-term care facilities in the New York metropolitan area, the College is the largest provider of comprehensive affordable dental care in New York State and in the nation. Through its new public health programs, the College is a national center for consumer information, education, and research into the causes and prevention of oral cancer. The College's distinguished faculty of more than 800 full- and part-time clinicians and researchers includes many who have made pioneering contributions in such areas as pain control, implant dentistry, and the correction of facial deformities.

THE GRADUATE SCHOOL OF ARTS AND SCIENCE

In 1866, NYU became the second American institution (after Yale University) to award a doctoral degree for academic work. Twenty years later, University chancellor Henry Mitchell MacCracken established the Graduate School at NYU, emphasizing both research excellence and the interconnection between school and city. This new vision of graduate training attracted ever-growing numbers of young women and men to doctoral programs. The first female graduate students entered the University in 1888. Today, women constitute over half of the Graduate School's 4,300 students. Over the last decade, the Graduate School has brought together a superb faculty, and now it is reclaiming its role as an academic pioneer. The Graduate School currently houses 45 programs that offer doctoral and master's degrees. Its achievements in the fields of anthropology, economics, Middle Eastern studies, philosophy, fine arts, French, mathematics, and neuroscience have earned international acclaim. In 1998, more National Science Foundation Graduate Research Fellows chose to study at NYU than ever before. The Graduate School has also become a national leader at linking programs together. It established such interdisciplinary activities as the Program in Africana Studies, joint degrees with NYU's School of Law, and the John W. Draper Interdisciplinary Master's Program in Humanities and Social Thought. The Graduate School is also planning to bring undergraduate and graduate education together through innovative B.A./M.A. programs. Mirroring the cultural diversity of New York City, today's Graduate School is a major international research center with students from more than 75 countries. There is little doubt that the contours and content of graduate education will continue to change in the coming years. NYU's Graduate School, which has embraced innovation throughout its history, is ready for these changes. Powered by its faculty, it is a place where research, teaching, and learning will continue to flourish.

THE SCHOOL OF EDUCATION

Founded in 1890 as the School of Pedagogy, the School of Education was the first professional school established at an American university devoted to teacher education. The School's early mission was to educate school administrators and prepare men and women for work in colleges of teacher education. By 1921, when the name changed to the School of Education, the School expanded its mission to educate teachers at all levels, offering undergraduate through doctoral degrees. At this time, when public education experienced tremendous change, the School extended its resources to the city and began using the public schools as laboratories for research to address education issues locally and, later, statewide. As the education field expanded, the School of Education responded with new programs in home economics, health, and arts education. The School introduced university-level studies, research, and doctoral programs in nursing and health professions. Today, through 13 departments, the School of Education prepares students for a variety of professions in human services, as educators, child psychologists, nutritionists, nurses, speech pathologists, and physical and occupational therapists. Degrees are also offered in communications, music and performing arts professions, and the visual arts. The School of Education provides students with practical experience through numerous field projects in the New York City schools, in such areas as health clinics, student teaching, tutoring programs, and art and music therapy practices. Continuing a tradition of serving the community, the School of Education houses research institutes and advocacy centers working to improve conditions in urban areas, including the NYU Institute for Education and Social Policy, the Child and Family Policy Center, the Hartford Foundation Institute for Geriatric Nursing, the Metropolitan Center for Urban Education, the Nordoff-Robbins Center for Music Therapy, and the Center for Urban Community College Leadership. Faculty and project staff provide educators and health care professionals with various continuing education and career development programs throughout the city.

THE LEONARD N. STERN SCHOOL OF BUSINESS UNDERGRADUATE

In 1899, representatives of the New York Society of Certified Public Accountants and New York University came together to plan a new school to educate individuals preparing for the requirements of the first Certified Public Accounting Law, passed by New York State to recognize accounting as a profession in the United States. In 1900, the School of Commerce, Accounts, and Finance was established. It was one of the first schools of business in the country, and Charles Waldo Haskins was its first dean. The School took the lead in formulating objective, scholarly standards of academic excellence. In doing so, it became a charter member of the American Assembly of Collegiate Schools of Business (AACSB), which is the sole professional accrediting agency for undergraduate and graduate degree programs in business. In addition, the undergraduate college was the first school to award the Bachelor of Science degree with a solid grounding in the liberal arts and sciences. By the end of the School's first decade, significant demand had arisen for graduate courses. These were offered at the School of Commerce, Accounts, and Finance's satellite division near Wall Street. In 1916, the Graduate School of Business Administration was established. The School also acquired a new home, Tisch Hall, funded by a generous gift from NYU trustee Laurence A. Tisch. In 1988, the undergraduate college and the graduate school received a major gift from an alumnus, Leonard N. Stern, chairman of the Hartz Group, Inc. In recognition of Mr. Stern's generosity, the New York University Board of Trustees combined the college and graduate school under the name Leonard N. Stern School of Business. As the 20th century drew to a close, advances in information technology and the forces of globalization radically altered the landscape of business. To prepare its graduates to effectively compete in the business world of tomorrow, the Undergraduate College remains committed to delivering the highest quality business education, combining the critical thinking and humanistic focus of liberal arts education with state-of-the-art training in business administration.

THE LEONARD N. STERN SCHOOL OF BUSINESS GRADUATE

The Leonard N. Stern School of Business was founded in 1900 as NYU's School of Commerce, Accounts, and Finance. By 1916 the demand for advanced business education led to the creation of the Graduate School of Business Administration, located on Wall Street. A few decades later, with 10,000 students, the School was the largest business educational institution in America. Master of Science degree programs in accounting and in quantitative analysis; M.B.A. joint-degree programs in law, journalism, politics, and French studies; and one of the nation's first majors in international business was added to the curriculum in the 1970s. In the next decade, the School created the Executive M.B.A. Program and the Berkley Center for Entrepreneurial Studies, and, in 1996, the Entertainment, Media, and Technology Program. In 1988, another gift transformed the entire institution when Leonard N. Stern (B.S. 1957, M.B.A. 1959), the chairman of the Hartz Group, Inc., and then a trustee of the University, gave $30 million to his alma mater—the largest single gift ever made to an American business school. This gift made it possible to unite the graduate and undergraduate business schools under the name Leonard N. Stern School of Business and build a facility to house them on the same campus. In 1992 the Management Education Center was completed and the graduate division moved from Wall Street to Washington Square. An additional donation of $10 million from alumnus Henry Kaufman (B.A. 1948, Ph.D. 1958), the noted economist and chairman of NYU's Stern Board of Overseers, renamed the facility the Henry Kaufman Management Center. Today's core M.B.A. curriculum has been revised to stress cross-disciplinary perspectives and globalization, an approach that better equips future leaders for an ever-changing marketplace. Stern's century-long commitment to quality has attracted many eminent teachers; among its faculty are Nobel laureates, members of the National Academy of Arts and Sciences, and titans of the business world. The School also has produced countless successful graduates, including more partners of the major accounting-consulting firms and more Wall Street executives than from any comparable institution.

THE INSTITUTE OF FINE ARTS

anked first in this country among graduate programs in the history of art, the Institute of Fine Arts can trace its origins to the founding of the University in 1832 and the painter and great inventor of the telegraph Samuel F. B. Morse. However, it wasn't until 1922 when the young scholar-architect Fiske Kimball, who was appointed the Morse Professor of the Literature of the Arts of Design, established a distinguished program in the history of art that fine arts as an academic discipline came into its own at the University. During this period, the foundation was laid for much of what is typical about the Institute today: its special relationships with New York's museums, its liberal use of the special expertise of visiting and adjunct faculty, and a core faculty of the highest quality. Academically part of the University's Graduate School of Arts and Science, the Institute is administered separately and has its own Board of Trustees, a Council of Friends, and a separately incorporated foundation dedicated to its support. In 1958, the Institute moved to its present home in the James B. Duke House, located at the corner of Fifth Avenue and 78th Street. Beginning in 1960, for the first time anywhere, the Institute began offering university training in conservation. The unique program comprises an intensive four-year curriculum that combines the demanding master's degree in history of art with scientific, practical, and historical training in conservation. The Institute's excellence is widely recognized and was commended by the National Endowment for the Humanities in 1973 as a national asset. It is unique in the world as a center of research and graduate study that combines the history of art, archaeology, conservation, and museum curatorship. It boasts a world-renowned international faculty and graduates who hold principal positions in universities and museums in the United States, Europe, and Asia.

THE COURANT INSTITUTE OF MATHEMATICAL SCIENCES

In 1934, Richard Courant emigrated from Germany and joined NYU to form the Center for Research and Graduate Education in Mathematics. He brought to the center a focus on applied mathematics, a sharp eye for outstanding mathematical talent, an emphasis on overlap of faculty research interests, and a commitment to securing government and foundation funds. With this vision, Courant was able to assemble a stellar faculty, and by the 1950s his Institute for Mathematics and Mechanics had risen to premier status. In 1965, the newly renamed Courant Institute of Mathematical Sciences moved into its own building, Warren Weaver Hall. Since World War II, the Institute has been best known for its work in applied mathematics. At the same time, it was taking a pioneering role in computer science. In 1952, the Atomic Energy Commission installed the UNIVAC computer at the Institute—the first mainframe computer to be located at a university. In the 1960s, the Institute established a division of computer science. This division became a full-fledged science department in 1971. Today, the Courant Institute consists of two departments—computer science and mathematics—that emphasize partial differential equations, geometric and probabilistic analysis, programming languages, parallel and distributed computing, applied mathematics, and scientific computing. Programs of application include plasma physics, biology, fluid dynamics, neural science, material science, and multimedia technology. Courant faculty have received a remarkable array of awards and honors. The Institute boasts 12 members of the National Academy of Sciences. Four faculty members have been awarded the National Medal of Science. Five members have received career awards from the National Science Foundation. And one has received an Academy Award from the Academy of Motion Picture Arts and Sciences. At Courant, education and research have always been closely intertwined. The institute offers degree programs in both mathematics and computer science, and each year students receive some 45 bachelor's degrees, 80 master's degrees, and 35 Ph.D.'s.

THE SCHOOL OF CONTINUING AND PROFESSIONAL STUDIES

The School of Continuing and Professional Studies (SCPS) at New York University was founded in 1934 as a separate school within the University. Formerly known as the School of Continuing Education, it was renamed the School of Continuing and Professional Studies in 1998. As the nation's largest private, university-based provider of continuing higher education, SCPS sets the pace for critical developments in lifelong learning. SCPS is committed to helping further careers, to enhancing professional qualifications, and to enriching the intellectual life of its students. A comprehensive choice of learning opportunities helps students understand and master the knowledge and skills they need to keep up and excel in a world where the only constant is change. Focusing on the most current topics and designed to be immediately applicable, the School's over 2,000 credit and noncredit courses, seminars, and workshops in more than 100 fields constitute a dynamic, innovative curriculum that is recognized nationally and internationally as a model of lifelong learning. Students at SCPS can choose the path that fits their needs with courses toward certificates, diplomas, and undergraduate and graduate degrees. SCPS also introduced a variety of undergraduate, graduate, and certificate courses on-line, allowing students the convenience of learning from their home or office. The courses for each program are planned under the guidance of boards of advisers consisting of leaders in each profession and taught by outstanding professionals in the field as well as by experienced academicians. Several nationally renowned institutes and centers—such as the Real Estate Institute; the Center for Hospitality, Tourism, and Travel Administration; the Center for Publishing; the Center for Direct Marketing; and the Center for Philanthropy—are housed at SCPS. The School's growth reflects the forces that are transforming the workplace—new technology, organizational restructuring, demographic shifts, and global competition have made continuing education and training a necessity, not a luxury.

THE ROBERT F. WAGNER GRADUATE SCHOOL OF PUBLIC SERVICE

The Robert F. Wagner Graduate School of Public Service was founded in 1938 as the Graduate Division for Training in Public Service. It was subsequently renamed the Graduate School of Public Administration and grew steadily through the years, adding doctoral and master's programs and launching formal concentrations in health policy, planning, and administration. In 1989 the school was renamed the Robert F. Wagner Graduate School of Public Service in honor of New York City Mayor Robert F. Wagner. Today, the Wagner School is the largest school of its kind in the country, offering the Doctor of Philosophy, the Master of Public Administration, the Master of Urban Planning, and the Master of Science in management, advanced management for clinicians, and performance and information systems auditing, as well as various advanced certificates. Committed to the values of public service and enriched by the academic excellence of New York University, the Wagner School delivers a comprehensive, practical education for those seeking to serve the public sector. Hailing from all over the world, students arrive at the Wagner School with a desire to serve the public and leave with the skills and experience to bring about change. Combining course work in management, finance, and policy with cutting-edge research and work experience, the Wagner education enables them to transform personal commitment into public leadership. The Wagner School prepares students to make government more effective, help nonprofit agencies thrive, and build bridges between the public and private sectors. The full-time faculty includes first-rate teachers, sophisticated researchers, and committed practitioners. With extensive ties to leading health, nonprofit, and government institutions, the adjunct professors bring firsthand knowledge into the classroom. Through the Capstone Program, students get hands-on experience in public service through commissioned, yearlong consulting projects for city agencies, nonprofits, and health organizations. New York University is a private university in the public service, and the Wagner School stands at the heart of this mission, linking the enormous resources of the University to the community, to New York City, and, by extension, to the great cities of this country and around the world.

THE SHIRLEY M. EHRENKRANZ SCHOOL OF SOCIAL WORK

Established as part of the Graduate School of Public Administration and Social Service (now the Robert F. Wagner Graduate School of Public Service) in 1953, the School of Social Work was launched as an autonomous school within NYU in September 1960. In 1994, the School was named the Shirley M. Ehrenkranz School of Social Work after its longtime dean, the late Shirley M. Ehrenkranz. Initially, only a full-time, two-year master's program was offered. The School later added baccalaureate, advanced certificate, and Ph.D. programs, becoming one of the few in the country to provide a continuum of social work education from the undergraduate through the doctoral levels. It was also the first school of social work in New York City authorized by the New York State Education Department to offer a Ph.D. degree. The Ehrenkranz School is one of the leading centers of professional training in direct social work practice. Graduates at all levels acquire the core knowledge and skills necessary to work directly with individuals, families, and groups. Concurrent practical experience is an integral component of professional social work education, and the School draws on the extraordinary diversity of more than 350 service agencies in the New York City metropolitan area and the tri-state region for its student placements. Students develop professionally in an intimate, supportive, and comfortable environment while having the resources of a major university and city at their disposal. Three 19th-century homes, located directly on historic Washington Square Park, are now the quarters of the Ehrenkranz School of Social Work's students and faculty. These stately residences have a distinguished history. The American artist Edward Hopper lived and worked in Number Three Washington Square North from 1939 to 1965, and portions of his studio are preserved in that building to this day.

THE TISCH SCHOOL OF THE ARTS

In 1965, charged with organizing NYU's various programs in acting, dance, design, and film and television into a new school of the arts, Dean Robert W. Corrigan established an Institute for Performing Arts and an Institute for Film and Television within a new School of the Arts at the University. The School quickly gained a reputation as a spirited, innovative laboratory for the arts. Not long after its founding, the School underwent a period of rapid programmatic growth: 12 independent departments were created, and the student body expanded from 500 in the late 1960s to 1,600 by 1980. In 1982, a major gift from Laurence Tisch, then chairman of the Board of Trustees at NYU, and his brother Preston Robert Tisch, a member of the board, made possible the acquisition and renovation of two buildings on campus. In recognition of that gift and the leadership of the family, the School was named in their honor. Today, the Tisch School of the Arts, comprising the Institute of Performing Arts, the Maurice Kanbar Institute of Film and Television, and the Jack H. Skirball Center for New Media and Film, is one of the nation's preeminent centers for professional training, scholarship, and research in the performing and cinematic arts. Nearly 3,000 undergraduate and graduate students pursue degrees in acting, dance, design, drama, musical theatre, performance studies, film and television, cinema studies, dramatic writing, photography, and interactive telecommunications. The Tisch School's undergraduate programs combine the artistic training of a professional school with the liberal arts education of a major university. Its graduate departments follow a conservatory model and are among the country's most challenging and innovative. Tisch School programs include the first within a university to offer undergraduate, master's, and Ph.D. degrees in the history, theory, and criticism of film; a pioneering interactive telecommunications program; the only academic program designed for collaborators in the creation of new musical theatre and opera; and an undergraduate drama program in which students receive their primary professional training from renowned theatres and actor training studios.

THE GALLATIN SCHOOL OF INDIVIDUALIZED STUDY

The Gallatin School of Individualized Study, a small, innovative college within New York University, gives students the opportunity to design a program of study tailored to their own needs and interests. Founded in 1972 as the University Without Walls and later named the Gallatin Division, it was considered an "experiment" in nontraditional education. Over the next two decades, the experiment was transformed into a finely tuned educational approach that has developed a national reputation for its unique combination of flexibility and high standards. The Gallatin School grew out of the educational reform movement of the late 1960s and early 1970s, a period when social forces were bringing new populations of students to higher education. For almost 30 years, the Gallatin approach has continued to attract a wide variety of bright, talented students with its flexible but academically rigorous curriculum; innovative, interdisciplinary approach to education; outstanding teachers and advisers; and small-college atmosphere. The key to Gallatin's educational approach is its faculty advisers. The adviser ensures that the student's program has depth, breadth, and coherence and that it is consistent with career and educational goals. Advisers also supervise and evaluate independent study and internship projects and advise graduate students on their theses. Undergraduates experience a thorough grounding in the history of ideas and great books, and graduate students pursue advanced study in interdisciplinary modes of thought. As a small college within a highly regarded research university, Gallatin provides its students with the best of both worlds. Its small size—700 undergraduates and 300 graduate students—creates a strong sense of community among students and faculty and allows for the development of lasting relationships with professors, advisers, and classmates. At the same time, Gallatin students have access to all of New York University with a wide variety of courses taught by world-renowned scholars, excellent facilities and research institutes, and all of the resources of New York City at their fingertips. Gallatin is a school for people who want to push the boundaries of a college education.

UNIVERSITY LIBRARIES

New York University could not have become a great university without building a great library. Before Bobst Library opened in 1973, the University had just over one million volumes kept in 30 different locations, with no central catalog. A generous gift from Elmer Holmes Bobst and his wife, Mamdouha, allowed New York University to build a new central research library.

Today, the striking, 12-story Elmer Holmes Bobst Library and Study Center, designed by Philip Johnson, is the flagship of a nine-library, 4.2 million-volume system that provides students and faculty members with access to the world's scholarship and serves as a center for the University community's intellectual life. The library houses more than to three million volumes, 19,000 journals, and more than three million microforms; it provides access to thousands of electronic resources; and it supports the teaching and research needs of 125 Ph.D. fields.

In addition to three specialized reference centers and eight floors of open book stacks, Bobst Library houses the Avery Fisher Center for Music and Media and the Electronic Resources Center. It is also home to significant special holdings such as the Fales Collection of English and American Literature, one of the best collections in English and American fiction in the United States. In addition, the library includes the University Archives and the Tamiment Institute/Ben Josephson Library, one of the nation's finest collections for scholarly research in labor history, socialism, anarchism, communism, and American radicalism. The Robert F. Wagner Labor Archives houses the Jewish Labor Committee Archives and the historical records of more than 130 New York City labor organizations. Beyond Bobst, the library of the distinguished Courant Institute of Mathematical Sciences focuses on research-level material in mathematics, computer science, and related fields, and the Stephen Chan Library of Fine Arts at the renowned Institute of Fine Arts supports the research and curricular needs of the institute's graduate programs in art history and archaeology.

The library continues to enhance its services to NYU students and faculty and to strengthen its research collections. The extraordinary growth of the University's academic programs in recent years, along with the rapid expansion of electronic information resources, has provided an impetus for new development in the New York University Libraries. A team of 28 subject specialists selects books, journals, and other materials for Bobst Library to reflect the needs of the University's teaching and research programs.

University Administration

L. Jay Oliva
B.A., M.A., PH.D.; HON.: D.H.L.,
LITT.D., LL.D., PH.D.
President

Harvey J. Stedman
B.A., M.A., PH.D.
Provost

Naomi B. Levine
B.A., LL.B., J.S.D.
*Senior Vice President for External
Affairs*

S. Andrew Schaffer
B.A., LL.B.
*Senior Vice President, General
Counsel, and Secretary of the
University*

Robert Berne
B.S., M.B.A., PH.D.
*Vice President for Academic and
Health Affairs*

Richard N. Bing
B.A., M.A., PH.D.
*Vice President for Budget and
Resource Planning*

Lynne P. Brown
B.A., M.A., PH.D.
*Vice President for University
Relations; Senior Assistant to the
President*

Robert Goldfeld
B.A., LL.B.
Vice President for Administration

David C. Koehler
B.S.
*Vice President for Development and
Alumni Affairs*

Anthony R. Marchionni
B.S., C.P.A.
Treasurer

Margo Post Marshak
B.A., M.A., J.D.
Vice President for Student Affairs

Harold T. Read
B.S., M.B.A.
Vice President for Finance

Deans

Michael C. Alfano
D.M.D., PH.D.
Dean, College of Dentistry

Jo Ivey Boufford
B.A., M.D.
*Dean, Robert F. Wagner Graduate
School of Public Service*

Mary Schmidt Campbell
B.A., M.A., PH.D.; HON.: D.F.A.,
PH.D.
Dean, Tisch School of the Arts

Frederick D. S. Choi
B.B.A., M.B.A., PH.D.
*Dean, Undergraduate College;
Vice Dean, Leonard N. Stern School of
Business*

George Daly
B.A., M.A., PH.D.
*Dean, Leonard N. Stern School
of Business*

George W. Downs
B.A., PH.D.
*Dean for Social Sciences, Faculty of
Arts and Science*

David F. Finney
B.A., M.A., ED.D.
*Dean, School of Continuing and
Professional Studies; Special Assistant
to the President*

Richard Foley
B.A., M.A., PH.D.
Dean, Faculty of Arts and Science

Robert M. Glickman
B.A., M.D.
*Saul J. Farber Dean, New York
University School of Medicine and
Post-Graduate Medical School*

Peter Lennie
B.SC. [HULL], PH.D. [CANTAB.]
*Dean for Science, Faculty of Arts
and Science*

Carol A. Mandel
B.A., M.A., M.S.L.S.
Dean of Libraries

Ann Marcus
B.A.; M.SC. [LONDON], ED.D.
Dean, School of Education

Thomas M. Meenaghan
B.S., M.S.W., PH.D.
*Dean, Shirley M. Ehrenkranz School
of Social Work*

Arthur H. Rubenstein
M.B.,CH.B. [WITWATERSRAND]
*Dean, Mount Sinai School of
Medicine (affiliated)*

Matthew S. Santirocco
B.A.; M.A. [CANTAB.], M.PHIL.,
PH.D.
Dean, College of Arts and Science

John E. Sexton
B.A., M.A., PH.D., J.D.
Dean, School of Law

Catharine R. Stimpson
B.A.; B.A., M.A. [CANTAB.], PH.D.;
HON.: D.H.L., HUM.D., LITT.D.,
LL.D.
*Dean, Graduate School of Arts
and Science*

E. Frances White
B.A., M.A., PH.D.
*Dean, Gallatin School of
Individualized Study*

NEW YORK UNIVERSITY BOARD OF TRUSTEES

New York University Institute of Fine Arts Board of Trustees

NEW YORK UNIVERSITY SCHOOL OF MEDICINE FOUNDATION BOARD

INDEX